Implementing Innovation

D0039307

Public Management and Change Series

Beryl A. Radin, Series Editor

Titles in the Series

Challenging the Performance Movement: Accountability, Complexity, and Democratic Values, Beryl A. Radin

Charitable Choice at Work: Evaluating Faith-Based Job Programs in the States, Sheila Suess Kennedy and Wolfgang Bielefeld

The Collaborative Public Manager: New Ideas for the Twenty-first Century, Rosemary O'Leary and Lisa Blomgren Bingham, Editors

The Dynamics of Performance Management: Constructing Information and Reform, Donald P. Moynihan

The Greening of the U.S. Military: Environmental Policy, National Security, and Organizational Change, Robert F. Durant

How Management Matters: Street-Level Bureaucrats and Welfare Reform, Norma M. Riccucci

Managing within Networks: Adding Value to Public Organizations, Robert Agranoff

Measuring the Performance of the Hollow State, David G. Frederickson and H. George Frederickson

Organizational Learning at NASA: The Challenger and Columbia Accidents, Julianne G. Mahler with Maureen Hogan Casamayou

Public Values and Public Interest: Counterbalancing Economic Individualism, Barry Bozeman

The Responsible Contract Manager: Protecting the Public Interest in an Outsourced World, Steven Cohen and William Eimicke

Revisiting Waldo's Administrative State: Constancy and Change in Public Administration, David H. Rosenbloom and Howard E. McCurdy

Implementing Innovation

FOSTERING ENDURING CHANGE IN ENVIRONMENTAL AND NATURAL RESOURCE GOVERNANCE

Toddi A. Steelman

Georgetown University Press/Washington, DC

Georgetown University Press, Washington, DC, www.press.georgetown.edu
© 2010 by Georgetown University Press. All rights reserved. No part of this book may be reproduced or utilized in any form or by any means, electronic or mechanical, including photocopying and recording, or by any information storage and retrieval system, without permission in writing from the publisher.

Library of Congress Cataloging-in-Publication Data

Steelman, Toddi A.
    Implementing innovation : fostering enduring change in environmental and natural resource governance / Toddi A. Steelman.
        p. cm. — (Public management and change series)
    Includes bibliographical references and index.
    ISBN 978-1-58901-627-9 (pbk. : alk. paper)
    1. Environmental policy—United States.   2. Conservation of natural resources—Government policy—United States.   3. Forest management—Government policy—United States.   4. Soil management—Government policy—United States.   I. Title.
    GE180.S73 2010
    333.72—dc22   2009024525

♾ This book is printed on acid-free, 100% recycled paper meeting the requirements of the American National Standard for Permanence in Paper for Printed Library Materials.

15 14 13 12 11 10   9 8 7 6 5 4 3 2
First printing

Printed in the United States of America

To Joey—you are still the one for me.

Contents

List of Illustrations
ix

Preface
xi

List of Abbreviations
xiii

CHAPTER 1
Innovation, Implementation, and Institutions   1

CHAPTER 2
The Evolution of Environmental and Natural Resource Governance:
Land, Water, and Forests   30

CHAPTER 3
Aligning Institutional Characteristics:
Implementing Innovation in Land Protection   70

CHAPTER 4
Intermittent Alignment of Institutional Characteristics:
Implementing Innovation in Watershed Management   101

CHAPTER 5
Misalignment of Institutional Characteristics:
Implementing Innovation in Forest Management   138

CHAPTER 6
Fostering Enduring Change   171

Index
201

Illustrations

Tables

1.1: Categories of Innovation   6

1.2: A Framework for Analyzing the Implementation of Innovation   17

3.1: Chronological Developments in Great Outdoors Colorado   73

3.2 Summary of Cultural, Structural, and Individual Characteristics Related to GOCO   95

4.1: Chronological Developments in Friends of the Cheat/ River of Promise   105

4.2 A Framework for Analyzing Watershed Innovation with Friends of the Cheat and River of Promise   131

5.1: Chronological Developments in Collaborative Stewardship on the Camino Real Ranger District   141

5.2: A Framework for Analyzing Forest Management Innovation on the Camino Real Ranger District   164

6.1: Summary of Individual, Structural, and Cultural Characteristics in Case Studies   173

6.2: Consistent Alignment, Intermittent Alignment, and Misalignment of Characteristics in Case Studies   186

6.3 Practical Implementation Lessons about Individuals, Structures, and Culture   193

ILLUSTRATIONS

Figures

1.1: Relationships among Individual, Structural, and Cultural Factors That Influence the Implementation of Innovation   18

2.1: Influences on Innovative Policy   31

2.2: Influences of Environmental and Natural Resource Governance on Innovations   38

3.1: Influences on Land Use Governance   71

4.1: Hierarchical Influences on Watershed Governance   102

5.1: Hierarchical Influences on Forest Governance   139

6.1: Consistent Alignment in Great Outdoors Colorado Case Study   187

6.2: Misalignment in Great Outdoors Colorado Case Study   187

6.3: Consistent Alignment in Friends of the Cheat/River of Promise Case Study   188

6.4: Misalignment in Friends of the Cheat/River of Promise Case Study   188

6.5: Consistent Alignment in the Camino Real and Collaborative Stewardship   189

6.6: Misalignment in the Camino Real and Collaborative Stewardship   189

6.7: Implementation Patterns That Foster Consistent Alignment in Individual, Structural, and Cultural Factors   190

6.8: Implementation Patterns That Contribute to Cultural and Structural Misalignment   191

6.9: Implementation Patterns That Contribute to Individual and Structural Misalignment   192

Preface

FOR THE LAST FIFTEEN YEARS I have been studying various innovations in environmental and natural resource governance. During this time I had been collecting my thoughts in what could be considered a manuscript in description but not in substance. Languishing on a shelf in my office, the manuscript taunted me for a greater investment of time, which was impossible to find given my overall workload.

When given the opportunity for a sabbatical in 2008, I wanted to reflect on what I had learned about these innovations in a more comprehensive way and rework the manuscript. What were some of the larger lessons that flowed from the numerous in-depth case studies in which I had been invested over the previous decade and a half? Consequently, the manuscript was reshaped around a simple question: Why were some of the innovations implemented while others were not? It is not enough just to come up with a clever idea—it actually has to be put into practice. So how do clever ideas get put into long-term practice?

Innovative public, nonprofit, and collaborative programs have been the object of much excitement and optimism among academics and practitioners seeking improvements in our way of life. Yet not all innovations thrive or even survive. Given that public agencies, nonprofit organizations, and philanthropic organizations invest millions of dollars in promoting innovative programs, it is imperative that we understand the conditions under which these innovations are likely to fulfill their promise. This book is important because it provides insight into the conditions that impede or facilitate successful innovations. If we understand these conditions, then we can better target funding, human resources, and political will to support innovations over the long term.

I owe a debt of gratitude to numerous people who were willing to participate in this book in many different ways. It seems unfair to put one person's name on the cover when so many people lent a hand in its creation. First, I wish to offer my thanks to the scores of people who were interviewed for this project. I was privileged to learn about these innovations from the individuals who participated in them firsthand. I thank them for sharing their stories and insights with me and allowing me to further share those stories and insights with a broader public. For the Great Outdoors Colorado case study, Floyd Ciruli, David Harrison, Chris Leding, Andrew Purkey, Ken Salazar, Will Shafroth, Tom Strickland, Sydney Macy, Chris Romer, Roy Romer, and Janis Wisman were particularly obliging in helping me understand how the program came to be and persist over time. For the Friends of the Cheat case study, I am indebted to Dave Bassage, who talked with me scores of hours about this case study. Keith Pitzer also was exceedingly generous with his time to ensure that I understood the opportunities and challenges faced since Dave Bassage's departure as executive director of the organization. Additional individuals were also essential to understanding the full scope of what Friends of the Cheat set out to do and has continued to do over time. These people include Greg Adolfson, Rick Buckley, Jennifer Pauer, Jim Snyder, Troy Titchnell, Bob Uram, Brent Wiles, and Sally Wilts. For the Camino Real case study, Crockett Dumas was very patient in reading and talking through my interpretation of Collaborative Stewardship. Likewise, Max Córdova was exceedingly charitable with his time and willingness to show me the beauty of northern New Mexico. Perspectives from other people were also indispensable in capturing the Camino Real case study, and those people include Ernest Atencio, Ike DeVargas, Pat Jackson, Carveth Kramer, Henry Lopez, Kay Mathews, Mark Schiller, Luis Torres-Horton, and Kirt Winchester.

Second, my research assistants, Donna Tucker and Karl Wunderlich, provided much needed support in collecting the data in the Great Outdoors Colorado and Camino Real case studies. It was a pleasure to work with such capable and dedicated students. The students in my doctoral-level seminar on natural resource governance also provided a helpful sounding board for many of the ideas moved forward in this book. Thank you to Caitlin Burke, Kathleen McGinley, and Jay Gerlach.

Third, I am thankful to the many colleagues who were willing to read previous drafts of this manuscript, sat through earlier presentations, and were patient with me while the ideas matured. Chris Leding, Dave Bassage, Keith Pitzer, and Crockett Dumas each read through their case study chapters to make sure I captured the details accurately. JoAnn Carmin, Peter deLeon, and Cass Moseley gave me detailed and unvarnished criticism on the later versions that made this a much better book. Craig Thomas organized a presentation at the University of Washington in spring 2008 that allowed me to articulate my ideas more clearly. Craig Thomas, Ann Bostrom, and Stephen Page provided practical advice and suggested areas ripe for improvement. Bill Ascher, Ron Brunner, and Andy Willard also read earlier versions and might not recognize the final product given the changes it has been through. Two peer reviewers through Georgetown University Press, as well as Public Management and Change series editor Beryl Radin, contributed helpful feedback. I thank you all for your willingness to engage in the project and lend your thoughts in a constructive way to assist me.

At the end of this process, I am humbled by those who choose to engage in innovative practices and weather the many ups and downs that come along with striving to improve the world in some way. I hope the insights here are helpful to those who practice and study innovation and contribute to the improvement of how we govern ourselves for the common good.

Abbreviations

AMD   acid mine drainage

BLM   Bureau of Land Management

EPA   U.S. Environmental Protection Agency

ESA   Endangered Species Act

GOCO   Great Outdoors Colorado

NCDWQ   North Carolina Division of Water Quality

NEPA   National Environmental Policy Act

NIMBY   Not in My Backyard

NPDES   National Pollutant Discharge Elimination System

NPS   National Park Service

NWPPC   Northwest Power Planning Council

SMCRA   Surface Mining Control and Reclamation Act

TMDL   total maximum daily load

TNC   The Nature Conservancy

TVA   Tennessee Valley Authority

USACOE   U.S. Army Corps of Engineers

USFS   United States Forest Service

USFWS   U.S. Fish and Wildlife Service

USOSM   U.S. Office of Surface Mining Reclamation and Enforcement

WVAML   West Virginia Abandoned Mine Lands

WVDEP   West Virginia Department of Environmental Protection

WVDMR   West Virginia Division of Mining and Reclamation

WVDNR   West Virginia Department of Natural Resources

Innovation, Implementation, and Institutions

THE PROBLEM WITH INNOVATION

A DEFINING TREND IN THE 1980s AND 1990s was the proliferation of seemingly innovative solutions to difficult environmental and natural resource problems. Innovation emerged in response to the inadequacy of traditional regulatory approaches to address a new generation of problems that to varying degrees involved complex and dynamic systems, great uncertainty, tangled political and jurisdictional boundaries, and a variety of control options.[1] Not surprisingly, these innovations raised the necessary question: How well have we fared in this new era of environmental and natural resource policy innovation?

Consider the following examples. In 1989 the North Carolina Division of Water Quality (NCDWQ) embarked on a bold effort to address nutrient pollution in the Tar-Pamlico River basin. Beginning in the late 1980s, massive fish kills in the Pamlico estuary on the North Carolina coast gained the attention of environmental managers. Algal blooms linked to high levels of pollution upstream in the Tar River caused the problem. The Tar River extends nearly 180 miles from central North Carolina to the coast and drains the collective flows from 2,300 miles of freshwater streams. On its journey from the interior of North Carolina to the Pamlico Sound, the river passes through seventeen counties, several cities, and extensive agricultural and forest lands. Multiple jurisdictions and wide geographic areas pose unique problems for environmental management because different agencies, landowners, and others have divergent and sometimes conflicting mandates, resources, and values that make it a challenge to impose and enforce standards from the top down. Facing numerous sources of pollution across a wide geographic expanse and numerous parties, the NCDWQ was reluctant to embark on traditional regulatory solutions. So in 1989, the NCDWQ began a series of bold policy innovations.

Instead of requiring limits on the various sources of nutrient pollution, the NCDWQ sought to develop a novel trading program between point and nonpoint sources. Using the power of the market, polluters could exchange permits to meet their respective targets, thereby finding the most cost-effective way to meet individual and overall regulatory goals. However, a well-functioning market never developed, and no trades took place.[2]

The NCDWQ adopted a second innovative pollution reduction strategy in 1994 to work with nonpoint sources of pollution in the Tar Pamlico Basin. Under a system of voluntary nitrogen and phosphorus reduction goals, the NCDWQ asked participants to decrease their pollution without requiring or enforcing regulatory action. As part of this second inventive strategy, pollution reduction goals were set and participants were asked to meet the requirements. Failed progress in voluntarily reducing pollution led to more stringent rules to achieve reduction goals two years after its implementation. To develop these rules, the NCDWQ decided on a third novel approach and called together a stakeholder group to establish regulations. The goal was to draw together those most affected by the new regulations and give them a say in how the rules were made and implemented. However, the stakeholder process was forced into an unrealistically short time frame. The technical nature of the task, coupled with the compressed time period, undermined public confidence in the regulations and the innovative participatory aspects of the policymaking process itself.[3]

To the south of North Carolina, the seven-square-mile strip of land between the Ashley and Cooper rivers in North Charleston, South Carolina, is home to another set of complex environmental problems, including the storage of hazardous wastes at historical and active industrial and commercial sites. The U.S. Environmental Protection Agency (EPA) identified the area as a potential target for a novel effort in Community-Based Environmental Protection, an EPA program that works with communities to protect and enhance environmental resources.[4] In conjunction with the South Carolina Department of Health and Environmental Control, the EPA assisted in the formation of a community action group to characterize the concerns of the residents and embark on plans to improve the quality of the land, water, air, and other resources in the area. Federal, state, and local agencies and organizations were called together to develop and guide the Community-Based Environmental Protection project. Funded by the EPA, facilitated by the EPA, and provided technical assistance by the EPA, the community action group came under criticism for not being more strongly grounded in local concerns and needs. The group experienced many difficulties, including overly structured bureaucratic processes, lack of community participation, and divergences in priorities about the objectives for the group and the region. Moreover, failure to work through community members resulted in a breakdown of trust and credibility among the more institutional members of the community action group and the local residents. As a consequence, most of the accomplishments in the project reflected EPA goals rather than those established by the community, and the group was difficult to maintain.[5]

In all of these cases the innovations themselves are bold. Markets for water pollution permits, voluntary strategies, coregulation, stakeholder groups, and community-based environmental protection are all relatively new approaches for remedying environmental and natural resource ills. But all failed to meet their objectives. North Carolina and South Carolina are not alone in their attempts at innovative environmental policy solutions to pressing and complex problems. In the last decade nearly twenty federal agencies, including the U.S. Forest Service (USFS), the Natural Resource Conservation Service, National Oceanic and Atmospheric Administration, Department of Energy, Bureau of Land Management (BLM), the EPA, and the U.S. Fish and Wildlife Service (USFWS), adopted innovative ways of approaching their environmental and natural resource management tasks. Undertaking innovative practices with great hope, practitioners, policymakers, agency officials, citizens, nonprofit organizations, academics, and industry often are bewildered when unforeseen consequences arise or desired outcomes go unfulfilled. Precious human, technical, and financial resources are squandered on failed innovative efforts with great opportunity cost to society at large. The question is why? Why are some innovations implemented, while others are not?

IMPLEMENTING INNOVATION IN AN INSTITUTIONAL CONTEXT

The short answer is that innovative practices are embedded in larger institutional processes that affect innovations' effectiveness, especially during the periods during which implementation occurs. Institutions are defined here as the structures, rules, laws, norms, and sociocultural processes that shape human actions.[6] There are inherent tensions between innovation and institutions. Innovations, by definition, are transitory. Institutions are not. How then do we establish new practices that can endure?

If institutional context matters during implementation, then the dominant ways of researching, understanding, and promoting innovation are wrong. Existing theory and practice fail to recognize these institutional opportunities and constraints. Current theories for understanding how to foster enduring change in the implementation of innovation are inadequate. I bring together public management, policy studies, implementation, and institutional theory to create a framework for understanding how innovation is implemented. Public management, policy studies, and implementation theory deal well with the concrete realities faced by real, live people in the innovation process. Institutional theory deals well with broader formal and informal forces that shape individual action, the structural parameters that constrain or facilitate innovation, and the cultural frames that influence response to change. These broad literatures do not adequately leverage the lessons from the others. The integration of these literatures results in a more comprehensive analytical framework for understanding opportunities and obstacles to innovation.

The integrated framework presented here suggests that there are ideal conditions that foster innovation over time. These include (a) individuals who are motivated and working within workplace social norms and the dominant agency or organizational culture that supports the innovation or the innovative practice; (b) structures that facilitate clear rules and communication, incentives that induce compliance with innovative practice, political environments that are open to innovation, and awareness of resistance and measures to address, mitigate, or otherwise neutralize opposition; and (c) strategies to frame problems to support innovative practice, capitalize on shocks or focusing events if they occur, and use of innovation to enhance legitimacy. Seldom are these ideal conditions satisfied, which is why innovation faces challenges in its implementation. Learning how to compensate when ideal conditions are not met is the key to fostering greater practical success. Likewise, becoming more sensitive to conditions that can thwart the chance of innovation's longer term success may help better prioritize how resources are expended.

The lessons that flow from this work challenge the conventional wisdom about the optimistic possibilities for innovation. Change is hard, especially within a long-established institutional context. There are limits to what individuals can accomplish on their own, and this runs counter to long-held cultural beliefs and scholarly research about entrepreneurism and innovation. Rather, the findings in this work suggest that for innovations to thrive, they must strategically compensate by building structural foundations to compete with the institutions they seek to change or replace. This finding counters conventional wisdom in the policy studies and public management literature about the role of entrepreneurs in innovation processes.[7] An appreciation for institutional forces causes us to rethink the role for policy entrepreneurs, given their ephemeral presence compared with the relative permanency of institutions. While policy entrepreneurs may be effective in setting agendas and forging or forcing policy windows to open, these actions may be only temporary unless structural supports are built that can compete with existing institutions or adaptive strategies are adopted to operate within overlapping and interconnected governance frameworks. By challenging conventional wisdom, I deal more realistically with the institutional obstacles that impede innovation and its longer term implementation.

WHAT IS INNOVATION?

Much like beauty, innovation is in the eye of the beholder. Underlying interest in innovation stems from an improved way of doing something, presumably to serve society better, but the scope or scale of change may cause different people to label something innovative while others might not. Some innovations are incremental; others are paradigm changing. Policy innovation is valued in our society because it means that someone has found a better way of problem solving. Laurence O'Toole defines policy innovation as "patterns of activities to achieve a new goal or improve the pursuit of an established one."[8] Everett M. Rogers famously characterized innovation from an individual's standpoint. For Rogers, an innovation is an idea, practice, or object that is perceived as new by the individual adopting it.[9] For others, innovative policies and programs are new to the entities adopting them, and they represent significant departures from previous activities and responses to problems.[10] In this respect, innovation incrementally can affect existing programs or policies, but it also can be the product of something entirely new. Some seek to use existing resources better; others seek to reinvent the processes of government.[11] Consequently, innovation is an end result as well as a process. For the purposes of this book, an innovation is a new program or process for the individuals adopting it.

People often think of innovation as technological improvement. As a technical exercise, it falls within the domain of invention and discovery and under the purview of the technocrat, manager, scientist, or expert who conceives or controls it. In this way the innovation is divorced easily from the institutional context that affects its adoption and sustained use. However, if innovation is understood as a new instrument, tool, or approach that is embedded within existing individual, structural, and cultural processes, then the connection to the broader institutional context is inescapable. While innovation can be understood as technological improvement, separating innovation from the broader circumstances where change must be tested and embraced is hazardous to the long-term survival of the original promise of the innovation.

Self-regulation, coregulation, initiated regulation, and *voluntary regulation* are four broad categories of innovative arrangements. The four categories are distinguished according to government involvement and the binding nature of the action stemming from the instrument, as indicated in table 1.1. Self-regulation occurs when an organized group regulates the behavior of its members.[12] Self-regulation does not involve government and is typified by situations where an industry, profession, or community group establishes codes of practice, guidelines, or other norms or rules to control or alter behavior. The actions taken by the group are not legally binding. For instance, the Chemical Manufacturers Association adopted a self-regulating program called Responsible Care in 1988.[13] Responsible Care consists of ten guiding principles that focus on environmental and safety responsibility as well as on public accountability. All Chemical Manufacturers Association members are required to participate in Responsible Care and must sign a commitment to do so. Likewise, the American Forest & Paper Association adopted the Sustainable Forestry Initiative, a self-regulatory program in 1995.[14] The Sustainable Forestry Initiative is a combination of environmental objectives and performance measures that integrate the business of forestry with the desire for sustained ecological diversity. Member companies that fail to meet the standards set through the Sustainable Forestry Initiative program are expelled from the American Forest & Paper Association. Self-regulation works through

CHAPTER 1

Table 1.1: Categories of Innovation

	Government Involved	**Government Not Involved**
Binding Action	*Coregulation* Actions are legally binding. Organized group jointly negotiates targets and strategies. Peer pressure and external government authority verify and ratify action. Government is involved. Government requires regulation. Regulation is decided by other parties or in conjunction with government.	*Initiated Regulation* Actions are legally binding. A group or individuals place an issue on the ballot for ratification by the public at large, in effect bypassing government. Government is not involved. Individuals outside of government require action and circumvent government to force action.
Nonbinding Action	*Voluntary Regulation* Actions are not legally binding. Individual entities agree to unilateral deeds or actions that have a positive regulatory outcome. There is no legal basis for coercion, but emphasis is placed on a custodial or stewardship ethic. Government is involved either as a member of a group or as establishing a framework for voluntary action.	*Self-Regulation* Actions are not legally binding. Organized group regulates members through peer pressure, internalized responsibility for compliance. No government involvement, but it may involve third-party (nongovernmental) certification.

peer pressure to uphold standards of behavior. Nongovernmental third parties also may participate in self-regulation by playing a watchdog role. While self-regulation has worked well in some circumstances, it can lack rigorous enforcement and employ inconsequential sanctions.[15] As observed by Peter Grabosky and John Braithwaite, "If self-regulation worked, Moses would have come down from the Mountain with the Ten Guidelines."[16]

Coregulation involves mandated regulations by government, but it allows other entities to influence the creation, promotion, implementation, or enforcement (or some combination) of the regulation.[17] Government engages directly in the coregulatory process by jointly negotiating targets and strategies and providing external verification or ratification or both. The resulting actions are legally binding. For instance, new rules resulting from a stakeholder group process are subjected to government approval and oversight. Likewise a business could influence specific regulations within a larger regulatory framework provided by the government. Like self-regulation, coregulation also works through peer pressure to uphold standards of behavior, but within a framework of government enforcement.

Initiated regulation involves legally binding actions initiated directly by citizens or interest groups.[18] The direct initiative is a process that enables citizens to bypass their state legislature by placing proposed statutes and, in some states, constitutional amendments on the ballot. Citizens, frustrated with stagnation in legislatures, apparently resort to more direct measures to influence policymaking, including environmental policy. Today twenty-four states have some form of initiative process in their constitution. A popular application of the initiative process since the 1980s has been on growth, open space, and quality-of-life issues. Between 1996 and 2004, voters across the United States approved 1,071 open space ballot measures authorizing $27.3 billion on open space conservation at the state, county, and municipal levels.[19] Issues about growth management, open space, and parks and recreation were placed on the ballot by citizens and interest groups who gathered the required number of signatures and other constitutional and statutory requirements needed to comply with the initiative process. Once passed, the actions are legally binding.

Voluntary regulation comes about when an individual or group undertakes a regulatory action unilaterally without any coercive action.[20] Government is involved in voluntary regulation in one of two ways. Government may be part of a group that encourages a voluntary action or establishes a framework or guidelines under which voluntary activities are played out, or government may follow the lead of other participants in a more collaborative process.[21] In both cases the actions taken by constituent members of the voluntary activity are not binding. The EPA's 33/50 and Green Lights/Energy Star programs are examples of voluntary agreements that involve the government establishing guidelines through which voluntary action takes place. Government, in the form of the EPA, provided frameworks for voluntary participation by industry in toxics reduction and energy savings. Various companies elected to participate voluntarily in the 33/50 program, which targeted seventeen priority chemicals with a goal of 33 percent reduction in releases and transfers of these chemicals by 1992 and a 50 percent reduction by 1995.[22] Green Lights is a voluntary pollution prevention program incorporated into EPA's Energy Star program. Following its inception Green Lights signed up 5 percent of all commercial office space to install energy-efficient lighting in less than three years.[23] Voluntary agreements also have been used in land protection and biodiversity conservation where government has no purview due to private property ownership.

Self-regulation, coregulation, initiated regulation, and voluntary regulation were increasingly popular in the 1980s and 1990s as alternative means to traditional environmental and natural resource regulation. The scholarly and practitioner literature is filled with stories describing new innovations in environmental and natural resource policy.[24] What we do not understand is why such innovations persist and what factors influence their perseverance. Public management research, policy studies, implementation theory, and neo-institutionalist literature are helpful for framing how to understand some of the challenges to and opportunities for innovation.

INNOVATION, IMPLEMENTATION, AND POLICY ENTREPRENEURS

I ask: Why are some innovations implemented, while others are not? Clearly, many authors have written about aspects of innovation. Much of this literature approaches innovation in an uncritical manner. Too little attention is given to whether innovations are actually implemented. Too much attention is showered on the heroic actions of the manager or entrepreneur in the process. Individual motivating factors are largely ignored. Policy and management scholars have failed to learn from each other, often writing about the same topic but unaware of each other's work. Almost universally the institutionalist perspective is ignored, leading to overly optimistic expectations for innovations' potential.

Much of what has been written about policy innovation focuses on how innovations appear, are chosen, or are diffused, while the complexities of implementing, evaluating, or terminating innovations have received significantly less attention.[25] In much of the policy literature, innovation begins when new ideas are placed on the agenda. This can occur when a new policy idea coincides with a favorable political environment and an appropriately framed problem definition.[26]

There are many types of catalysts that can induce policy change. These triggering actions go by many different names, including focusing events, external shocks, and windows of opportunity.[27] Specific events also can precipitate change or innovation in the policy arena. These could be natural disasters, venue shifts, or new scientific information.[28]

Subsystems and macro politics set the stage for innovation to occur at the national level.[29] Subsystems can be characterized as iron triangles, issue niches, or issue networks, while macro politics is the domain of Congress and the presidency. The two arenas are connected through an interlocking web of federated institutions and interactive jurisdictions. Large-scale innovation occurs when equilibrium is disrupted by a punctuation or focusing event in the macro political environment. National events, such as court rulings or changes in administration, create opportunity for action and the promotion of innovative ideas to key constituencies, including interest groups and government officials. The media are used strategically to promote ideas beyond the elites—where the idea initially takes hold. With respect to environmental and natural resource issues, in recent years the politics of punctuation has created opportunities for innovation within the subsystems where the politics of equilibrium previously dominated. Symbolic images and the language of market and democracy have been used widely to promote many environmental and natural resource innovations that embraced decentralized, individualistic choices. These broad-scale factors have created favorable conditions at state and local levels for innovation to occur throughout the federated system of governance.

The scholarly work on who initiates or promotes innovative activities focuses dominantly on those who hold formal political power, namely, governmental actors. Great emphasis also is placed on the role of the policy entrepreneur, especially policy entrepreneurs within government.[30] Policy entrepreneurs are influential individuals internal or external to an agency who work to get innovative ideas on the agenda. They are held up as paragons of policy change.[31] As summarized by Nancy C. Roberts and Paula J. King, these entrepreneurs "advocate new ideas and develop proposals; define and reframe problems; specify policy alternatives; broker the ideas among the many policy actors, mobilize public opinion and help set the decision making agenda."[32] With conviction, energy, and creativity, policy entrepreneurs can transform the policy status quo. Likewise, attention is given to networks of professional policy practitioners or entrepreneurs who spread ideas to new places thereby replicating innovation to different locales. Scholarship about policy entrepreneurs often focuses on their roles placing issues on the policy, and especially, the state and federal legislative, agenda. Their role in implementation is much less well understood, if not neglected.

The public management literature tends to emphasize the individual manager.[33] Sometimes referred to as the "hero" model of leadership in New Public Management, this literature emphasizes the role of the entrepreneur in fostering innovation.[34] Research tends to focus on managerial characteristics as predictors of innovation adoption or implementation.[35] Managers influence organizational culture by motivating, enabling, building capacity, controlling resources, and scouring the environment, but this is limited to the activities within their purview and control. There is an overall failure to acknowledge the broader structural and cultural forces at play that can facilitate or obstruct the longer term success of the innovation.

As has already been noted, scholars have arguably made more theoretical headway in explaining how innovations emerge, are chosen, or are diffused than in understanding how they are implemented.[36] While the study of implementation has stymied scholars, it nonetheless is a critical part of public management and policy studies that provides valuable insights into the persistence of innovation.[37] Rarely have the innovation and implementation literatures been joined.

INNOVATION AND IMPLEMENTATION

Three generations of implementation studies have shifted back and forth in epistemological stance and methodological approaches between top-down and bottom-up perspectives.[38] More recently, scholars have laid out contingency theories of implementation in which both bottom-up and top-down processes work simultaneously.[39] In this view, effective implementation of innovation is a function of multiple interrelated activities and capabilities. The challenge is to identify and understand the factors that are relevant to the specific innovation and to see whether they help to explain the potential for innovation success or failure.

From the top-down perspective, effectively implementing an innovative policy is a function of aligning formal structures and incentives. Implementation is a rational administrative process with a formal institutional structure, focused information, and resource allocation central to the policy goal.[40] Minimizing communication distortions between principals and agents helps to remedy problems;[41] targeted incentives and accountability mechanisms influence implementation compliance.[42] However, the complexity of environmental and natural resource governance creates problems for aligning these structures and processes. The federated system of governance rests within international, national, state, regional, and local structures and involves a variety of public, private, and nongovernmental actors all working at different levels. The nested structure provides a framework for understanding how the variety of public, private, and nongovernmental institutions functions together in a complex system.

Beginning predominantly in the late 1960s and 1970s, the number of environmental laws and regulations began to increase markedly (these dynamics are detailed more extensively in chapter 2). As the number of statutes proliferated, the administrative complexity required for the implementation of the laws also increased.[43] Actors emerged at every level within the system, with some gaining greater prominence at times than others. For instance, prior to the 1960s, actors at the federal or national level dominated the environmental governance landscape. Beginning in the 1960s and 1970s, more actors emerged on the federal and national level, as well as some grassroots actors at the local level. In the 1980s, the Reagan era resulted in a greater delegation of power to the states while also creating an additional incentive for greater interest-group action at the state level. In the late 1980s and throughout the 1990s, a variety of local organizations proliferated to flesh out the bottom-most level in the structure; altogether this increasing complexity made it difficult to align structures, incentives, and processes from the top down to ensure implementation.[44]

These intergovernmental aspects of environmental and natural resource governance have great implications for innovation.[45] Innovation occurs in situations involving numerous actors from multiple levels of governmental and nongovernmental domains, but the complexity of these interdependent systems is overlooked. The need to integrate across these fragmented systems has given way to the need to collaborate. While contributing to complexity, U.S. federalism is also an enduring model of collaborative problem solving.[46] The capacity to achieve effective, innovative outcomes depends on the ability to establish meaningful relationships with other institutions of governance. Innovation often means that public managers need to work creatively and cooperatively across bureaucratic domains.[47] Effective implementation therefore may lead us to ask what factors sustain and support these types of innovative activity.[48]

Suggesting that there are different conditions under which innovative approaches might best be implemented, Peter May and others focus on structural aspects of policy design to facilitate coordination for implementation. When there are fundamental tensions among layers of government over goals or means of reaching goals, top-down, coercive implementation designs are needed. When there are no fundamental dis-agreements with policy aims, coercion is not necessary and more cooperative designs are employed. According to May and others, in situations of tension between layers of government, the onus is on higher-level governments to create innovative ways of operating and impose them on lower levels. In contrast, when there is little tension, local government can experiment with cooperative intergovernmental policies.[49] Accordingly, local governments then are left to devise innovative solutions to their own problems.

The nested governance structures in a federated system create both opportunities and obstacles for innovation. We know that the conservative nature of the U.S. politi-cal system, which often favors the status quo, makes it difficult for change to emerge in the first place.[50] Even if an innovation takes hold, interests vested in the status quo, also known as policy monopolies, can obstruct change. The dynamics of federalism, separation of powers, and jurisdictional overlap can provide great obstacles to new ideas, policies, and change. Conversely, due to the multiple policy venues available in a federated system, if an attempt at innovation is stymied in one place, it may be successful in another.

In light of this complexity of nested governance structures, it is striking that the literature on innovation focuses almost exclusively on the federal or state level. For instance, states as a subset of participants in the innovation game are modeled exten-sively in the innovation literature, especially the propensity to adopt from or diffuse innovation to other states.[51] But states do not act in a vacuum and rather are part of an increasingly complex web of governance with interdependent parts. Causal models that define specific relationships among dependent and independent variables drive much of this work.[52] More is understood about the dynamics within state-level in-novation and diffusion than at other levels within intergovernmental systems.

The public management literature has emphasized the presence of networks and network structure that integrate across jurisdictions.[53] These authors often take the bottom-up view of considering what factors facilitate or impede innovation from the manager's perspective. Top-down implementation theory suggests that administrative rules; human and financial resources; communication and information exchange; and benefit, sanction, and monitoring structures should support compliance with an innovative effort. Surely these factors need to be taken into account in a framework that seeks to explain how innovation is effectively implemented. However, the rational top-down implementation model loses some of its precision within the complex world of intergovernmental organization and federated institutions that typify environmental and natural resource governance.

Top-down implementation theory can be contrasted to bottom-up implementa-tion theory. Bottom-up theorists urge consideration of the individual perspective in the implementation process. Relationships in working environments take the form of norms and arise as a result of previous experience. Organizational culture, social norms, and a desire to preserve harmony in the workplace shape individual actors' predisposition toward change.[54] Within a federated system of governance, the degree of congruence between dominant values within a federal or state agency and lower levels of government will affect the degree of shared understanding generated for a given policy. Accordingly, analysis needs to focus on the informal rules, experience with and perceived legitimacy of proposed actions, and workplace consensus about predisposition to change.

The perspectives of individual participants in innovation processes are largely ignored. These perspectives are important to consider since they color the way that individuals will interact and shape the motivation for participation. The power to implement an innovation rests ultimately with those most closely affected by the innovation. Consider for instance that in the policy entrepreneur literature the predisposition toward innovation is assumed to be favorable, and uniformly so. Policy entrepreneurs work with others to adopt the innovation, abide by it, or at a minimum not to reject the idea or obstruct it. Likewise, it is assumed that the innovation is treated as a welcomed change, not something that can pose a threat to an established operating order. New policy directions often are likely to create friction. However, many studies assume that an innovation is adopted wholesale without significant adaptations and promoted through a bureaucratic structure where the predisposition to genuine innovation is arguably less likely. Since "one person's innovation is another person's destruction," innovation is fraught with policy termination problems, but seldom are these addressed.[55]

Many policy authors do not consider motivation or behavioral aspects that may provide individual incentives for innovation. Sabatier and Jenkins-Smith are notable in the attention that they pay to perspective and their emphasis on the role of belief systems and core values, and how these affect various interactions in their theory of policy change and learning.[56] They theorize that belief systems are resistant to change except under specific conditions of external shocks, directives from superiors, or compelling empirical evidence that will alter beliefs.

In contrast, public management research has devoted considerable attention to understanding the factors that influence manager perspective and behavior. Bardach focused on behavior and process as keys to creativity in innovative activity, including collaboration.[57] This approach stands in stark relief to Osborne and Gaebler's structural emphasis on formal reorganization. Bardach suggests that altering the working relationships among individuals in organizations might be a better way to proceed. Others see shared beliefs, values, and attitudes as well as other individual motivational factors such as access to information, financial, and technical resources, the chance to be part of a network and work with others, and the opportunity to influence policy as important factors for managers.[58]

For bottom-up theorists, individuals respond to or behave according to cues that influence the priorities that they take into account. Individual actors will be predisposed toward change depending on their organizational culture, social norms, and desire to preserve harmony in the workplace. In the realm of environmental and natural resource policy, both top-down and bottom-up factors must be considered with the nested structure of governance systems influenced by multiple actors at various levels. For top-down implementation theorists, this means focusing on administrative and communication structures and whether they are aligned to support change on the ground. The probability of innovation being implemented therefore increases when top-down and bottom-up factors are mutually supportive.

INNOVATION AND INSTITUTIONAL THEORY

Institutional theory does not address innovation directly, but it does address change. Three branches of institutionalism identify different processes that foster change. Rational choice institutionalism emphasizes the individual's role in innovation processes. Historical institutionalism explores the arenas and structures within which innovation may happen. Sociological institutionalism considers the larger cultural and cognitive aspects that frame the institutional structures within which innovation takes place.

Rational choice scholars see institutions as intentionally created by individuals to achieve cooperative solutions to collective-action dilemmas.[59] Institutions persist when they provide more benefits to the relevant actors than alternative institutional forms. They evolve and are altered by human beings.[60] Consequently, innovation is most likely to occur when there is discontent with the status quo, coupled with the perception that change will leave the individual better off than the status quo.[61] Individuals will seek to innovate when the benefits to them outweigh the costs of effecting change.

Historical institutionalists focus on the impact of power struggles on institutional outcomes and the way these outcomes shape further rounds of political struggles over policy and rules.[62] This makes historical institutionalism particularly useful for analyzing innovation because it suggests the need to focus on specific arenas where change can occur. As opposed to rational choice scenarios of freely contracting individuals seeking innovations that improve the status quo, historical institutionalists see a world in which institutions give some interests disproportionate access to the decision-making process, resulting in those groups with access winning out over those without it.[63] While individuals may be discontented with a given situation and seek to innovate, these efforts may be obstructed by larger power dynamics and vested interests. In contrast to rational choice institutionalism, historical institutionalists see a world where the individual's ability to effect change is constrained by historical inertia. Institutions themselves are significant barriers to innovation, as their persistence through the historical landscape influences development along certain "paths," structuring responses to new challenges.[64] Critical choice junctures and developmental pathways cause institutions to evolve in ways constrained by past trajectories, and as vested interests develop, innovation becomes costly, thereby limiting future choices.[65] The implication is that individuals seeking change in the status quo must operate within a historical institutional structure, which is characterized by substantial inertia and tendencies toward maintaining that status quo.

Sociological institutionalists define institutions to include not just formal rules, procedures, and norms but also symbol systems, cognitive scripts, and moral templates that provide the "frames of meaning" guiding human action.[66] Sociological institutionalists provide a counterargument to rational choice institutionalists, who claim that most institutional forms and procedures are adopted simply because they are the most efficient means to an end or the product of a strategic analysis of cost and benefits, in part due to the concept of "embeddedness." Embeddedness encompasses the idea that once individuals establish a routine, they tend to stick with it; hence, it becomes embedded in a cognitive, cultural, structural, or political context. Potential avenues for effecting change come through two primary means—framing events or shocks. Goffman defines a frame as a "schemata of interpretation" that allows individuals or groups "to locate, perceive, identify, and label" events and occurrences enabling the production of meaning, organizing experiences, and guiding actions.[67] Symbolic communication, such as nationalist or ethnic rhetoric, can provide the basis for collective action. Framing also has been used in the policy literature to shape action or change policy direction.[68] Endogenous or exogenous shocks to the system may disrupt existing cognitive processes and provide a window for fostering a change in thinking and hence innovation.[69] This is consistent with those who believe that major crises provide the impetus for public-sector innovation.[70] Consider that the disaster literature capitalizes on these sociological constructs as explanatory variables for understanding how change is initiated.[71] In the absence of shocks to the system, alternative courses of action may be limited to existing institutional templates, restricting the range of innovative possibility. From the sociological perspective, "individuals are viewed as 'embedded' in so many social, economic, and political relationships beyond their control and even cognition that it is almost absurd to speak of utility-maximizing and rational behavior in a strictly economic sense."[72] Because of the importance of these relationships, innovations may be chosen because of their perceived legitimacy, rather than their efficiency in achieving desired outcomes. According to sociological institutionalists, organizations adopt a new institutional practice, not because it enhances the means-ends efficiency of the organization, but because it enhances the social legitimacy of the organization to outsiders. For instance, an organization may adopt new practices such as cost-benefit analysis or collaboration not because they will necessarily make work more efficient, but because they are socially accepted practices that enhance the status and legitimacy of the organization. Not using these practices will delegitimize the organization in the view of outsiders.

Much of the work on institutionalism has not been applied to natural resource governance. Elinor Ostrom's work is an exception. Among other things, she elaborates on the interconnected nature of rulemaking structures and how this affects resource management.[73] She identifies operational rules, collective choice rules, and constitutional rules that apply to three levels of decision making about environmental resources. Operational rules structure the day-to-day decisions about how to appropriate resources, provide information, monitor actions, and enforce rules. These are the day-to-day decisions made by people on the ground most closely connected to the resources in question. Collective choice rules affect the policy and management decisions that determine the operational rules for managing a resource. These rules provide a framework for how the processes related to the formation of the policy about the resource in question should be managed. Constitutional rules determine who is eligible to participate and the specific governance structure to be used in crafting collective choice rules. All sets of rules interact and structure activity at another level.[74]

Given the interconnected nature of the system of rules and the crucial role that some levels play in effecting change at other levels, it is impossible to treat a change or innovation at one level independently from another level. Two points are especially salient when innovative practices are considered. First, establishing rules at one level without putting into place complementary rules at the other levels produces an incomplete system. So, for instance, innovation at the collective level might not be successful in the long run if it is not supported by constitutional-level changes. Second, Goodin notes that rules at each successive level of the hierarchy are increasingly costly to change.[75] Consequently, innovation at the collective level may be more feasible than innovation required at the constitutive level. This is because extensive commitments (infrastructure, staffing, budgets, programs) are made based on the expectation that the rules will continue, which dramatically increases the cost of modifying arrangements, particularly at the higher levels. Also, efforts to change rules higher in the hierarchy require greater levels of consensus among actors. Thus, it is important to recognize the interdependent complexities among the nested levels of governance and how other levels might facilitate or impinge on the innovation's long-term prospects.

From an institutional perspective then, the probability of implementing innovation increases when different levels of decision making are mutually supportive and all three processes are aligned.[76] For rational choice institutionalists this means focusing on individuals and their perceptions. Innovation is most likely to happen when individuals perceive themselves as deprived (cost > benefit) under the status quo and as likely better off by change. The impetus for innovation rests on the discontented individuals who are free to devise alternative possible solutions. Organizations can facilitate collective action among these individuals by providing incentives and resources to alter the cost-benefit calculus to encourage innovation. For historical institutionalists, institutions channel the flow of ideas, create incentives for political actors, and help determine the political meaning of policy choices, thereby shaping the potential for innovation to take hold. Consequently, there must be an opening in the political structure that allows marginalized groups to gain access to power and influence the system. Innovation most likely will be "bounded" within the structural context within which it occurs and spread only to the extent that it is supported by the broader context.[77] For sociological institutionalists the determining factors that influence innovation are the cognitive frames that shape what types of information are perceived relevant to the individual, and the cultural constraints that lead an individual to question if change is even possible. Shocks to the system provide the opportunity for learning from this perspective. Framing processes can condition people's perception that they are aggrieved and that by acting collectively they can improve the situation. So the probability of innovation is contingent on individuals with an incentive to change working through structures that are open to change with frames or shocks that facilitate or catalyze action.

While far from exhaustive, these applications of neo-institutional concepts to the dynamics of innovation are intended to expand the conceptual tool set for understanding environmental and natural resource governance. No doubt those who study each of these branches of institutionalism in depth will find fault with some of the specifics of this synthesis. However, this should not discredit the utility of the institutional approach as it is applied to this new context of environmental and natural resource governance. The better we understand the dynamics of innovation, implementation, and institutions, the better we may be equipped to understand why some innovative practices fail while others succeed.

FRAMEWORK FOR ANALYSIS

Public management, policy studies, implementation, and institutional theory provide insights into understanding how innovation might be implemented. In table 1.2, these factors are combined under three macro categorizations according to individual, structure, and culture. These factors are arranged in figure 1.1 to illustrate how individuals are influenced by the structures that surround them and how culture influences both structure and individuals.

The factors are derived from the literature review in the previous section. For individuals these factors include the following: *motivation, norms and harmony,* and *congruence.* Motivation represents the stimulus that drives individuals to alter the status quo situation. Drawing from rational choice institutional theory and policy and management theory, motivation takes into account what drives a policy entrepreneur or leader to effect change. Theory suggests that discontented actors are often the ones who are motivated to undertake change. Likewise, these individuals must be free to devise alternative possible solutions. This suggests that they must have some level of authority to undertake change.

Norms and harmony take into consideration individuals' desire to preserve good working relationships. Bottom-up implementation theory and sociological institutionalism suggest that if workplace norms are consistent with the implementation of the innovation, then workplace harmony will be preserved, making it easier for the individual to go along with the innovative practice. If the innovation is inconsistent

Table 1.2: A Framework for Analyzing the Implementation of Innovation

Individuals	Structures	Culture
Motivation: The impetus for innovation rests with discontented individuals who are free to devise alternative possible solutions (rational choice institutionalism; policy/management entrepreneur literature)	*Rules and communication:* Administrative rules, communication, and information exchange support compliance (top-down implementation theory)	*Shocks:* Shocks to the system provide the opportunity for alternative courses of action (sociological institutionalism; management and policy studies; agenda-setting literature)
Norms and Harmony: Social norms and a desire to preserve harmony in the workplace shape individual actors' predisposition toward change (bottom-up implementation theory; sociological institutionalism)	*Incentives:* Organizations provide incentives and resources to alter the cost-benefit calculus to support innovation (rational choice institutional theory; top-down implementation theory)	*Framing:* Framing processes can condition people's perception that they are aggrieved and that by acting collectively they can improve the situation (sociological institutionalism; management and policy studies)
Congruence: Congruence between dominant values within a federal or state agency and lower levels of government will affect individual support for a given innovation (bottom-up implementation theory; sociological institutionalism)	*Opening:* The political structure allows marginalized groups an opportunity to foster change (historical institutionalism; common property literature)	*Legitimacy:* New practices enhance the social legitimacy of the organization (sociological institutionalism)
	Resistance: Inertia in the existing institution creates resistance to new practices. Efforts may be obstructed by larger power dynamics and vested interests (historical institutionalism; punctuated equilibrium theory)	

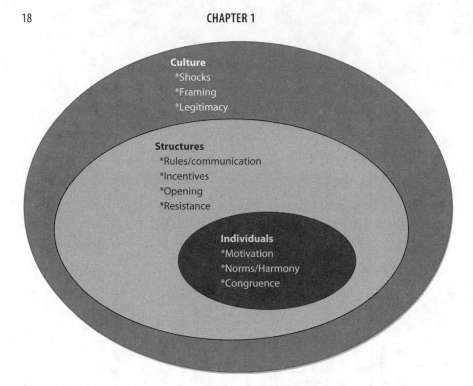

Figure 1.1: Relationships among Individual, Structural, and Cultural Factors That Influence the Implementation of Innovation

with workplace norms, then individuals who desire to pursue an innovative practice may find themselves in disharmony with fellow workers.

Congruence implies that individuals perform within the culture of an agency or organization and that a dominant culture permeates expectations within that nested structure. If individual values are incongruent with the dominant agency values, then this can create difficulty for the individual to support innovative practice.

Structure includes *rules and communication, incentives, opening, and resistance.* Rules and communication are derived from top-down implementation theory, which suggests that the structures within which innovation takes place should provide clear administrative support for innovative practice. If the administrative structure fosters clear lines of communication, written rules, and unambiguous information exchange, then there is a greater chance for the implementation of that innovation. Incentives draw from rational choice institutionalism and top-down implementation theory, which imply that the individual cost-benefit calculus to participate in innovative practice can be shaped toward compliance with the right incentives. If the structure provides the right incentives, then the innovation stands a better chance of being implemented over time. Drawing from historical institutionalism and common property literature, opening suggests that the political structure must be open to change and that the opportunity to open the political structure is not equal for all individuals or groups. If the political opportunity structure is closed to select groups, then opening the political structure can be challenging. Once opened, it is easier to create change at operational levels in the political structure than collective or constitutive levels. If change is effected at a collective or constitutive level, it may be longer lasting than change at the operational level. Resistance includes inertial forces that hinder change. Innovations are not brought into a world free of existing structures and power dynamics. Vested interests often seek to preserve the status quo. Historical institutionalism and punctuated equilibrium theory address the power dynamics, interest groups, and policy monopolies within existing structures that can obstruct change.

Culture entails *shocks*, *framing*, and *legitimacy*. Shocks refer to catalytic events that provide opportunity for reimagining the possibility for change. Sociological institutionalists suggest that we are all embedded in frames of reference that we do not question. A shock may provide the impetus to look at the world differently and motivate change. The public management and policy studies literature is replete with similar concepts, such as focusing events, external shocks, and windows of opportunity that embody the same phenomenon. Framing is a second and alternative pathway for breaking out of a traditional cultural worldview. Coming from sociological institutionalism, but also embraced in the public management and policy studies literature, framing implies that broader problem definitions and alternatives can be shaped to incite action. Often frames are invoked to make people feel aggrieved or deprived, thereby providing the impetus to take action. Finally, legitimacy, as proposed by sociological institutionalists, suggests that innovative practices may be adopted and maintained because they validate the organization or agency in a meaningful way within the broader culture within which the organization operates.

The hypothesis posited here suggests that when the individual, structural, and cultural categories are aligned and sustained, then the probability increases that innovation is implemented. When the categories are misaligned and/or unsupported at one or more level in the hierarchy, then the probability decreases for innovation. Implicit in the literature from which the framework is crafted is the relative equal importance of the three categories of factors—individual, structure, and culture. A systematic application of the framework tests the veracity of this assumption.

I apply the framework detailed above to three case studies of innovation. The case studies were selected based on a continuum of implementation efficacy—long-term implementation success, intermittent implementation success, and long-term implementation failure. The length of implementation efficacy functions as a dependent variable that allows the investigation of the independent variables—individual, structural, and cultural processes—on these outcomes. Three patterns of implementation response emerged from the data—the persistent alignment of individual, structural, and cultural processes; intermittent alignment of individual, structural, and cultural processes; and misalignment of individual, structural, and cultural processes. The patterns illustrate why some innovations persist and are implemented over time, while others are not. The empirical chapters are presented according to these patterns.

APPROACH, CASE STUDIES, AND ORGANIZATION

The case studies selected for inclusion were chosen from the many I investigated over the previous fifteen years. To help focus my search, I settled on identifying innovative practices that had been in existence for at least a decade. I defined "innovative practice" as something that was perceived as new by the entities adopting it while also representing a significant departure from previous activities and responses to problems. "Innovative practice" became my unit of analysis. The cases are "typical" in that I did not control for organizational type, substantive focus, or the level of implementation. Rather, I sought cases that took innovative approaches over ten years and had variation in the dependent variable—persistence of innovation over time. This allowed me to make inferences about the independent variables of individual, structural, and cultural factors.

Chapter 2 details the historical evolution of the nested structures in the environmental and natural resource governance system. The innovations that occurred in the 1980s and 1990s were predicated on the patterns of participation and changes to decision making that emerged prior to the 1960s and during the 1960s and 1970s. Against this backdrop of national context, I also detail three specific governance subsystems that relate to the three case studies discussed. These subsystems include the land protection governance system, the watershed governance system, and the forest governance system. This background is included in chapter 3 so that the case study chapters (3, 4, and 5) can focus exclusively on the narrative flow and framework analysis without disrupting the flow with the historical contextual details.

Chapters 3 through 5 utilize the framework and document cases where I saw the persistent alignment of individual, structural, and cultural processes; intermittent alignment of individual, structural, and cultural processes; and misalignment of individual, structural, and cultural processes. Each of these chapters follows the same organizational structure. I present a narrative description of the innovation and then use the analytical framework to illustrate how individual, structural, and cultural characteristics play a role in the implementation of the innovation (or not).

Chapter 3 explores a case study where an innovation emerged and persisted over time. This is due in part to the persistent alignment of individual, structural, and cultural characteristics. As early as the 1980s, Colorado was on its way to experiencing a crisis in protecting its valuable open spaces and scenic lands. Too few resources devoted to protecting and preserving open spaces, growing populations, and rapid development threatened the vistas, amenities, and values that were quintessentially Coloradoan. A group of activists—Citizens for Great Outdoors Colorado—recognized this threat and the inability of the state legislature to address it. Using Colorado's initiative process, the group created a new quasi-regulatory structure to carry out land protection efforts that became known as Great Outdoors Colorado (GOCO). The GOCO program emerged out of an initiated regulatory effort that was placed on the statewide ballot in 1992. Passing with 58 percent of the popular vote, GOCO takes half of the net proceeds from lottery sales and devotes these financial resources to open space protection and enhancement through a competitive grant process. As of 2009, GOGO has invested more than $575 million in over 2,800 projects that have protected 850,000 acres of open space throughout Colorado.[78]

GOCO is illustrative of the way the initiative process was used elsewhere in the 1990s and 2000s to diffuse power to a broader set of participants and open up new avenues for environmental and natural resource decision making. Little did Citizens for GOCO know that they were at the forefront of a trend that would continue through the 1990s and into the 2000s. The GOCO amendment was but one of thirty-five initiatives placed on the Colorado ballot throughout the 1990s.[79] The use of the initiative, in Colorado and other states, became an increasingly popular policy tool in the 1990s, especially for environmental and natural resource policy. In Colorado, the number of initiatives on the ballot in the 1990s surpassed the total number that was on the ballot in the 1970s and 1980s combined.[80] Since the initiative process was adopted in Colorado in 1910, 175 initiative and referenda have been on the ballot.[81] Of the 175, 124 of those were placed on the ballot from 1970 to 2000.[82] In Colorado the initiative process works by placing a constitutional amendment on the ballot by the electorate through a petition drive. Today twenty-four states have some form of initiative process in their constitution.

The dominant methods of data collection for the GOCO case study were archival document review and in-person and telephone interviews. The basis for the case study emerged from a research project in 1998 involving in-depth interviews with twenty-nine employees of county, city and town governments, nonprofit organizations, special districts, and statewide organizations who were grant applicants to GOCO. The interviews were tape-recorded and transcribed to facilitate analysis. In some instances, notes were taken when tape-recording was prohibited. All interviewees verified the transcripts to ensure accuracy. Four GOCO staff were interviewed on several occasions over a period of eighteen months between 1998 and 2000. Once the idea for this book germinated, I followed up with additional individuals who were formative in the creation of GOCO. Using a snowball sample, nine key informants were interviewed during between 1998 and 2001. These interviews were also transcribed and sent back to the interviewees for verification. Additional follow-up interviews were conducted via telephone in 2008. GOCO documents and records from 1992 to 2008 were reviewed, including historical documents from GOCO's archives, legislative histories, newspaper articles, and websites. My research assistant, Karl Wunderlich, was essential in helping me with the interviewing and archival document retrieval in the early stages of this project.

Chapter 4 illustrates how the intermittent alignment of individual, structural, and cultural processes leads to success at times and retrenchment at others. This chapter details Friends of the Cheat, a watershed group in West Virginia, and their innovative approach to mitigating acid mine drainage—an agreement called the River of Promise. Emerging after a mine disaster in 1994, Friends of the Cheat orchestrated a voluntary agreement with signatories committing resources to address the challenges of widespread non–point-source pollution from multiple polluters throughout their watershed. Problems with individual and structural processes have led Friends of the Cheat to be less effective at times than others. Nonetheless, Friends of the Cheat recovered from many of their challenges to continue to work on the persistent problem of acid mine drainage in their watershed. As of 2009, the group has completed ten watershed remediation projects, has additional ongoing projects, and has channeled millions of dollars in projects and studies to the watershed to assist in the long-term effort of watershed remediation. Regular monitoring indicates improvements in water quality at various places throughout the watershed. Biologists report recovering fish populations. Community residents recount anecdotal stories of seeing fish-eating species like osprey and other river-dwelling critters, such as beaver and river otter, which had disappeared from the river decades ago.

Friends of the Cheat is illustrative of other groups who have been part of the watershed movement in the 1980s and 1990s. Many of these groups were formed in response to persistent problems with water quality or water quantity issues for which traditional regulatory approaches had limited responses. Often working with government agencies, watershed groups have used different innovative approaches, including coregulation, voluntary regulation, and self-regulation to address the problems in their respective watersheds.

Several methods were employed to investigate and craft this case study. I was involved with Friends of the Cheat as a participant observer during its inception in 1994–1995. I was an original member of the board of directors until 1996. My formal role in the organization waned over the years as my researcher role waxed. Since 1995 I have kept a journal on my interaction with Friends of the Cheat. Formal methods of data collection for this case study include archival review, in-person interviews, and annual site visits (sometimes more than once a year) from 1995 to 2009. I conducted in-person interviews multiple times from 1995 to 2008 with the three executive directors and support staff. I also conducted in-person or telephone interviews with eight informants with key perspectives about the innovation. Individual interviews were circulated back to interviewees in some cases for verification. In other cases I sent a synthesized narrative account of the history and development of Friends of the Cheat to the key informants and asked them to verify whether my summary accurately reflected their lived experience. Corrections were made based on the feedback I received. Friends of the Cheat documents and records from 1995 to 2008 were reviewed including historical documents from Friends of the Cheat archives, correspondence, newsletters, newspaper articles, and websites.

Chapter 5 tackles a case of misalignment in individual, structural, and cultural processes as a way to explain the failure of implementation over time. In the late 1980s and early 1990s, conflict over failure to respect and serve local Hispano and environmental communities led to stalemate in timber management on the Camino Real Ranger District (Camino Real) in New Mexico's Carson National Forest. The arrival of a new district ranger on the Camino Real in 1990 led to an outreach effort in 1991 known as "horseback diplomacy" to understand how the needs of local communities could better be met by the district. A variety of innovative forest management practices emerged from these discussions and came to be collectively known as "Collaborative Stewardship." These voluntary efforts have faded with time and represent the only case of an innovation that has not lasted into the writing of this book.

The Camino Real and Collaborative Stewardship are illustrative of broader trends toward community forest management that began to surface in the late 1980s. Many communities were discouraged by the gridlock on national forests at the time and sought alternative management practices that could allow them to restore human and ecological communities alike. Community forestry practitioners have continued to be frustrated with the difficulties in working with the USFS, whose bureaucratic structure and practices do not fit well with the needs of local communities.

The dominant methods of data collection for this case study were archival document review; in-person, telephone, and e-mail interviews; and site visits. In 2000–2001, my research assistant, Donna Tucker, and I conducted thirteen in-person interviews with key informants associated with the innovations happening on the Camino Real. These interviews were tape-recorded and transcribed and returned to the interviewees for verification. Syntheses of an integrated narrative account of the Camino Real case study were returned to key participants in the process for their verification. Corrections were made based on the feedback from these individuals. In addition, we conducted trips to field sites in 2001 and 2002 and used photographic documentation to capture the people, processes, and outcomes from their work. Documents and records from 1997 to 2005 were reviewed, including historical documents from USFS archives, correspondence, newsletters, newspaper articles, and websites. Other academic- and research-oriented products were also helpful in triangulating the findings in this case study. Additional follow-up telephone interviews were conducted in 2008.

Chapter 6 synthesizes the findings of chapters 3 through 5 and revisits the framework presented in chapter 1. Theoretical lessons are presented, and I illustrate how the findings from the case studies both challenge and support the conventional wisdom about individual, structural, and cultural processes related to implementing innovation. More practical lessons also are detailed. These practical lessons are intended for practitioners and researchers who are interested in the applications that flow from the analytical framework and case studies. The intended purpose is to demonstrate the power of a more integrated framework for analyzing and diagnosing the challenges that face not only devising an innovative practice but implementing it over time in a dynamic environment.

This study has clear limitations. The empirical research is derived from three in-depth case studies, which I selected based on the dependent variable to create variation in the patterns of implementation response. This strategic selection introduces bias in the sample. While these case studies are rich in detail, they are not necessarily generalizable to a broader population. Nonetheless, the selection was intentional to build an argument, advance understanding, and put forward a model that can be refuted, verified, or improved upon by others. Alternative explanations for success and failure in implementing innovation are also possible. Even with these shortcomings, this study is offered in the spirit of moving our understanding of environmental and natural resource governance forward to better serve the public good.

NOTES

1. Daniel J. Fiorino, *The New Environmental Regulation* (Cambridge, MA: MIT Press, 2006).

2. North Carolina Department of Water Quality, North Carolina Non Point Management Program, http://h2o.enr.state.nc.us/nps/tarpam.htm (accessed September 19, 2002).

3. Lynn Maguire and E. Allen Lind, "Public Participation in Environmental Decisions: Stakeholders, Authorities and Procedural Justice," *International Journal of Global Environmental Issues* 3, no. 2 (2003): 133–48.

4. U.S. EPA, *Community Based Environmental Protection: A Resource Book for Protecting Ecosystems and Communities*, EPA 230-B-96-003 (September 1997); and U.S. EPA, *People, Places and Partnerships: A Progress Report on Community Based Environmental Protection*, EPA-100-R-97-003 (July 1997).

5. Industrial Economics, "Evaluation of Community-Based Environmental Protection Projects: Accomplishments and Lessons Learned" (Washington, DC: EPA Office of Planning, Analysis and Accountability and Office of Policy, Economics and Innovation, February 2001).

6. Kathleen Thelen and Sven Steinmo, "Historical Institutionalism in Comparative Politics," in *Structuring Politics: Historical Institutionalism in Comparative Analysis*, ed. Sven Steinmo, Kathleen Thelen, and Frank Longstreth (Cambridge: Cambridge University Press, 1992); Peter Hall, *Governing the Economy: The Politics of State Intervention in Britain and France* (New York: Oxford University Press, 1986); and B. Guy Peters, *Institutional Theory in Political Science: The New Institutionalism* (London: Pinter, 1999).

7. John W. Kingdon, *Agendas, Alternatives and Public Policies*, 2nd ed. (New York: Longman, 1995); Frank R. Baumgartner and Bryan D. Jones, *Agendas and Instability in American Politics* (Chicago: University of Chicago Press, 1993); Michael Mintrom, "Policy Entrepreneurs and the Diffusion of Innovation," *American Journal of Political Sciences* 41, no. 3 (1997): 738–70; and Tom Birkland, *After Disaster: Agenda Setting, Public Policy and Focusing Events* (Washington, DC: Georgetown University Press, 1997).

8. Laurence O'Toole Jr., "Implementing Public Innovations in Network Settings," *Administration and Society* 29, no. 2 (1997): 116.

9. Everett M. Rogers, *Diffusion of Innovations*, 4th ed. (New York: Free Press, 1995).

10. Robert E. Deyle, "Conflict, Uncertainty, and the Role of Planning and Analysis in Public-policy Innovation," *Policy Studies Journal* 22 (1994): 457–73; and Jack L. Walker, "The

Diffusion of Innovations among the American States," *American Political Science Review* 63 (1969): 880–99.

11. David Osborne and Ted Gaebler, *Reinventing Government* (Boston: Addison-Wesley, 1992).

12. Neil Gunningham and Peter Grabosky, with Peter Sinclair, *Smart Regulation: Designing Environmental Policy* (Oxford: Clarendon Press, 1998), 50–51.

13. Ronnie Garcia-Johnson, *Exporting Environmentalism: U.S. Multinational Chemical Corporations in Brazil and Mexico* (Cambridge, MA: MIT Press, 2000).

14. Sustainable Forestry Initiative, "The SFI Program: A Bold Approach to Sustainable Forest Management," www.afandpa.org/forestry/sfi/menu.html (accessed on January 3, 2002).

15. Toddie Steelman and Jorge Rivera, "Voluntary Environmental Programs in the United States: Whose Interests Are Served?" *Organization and Environment* 19, no. 4 (2006): 505–26.

16. Peter Grabosky and John Braithwaite, *Of Manners Gentle: Enforcement Strategies of Australian Business Regulatory Agencies* (Melbourne: Oxford University Press, 1986), 184.

17. Gunningham and Grabosky, *Smart Regulation*, 50–51.

18. The initiative process is in contrast to the referendum process, which is instigated by the state legislature.

19. Peter S. Szabo, "Noah at the Ballot Box: Status and Challenges," *BioScience* 57, no. 5 (2007): 424–27.

20. Gunningham and Grabosky, *Smart Regulation*, 56–57.

21. Tom Koontz, Toddi Steelman, JoAnn Carmin, Katrina Korfmacher, Cass Moseley, and Craig Thomas, *Collaborative Environmental Management: What Roles for Government?* (Washington, DC: Resources for the Future, 2004).

22. U.S. EPA, "33/50 Program: The Final Record," Washington, DC: EPA Office of Pollution Prevention and Toxics, EPA-745-R-99-004 (March 1999).

23. Gunningham and Grabosky, *Smart Regulation*, 58.

24. Fiorino, *New Environmental Regulation*; Ben Cashore, Graeme Auld, and Deanna Newsom, *Governing through Markets: Forest Certification and the Emergence of Non State Authority* (New Haven, CT: Yale University Press, 2004); Aseem Prakash and Matthew Potoski, *The Voluntary Environmentalists: Green Clubs, ISO 14001, and Voluntary Environmental Regulation* (Cambridge: Cambridge University Press, 2006); Julia Wondolleck and Steve L. Yaffee, *Making Collaboration Work: Lessons from Innovation in Natural Resource Management* (Covelo, CA: Island, 2000); Doug S. Kenney and William B. Lord, *Analysis of Institutional Innovation in the Natural Resources and Environmental Realm: The Emergence of Alternative Problem-solving Strategies in the American West*, Research Report 21 (RR-21) (Boulder: University of Colorado School of Law, Natural Resources Law Center, 1999); Gunningham and Grabosky, *Smart Regulation*; Mark Poffenberg, *Communities and Forest Management in Canada and the United States* (Berkley, CA: Working Group on Community Involvement in Forest Management, 1998); DeWitt John, *Civic Environmentalism: Alternatives to Regulation in States and Communities* (Washington, DC: Congressional Quarterly Press, 1994); Kathy K. Dhanda, "A Market-Based Solution to Acid Rain: The Case of the Sulfur Dioxide Trading Program," *Journal of Public Policy & Marketing* 18, no. 2 (1999): 258–63; B. D. Solomon and Lee Russell, "Emissions Trading Systems and Environmental Justice," *Environment* 42, no. 8 (2000): 32–46; Sheldon Kamieniecki, "Forming Partnerships in Environmental Policy," *American Behavioral Scientist* 43, no. 1 (1999): 107–24; Richard A. Kerr, "Acid Rain Control: Success on the Cheap," *Science* 282, no. 5391 (1998): 1024–28; and Gary C. Bryner, "Market Incentives in Air Pollution Control," in *Flashpoints in*

Environmental Policy Making: Controversies in Achieving Sustainability, ed. Sheldon Kamieniecki, George A. Gonzalez, and Robert O. Vos (Albany: SUNY Press, 1997), 85–107.

25. Kingdon, *Agendas, Alternatives and Public Policies*; Baumgartner and Jones, *Agendas and Instability*; Paul A. Sabatier and Hank C. Jenkins-Smith, "The Advocacy Coalition Framework: An Assessment," in *Theories of the Policy Process*, ed. Paul A. Sabatier (Boulder, CO: Westview, 1999), 117–66; Scott P. Hays and Henry R. Glick, "The Role of Agenda Setting in Policy Innovation: An Event History Analysis of Living-Will Laws," *American Politics Quarterly* 25, no. 4 (1997): 497–517; Francis S. Berry and William D. Berry, "Innovation and Diffusion Models in Policy Research," in Sabatier (1999), 169–200; Mintrom, "Policy Entrepreneurs and the Diffusion of Innovation"; Jeffrey L. Pressman and Aaron Wildavsky, *Implementation: How Great Expectations in Washington Are Dashed in Oakland; Or, Why It's Amazing That Federal Programs Work at All, This Being a Saga of the Economic Development Administration as Told by Two Sympathetic Observers Who Seek to Build Morals on a Foundation of Ruined Hope*, 3rd ed. (Berkeley, CA: University of California Press, 1984); and Laurence O'Toole Jr., "Implementing Public Innovations in Network Settings," *Administration and Society* 29, no. 2 (1997): 115–39.

26. Kingdon, *Agendas, Alternatives and Public Policies*; and Tom Birkland, *After Disaster: Agenda Setting, Public Policy and Focusing Events* (Washington, DC: Georgetown University Press, 1997).

27. Marcia L. Godwin and Jean R. Schroedel, "Policy Diffusion and Strategies for Promoting Policy Change: Evidence from California Local Gun Control Ordinances," *Policy Studies Journal* 28 (2000): 760–76; Baumgartner and Jones, *Agendas and Instability in American Politics*; and Kingdon, *Agendas, Alternatives and Public Policies*.

28. Birkland, *After Disaster*; Sarah B. Pralle, "Venue Shopping, Political Strategy, and Policy Change: The Internationalization of Canadian Forest Advocacy," *Journal of Public Policy* 23 (2003): 233–60; and Tanya Heikkila and Andrea K. Gerlak, "The Formation of Large-scale Collaborative Resource Management Institutions: Clarifying the Roles of Stakeholders, Science, and Institutions," *Policy Studies Journal* 33 (2005): 583–612.

29. Baumgartner and Jones, *Agendas and Instability*; and Hays and Glick, "Role of Agenda Setting in Policy Innovation."

30. Kingdon, *Agendas, Alternatives and Public Policies*; Nancy C. Roberts and Paula J. King, "Policy Entrepreneurs: Their Activity, Structure and Function in the Policy Process," *Journal of Public Administration Research and Theory* 1, no. 2 (1991): 147–75; Baumgartner and Jones, *Agendas and Instability*; Mintrom, "Policy Entrepreneurs and the Diffusion of Innovation"; and Michael Mintrom and Sandra Vergari, "Policy Networks and Innovation Diffusion: The Case of State Education Reforms," *The Journal of State Politics* 60 (1998): 121–48.

31. Michael Mintrom, *Policy Entrepreneurs and School Choice* (Washington, DC: Georgetown University Press, 2000).

32. Roberts and King, "Policy Entrepreneurs," 148.

33. Gerald T. Gabris, Robert T. Golembiewski, and Douglas M. Ihrke, "Leadership Credibility, Board Relations, and Administrative Innovation at the Local Government Level," *Journal of Public Administration Research and Theory* 11 (2000).

34. Osborne and Gaebler, *Reinventing Government*; and Francis Berry, "Innovation in Public Management: The Adoption of Strategic Planning," *Public Administration Review* 67, no. 3 (1994): 322–30.

35. For instance, see Fariborz Damanpour and Marguerite Schneider, "Characteristics of Innovation and Innovation Adoption in Public Organizations: Assessing the Role of

Managers," *Journal of Public Administration Research and Theory* 19, no. 3 (2009): 495–522; and Fariborz Damanpour and Marguerite Schneider, "Phases of the Adoption of Innovation in Organizations: Effects of Environment, Organization and Top Managers," *British Journal of Management* 17 (2006).

36. O'Toole, "Implementing Public Innovations in Network Settings"; and Peter deLeon and Linda deLeon, "What Ever Happened to Policy Implementation? An Alternative Approach," *Journal of Public Administration Research and Theory* 12 (2002).

37. Paul Berman, "Thinking about Programmed and Adaptive Implementation: Matching Strategies to Situations," in *Why Policies Succeed or Fail*, ed. Helen M. Ingram and Dean E. Mann (Beverly Hills, CA: Sage, 1980); Daniel A. Mazmanian and Paul A. Sabatier, *Implementation and Public Policy* (Lanham, MD: University Press of America, 1989); Malcolm L. Goggin, Ann O'M. Bowman, James P. Lester, and Laurence J. O'Toole Jr., *Implementation Theory and Practice: Toward a Third Generation* (Glenview, IL: Scott, Foresman, 1990); and deLeon and deLeon, "What Ever Happened to Policy Implementation?"

38. Robert T. Nakamura and Frank Smallwood, *The Politics of Policy Implementation* (New York: St. Martin's, 1980); Berman, "Thinking about Programmed and Adaptive Implementation"; Mazmanian and Sabatier, *Implementation and Public Policy*; Pressman and Wildavsky, *Implementation*; Martha Derthick, *New Towns, In-Town* (Washington, DC: Urban Institute, 1972); and Eugene Bardach, *The Implementation Game* (Cambridge, MA: MIT Press, 1977).

39. Helen Ingram, "Implementation: A Review and Suggested Framework," in *Public Administration: The State of the Art*, ed. Naomi B. Lynn and Aaron Wildavsky (Chatham, NJ: Chatham House, 1990); Richard E. Matland, "Synthesizing the Implementation Literature: The Ambiguity-Conflict Model of Policy Implementation," *Journal of Public Administration Research and Theory* 5, no. 2 (1995): 145–74; Denise Scheberle, *Federalism and Environmental Policy* (Washington, DC: Georgetown University Press, 1997); and deLeon and deLeon, "What Ever Happened to Policy Implementation?"

40. Mazmanian and Sabatier, *Implementation and Public Policy*.

41. Michael Lipsky, "Standing the Study of Policy Implementation on Its Head," in *American Politics and Public Policy*, ed. Walter D. Burnham and Martha W. Weinberg (Cambridge, MA: MIT Press, 1978).

42. Goggin et al., *Implementation Theory and Practice*; and Ray J. Burby, Peter J. May, and Robert C. Paterson, "Improving Compliance with Regulations," *Journal of the American Planning Association* 64 (1998): 324–35.

43. Peter May, Ray J. Burby, Neil J. Ericksen, John W. Handmer, Jennifer E. Dixon, Sarah Michaels, and D. Ingle Smith, *Environmental Management and Governance: Intergovernmental Approaches to Hazards and Sustainability* (London: Routledge, 1996).

44. Fiorino, *New Environmental Regulation*.

45. May et al., *Environmental Management and Governance*.

46. Robert Agranoff and Michael McGuire, *Collaborative Public Management: New Strategies for Local Governments* (Washington, DC: Georgetown University Press, 2003).

47. Eugene Bardach, *Getting Agencies to Work Together: The Practice and Theory of Managerial Craftsmanship* (Washington, DC: Brookings, 1998); and Eugene Bardach, "Developmental Processes: A Conceptual Exploration," in *Innovation in Government: Research, Recognition, and Replication*, ed. Sandford Borins (Washington, DC: Brookings, 2008), 113–37.

48. Guy Peters, *The Future of Governing: Four Emerging Models*, 2nd ed. (Lawrence: University Press of Kansas, 2001).

49. May et al., *Environmental Management and Governance.*

50. Baumgartner and Jones, *Agendas and Instability.*

51. Francis S. Berry and William D. Berry, "State Lottery Adoptions as Policy Innovations: An Event History Analysis," *American Political Science Review* 84 (1990): 395–441; Mintrom and Vergari, "Policy Networks and Innovation Diffusion"; Hays and Glick, "The Role of Agenda Setting in Policy Innovation"; Virginia Gray, "Innovation in the States: A Diffusion Study," *American Political Science Review* 67 (1973): 1174–85; and John Walker, "The Diffusion of Innovations among the American States," *American Political Science Review* 63 (September 1969): 880–99.

52. Gray, "Innovation in the States"; and Berry and Berry, "Innovation and Diffusion Models in Policy Research."

53. Bardach, *Getting Agencies to Work Together*; Agranoff and McGuire, *Collaborative Public Management*; and Rosemary O'Leary and Lisa B. Bingham, *The Collaborative Public Manager: New Ideas for the Twenty-first Century* (Washington, DC: Georgetown University Press, 2009).

54. Paul Berman, "The Study of Macro- and Micro-Implementation," *Public Policy* 26, no. 2 (1978): 157–84; Daniel Press, "Local Environmental Policy Capacity: A Framework for Research," *Natural Resources Journal* 38, no. 1 (1998): 29–52; Jerry Delli Priscoli, "Implementing Public Involvement Programs in Federal Agencies," *Citizen Participation in America: Essays on the State of the Art,* ed. Stuart Langton (Lexington, MA: Lexington, 1978); and Robert T. Nakamura and Frank Smallwood, *The Politics of Policy Implementation* (New York: St. Martin's, 1980).

55. Garry Brewer, "On the Theory and Practice of Innovation," *Technology in Society* 2 (1980): 337–63.

56. Sabatier and Jenkins-Smith, "The Advocacy Coalition Framework."

57. Bardach, *Getting Agencies to Work Together.*

58. Rachel Fleishman, "To Participate or Not to Participate? Incentives and Obstacles for Collaboration," in *The Collaborative Public Manager,* ed. Rosemary O'Leary and Lisa Bingham (Washington, DC: Georgetown University Press, 2008), 31–52.

59. Paul Hall and Rosemary Taylor, "Political Science and the Three New Institutionalisms," *Political Studies* 44 (1996): 936–57; and Kathleen Thelen, "Historical Institutionalism in Comparative Politics," *Annual Review in Political Science* 2 (1999): 369–404.

60. Douglass C. North, *Institutions, Institutional Change, and Economic Performance* (Cambridge: Cambridge University Press, 1990).

61. Margaret Levi, "A Logic of Institutional Change," in *The Limits of Rationality,* ed. Karen S. Cook and Margaret Levi (Chicago: University of Chicago Press, 1990), 402–18.

62. Hall and Taylor, "Political Science and the Three New Institutionalisms."

63. Thomas A. Koelble, "The New Institutionalism in Political Science and Sociology," *Comparative Politics* 27 (1995): 231–44.

64. Hall and Taylor, "Political Science and the Three New Institutionalisms."

65. Thelen, "Historical Institutionalism in Comparative Politics."

66. Hall and Taylor, "Political Science and the Three New Institutionalisms."

67. Erving Goffman, *Frame Analysis: An Essay on the Organization of Experience* (London: Harper and Row, 1974), 21.

68. Donald A. Schön and Martin Rein, *Frame Reflection: Toward the Resolution of Intractable Policy Controversies* (New York: Basic, 1994).

69. Ronald Jepperson, "Institutions, Institutional Effects, and Institutionalism," in *The New Institutionalism in Organizational Analysis*, ed. Walter W. Powell and Paul J. DiMaggio (Chicago: University of Chicago Press, 1991), 143–63.

70. James Q. Wilson, "Innovation in Organization: Notes Toward a Theory," in *Approaches to Organization Design*, ed. James D. Thompson (Pittsburgh, PA: University of Pittsburgh Press, 1966); and Martin A. Levin and M. Bryna Sanger, *Making Government Work: How Entrepreneurial Executives Turn Bright Ideas into Real Results* (San Francisco: Jossey-Bass, 1994).

71. Birkland, *After Disaster*.

72. Koelble, "The New Institutionalism in Political Science and Sociology."

73. Elinor Ostrom, *Governing the Commons* (Cambridge: Cambridge University Press, 1990); and Elinor Ostrom, Roy Gardner, and James Walker, *Rules, Games and Common Pool Resources* (Ann Arbor: University of Michigan Press, 1994).

74. Ostrom, *Governing the Commons*, 192. As stated by Ostrom, "Decisions made in constitutional-choice situations indirectly affect operational situations by creating and limiting the powers that can be exercised within collective-choice arrangements (creating legislative and judicial bodies, protecting rights of free-speech and property, etc.) and by affecting the decision regarding who is represented and with what weight in collective-choice decisions."

75. Robert Goodin, *Institutions and Their Design* (Cambridge: Cambridge University Press, 1996).

76. Doug McAdam, Sidney Tarrow, and Charles Tilly, "Toward an Integrated Perspective on Social Movements and Revolution," in *Comparative Politics: Rationality, Culture and Structure*, Mark Irving Lichbach and Alan S. Zuckerman (New York: Cambridge University Press, 1997), 142–73.

77. Margaret Weir, "Ideas and the Politics of Bounded Innovation," in *Structuring Politics: Historical Institutionalism in Comparative Analysis*, ed. Sven Steinmo, Kathleen Thelen, and Frank Longstreth (Cambridge: Cambridge University Press, 1992), 188–216.

78. Great Outdoors Colorado, "Accomplishments," www.goco.org/Results/Accomplishments/tabid/115/Default.aspx (accessed February 22, 2009).

79. Stan Elofson, "Initiatives and Referenda in the 1990s—An Update," Colorado Legislative Council Staff Legislative Brief, Number 99-2, 1999, www.state.co.us/gov%5Fdir/leg%5dir/lcsstaff/research/issuebrf-99-2.htm (accessed March 27, 2001).

80. Ibid.

81. National Conference of State Legislators, "Initiative States Ranked in Order of Use, 1898-1999," 2000, www.ncsl.org/programs/legman/elect/inrank.htm (accessed March 28, 2001).

82. Ibid.; and Elofson, "Initiatives and Referenda in the 1990s—An Update."

CHAPTER 2

The Evolution of Environmental and Natural Resource Governance

Land, Water, and Forests

PUBLIC MANAGEMENT RESEARCH, POLICY STUDIES, and institutional theory all recognize the importance of hierarchy within governance and how one level can influence the operation at another level. Policy studies literature, such as the advocacy coalition framework and punctuated equilibrium theory, suggests that there may be, but not always, influences from international, national, state, and/or local arenas on a policy innovation. Public management scholars explore the roles of networks, collaboration, and possibilities for integrating various participants from across different levels and aspects of governance. Likewise, implementation theory refers to top-down and bottom-up forces that can influence policy. Institutional theory recognizes the nested effect that constitutive, collective, and operational rulemaking have on individual actors. Accordingly, these levels are incorporated into an analytical framework to account for hierarchical pressures that can shape any attempt at policy innovation, as detailed in figure 2.1.

The historical context documented here conveys the increasingly complex and interrelated relationships throughout the governance hierarchy related to environmental and natural resource problems. Over time we have seen shifts not only in the types of people involved in environmental and natural resource policymaking but also in the types of values that are pursued, the strategies and tactics used, the venues for taking action, and the outcomes desired. Implicit in these shifts in people, values, strategies, venues, and desired outcomes are reallocations in the balance of power within our local, state, and national governance structures. Also present is an increasingly complicated web of constitutive, collective, and operational decision-making rules and norms that influence action. Innovations must be integrated into this structure and

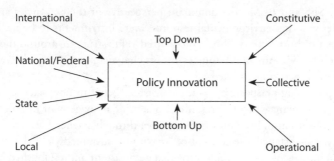

Figure 2.1: Influences on Innovative Policy

harmonized to some degree if they are to thrive. If the institutional context is important, then understanding the historical background that gave rise to these changes is crucial to assessing the challenges faced by innovation in today's social environment. I begin here by providing a broad overview of the trends nationally and then turn to more specific treatment of the land, water, and forest governance subsystems that relate to the three case studies in chapters 4, 5, and 6. The initial treatment of broad trends can be traced over three eras in environmental and natural resource governance—the pre-1960s, the 1960s and 1970s, and the 1980s and 1990s.

THE EVOLUTION OF THE NATIONAL ENVIRONMENTAL AND NATURAL RESOURCE GOVERNANCE SYSTEM

Until the 1960s environmental problems were defined dominantly as commodity management problems.[1] When defined as commodity management, the goals for resource professionals were clear and focused on maximizing production of the commodities in question. How do we grow enough wood to meet the needs of an industrializing society? How do we manage wildlife to ensure viable hunting populations? What incentives can we provide to encourage mineral exploration and settlement of the public domain? What recreation experiences should be provided to the public?

Pre-1960s

The dominant actors in this era were the federal public land management agencies— the United States Forest Service (USFS), the Bureau of Land Management (BLM), the United States Fish and Wildlife Service (USFWS), and the National Park Service (NPS)—and their constituencies: timber companies, ranchers, hunters and fishers, and recreationists.[2] These agencies were granted administrative authority to govern resources under executive privilege or, in some cases, through organic acts, as in the case of the USFS and BLM. The dominant perspective of these agencies and their constituencies was that environmental resources were instruments to be utilized for the betterment of humankind. This homogenized value structure around the instrumental value of environmental resources meant that management goals were clear and, for the most part, uncontested.

Another prevailing perspective was the consistent belief in how science could be used to aid in the management of resources. Scientific management or efficiency in the exploitation of natural resource commodities through science-based technology ruled the day. For instance, the concept of "maximum sustained yield" led to linear, deterministic models of causality and provided a consistent and established basis for making decisions about how commodities could be managed.[3] Many undergraduate and graduate schools supported this conception of science in their curricula, and few other competing or alternative paradigms were taught in various schools of natural resource management. The certainty of this science and a desire for efficiency in management resulted in the establishment of classic bureaucratic structures.[4] The twin beliefs in the instrumental value of resources combined with a static and orthodox understanding of "science" led to the bureaucratic institutionalization of these values. Placing their faith in this science as well as the "gospel" of efficiency, many environmental and natural resource agencies were typified by organizational structures and institutional norms that supported and reinforced these values with hierarchical, bureaucratic systems; defined and compartmentalized jurisdictions; detailed rules; and clear lines demarcating the agency from its surrounding environment.[5]

Thus, defining the problem as commodity management resulted in and from three distinct trends—valuing resources as instruments, the creation and reinforcement of a science that allowed resources to be managed as instruments, and institutional infrastructure that channeled and supported these values. The upshot of all of this was the rise to authority of those with technical expertise and scientific management resources. While professional and technical experts were accorded authority, those with control over the resources were the constituencies most affected by commodity management—resource-oriented trade associations that represented timber companies, mining enterprises, ranchers, hunters and fishers, and, to a lesser extent, recreationists.[6] The "capture" of various agencies and the "iron triangles" of influence between trade groups, agencies, and politicians typified relationships among and between those with power.[7] Decisions often were not challenged because agency managers established informal working relationships with the constituencies most affected by the decisions. Early conservationist and preservationist groups were established prior to the 1960s, but their role in politics was limited.[8] The Hetch-Hetchy Dam controversy in 1955 was a main catalyzing event in re-politicizing the Sierra Club. Relationships among actors and within institutions of management, for the most part, were stable. Agency "regulatory" focus was largely of a collaborative nature in which access was tightly controlled.

1960s and 1970s

Beginning in the 1960s many of the conditioning factors influencing the previous dominant trends in environmental and natural resource governance began to change. New problems were surfacing while the old problems were being recast in different ways. Environmental pollution and its poisonous concerns rose on the national agenda. New constituencies were focused on noncommodity values associated with environmental resources and posed a challenge to previously existing problem definitions.[9] The problems identified by these new constituencies pointed to the complex origins and consequences associated with new technologies, growing consumption, burgeoning populations, and the cumulative impacts on both human health and natural environments.[10] As new interests arose and asserted themselves, the problems that needed attention expanded and changed, and the previous clarity that had existed about management goals began to fade.

The number and type of participants in this emerging era of environmental and natural resource governance were drastically different from those that prevailed in the previous era. The principal participants in the prior era had been commodity managers and their constituencies. In this new era entities concerned with a broader scope of values harnessed and enlarged their existing memberships and politicized their missions, as in the case of Sierra Club and the National Audubon Society, or emerged as new groups outright, as in the case of the World Wildlife Federation (established 1961), Environmental Defense Fund (established 1967), Friends of the Earth (established 1969), the Natural Resources Defense Council (established 1970), Environmental Action (established 1970), League of Conservation Voters (established 1970), Sierra Club Legal Defense Fund (established 1971), Greenpeace (established 1971), Environmental Policy Institute (established 1972), and Sea Shepherd Society.[11] These nonprofit groups and other national groups provided a formidable challenge to the traditional commodity management agencies and actors. Individual activists such as Lois Gibbs and Rachel Carson also materialized to put faces on a growing grassroots movement of people concerned about toxic and hazardous waste and the subsequent impacts on their quality of life.[12]

Underlying this proliferation in new actors was a change in how environmental and natural resources were valued. As personal incomes rose following World War II, so did societal expectations for environmental quality. This heightened awareness of the intrinsic value of environmental and natural resources began to muddy the waters of what values should be given precedence by environmental managers.[13] The previously homogenized value structure around environmental resources became increasingly heterogeneous. Not only were commodity values called into question as a management focus but concerns also arose about the effects of water and air pollution.

In response to the growing concern about pollution, Congress and President Richard Nixon established a new agency, the EPA, to address these issues—partially to neutralize Ed Muskie's campaign for the presidency. The attention was in response to a changing public mood where the environment began to be perceived as a public good. The EPA emerged out of an executive order issued by President Nixon in 1969. Congress did not issue a legislative mandate for the agency as a whole. Rather, the agency's mandate emerged piecemeal and became the sum of individually authorized programs. These early regulatory efforts targeted easily identifiable and tractable sources, such as smokestack and effluent pipe polluters (point sources), and used mostly command-and-control regulations that imposed technological fixes. Technology-based standards, performance-based standards, and process-based standards were determined for specific industrial sectors.[14] Technology standards involve design or specifications for a particular industrial process, like a scrubber on smoke stacks. Performance standards, in contrast, are outcome-focused and elaborate on a company's duty in terms of the problem it must solve or the goal it must achieve. Process-based standards outline procedures for achieving a desired result; for instance, the processes followed in managing hazardous materials. Sanctions applied to those who did not adhere to the standards mandated by law. Different media, like air, land, and water, were compartmentalized under separate regulations within different agency jurisdictions.

On the natural resource management side, things also were changing. The three pillars on which the commodity management philosophy was built were being chipped away. The primacy of managing for instrumental commodity values was questioned. Some scientists saw environmental and natural resource processes as being defined better as nonlinear, stochastic relationships with unpredictable outcomes, thereby providing an alternative management paradigm to the previously monolithic stable of options for resource professionals.[15] This changing conception of science pointed to the need for organizational structures and institutional norms to accommodate the ambiguity and uncertainty in this new era of management.[16]

Accompanying this shift in the scientific management paradigm was a growing lack of trust and confidence by the public in traditional environmental and natural resource management individuals and institutions.[17] A growing segment of U.S. society did not see their values reflected in the decisions by environmental and natural resource managers. However, challenging the existing power structure held by natural resource agencies, managers, and their constituencies was a daunting task. The resources that allowed natural resource agencies, managers, and constituencies to maintain their hold on power were their scientific expertise and bureaucratic institutions. Thus, the new actors devised strategies that could counter or trump these resources. The courts and Congress were the chosen arenas to do battle. Marshalling their power in the form of national environmental groups, their own scientific expertise, grassroots support, lawsuits, and new legislation, these actors began to challenge and change the basis on which discussions about environmental management took place. Case law, such as *Scenic Hudson Preservation Conference v. FPC* (1965) and *Sierra Club v. Morton* (1972), gave precedence to new principles by establishing that private citizens and organization had standing in court to protect environmental values or provided stronger ground for multiple use claims, as in the case of *Udall v. Federal Power Commission* (1967).[18] New statutes mandated that agencies manage for multiple resources, such as the Multiple Use Sustained Yield Act of 1960, as well as established procedural protocols for planning and allowing the public to have a voice in these processes, as in the National Environmental Policy Act (NEPA) (1969), the Coastal Zone Management Act (1972), the Federal Land Policy and Management Act (1976), and the National Forest Management Act (1976). Confrontation between the differing sides typified interaction.

In the 1970s many changes were taking place. New institutions emerged, as in the case of the EPA and Council on Environmental Quality and active nonprofit organizations. In the area of commodity management, the stability that once had characterized the relationship between commodity managers and their constituencies began to change. As the number of interests concerned about environmental and natural resources grew, the interests that were well served by the existing regulatory structure grew smaller. The relevant political actors concerned about environmental and natural resource management were broadened to include national commodity groups but also national environmental and conservation groups, as well as some local grassroots groups. As such, the power base was broadened and diversified. These new groups held different expectations about who should hold power and how decisions should be made about environmental resources. Those traditionally in power, meaning commodity managers, had maintained their power based on scientific and technical expertise. But people began to see that this form of scientific and technical expertise did not serve their interests well, since their institutions for managing resources covered only a narrow part of a much broader spectrum of concern. Management institutions that had served commodity managers and their constituencies were becoming brittle and vulnerable to change. To bring reality in line with changing expectations about who should make decisions and how they should be made, nontraditional actors began to challenge the decisions made by those with formal power through the courts and through Congress. To effect change, new anticommodity constituencies needed to go outside the existing bureaucracies to establish a new basis for challenging this power. For the most part, these battles took place at the national level.

1980s and 1990s

If action during the 1960s and 1970s was characterized as taking place predominantly at the national level, one of the hallmarks of environmental and natural resource governance in the late 1980s and 1990s was the refocusing of management decisions to more decentralized levels and greater public involvement in decisions.[19] The problem in the previous eras centered on how commodities and then noncommodities would be managed, as well as the need to tackle pollution problems. In the 1980s and 1990s the problem shifted to the appropriateness of existing agencies to deal with environmental and natural resource governance and management. Initially air and water pollution were defined as point sources coming from smokestacks or pipes into waterways. Now the dominant problems were typified by nonpoint polluters or problems that needed voluntary collective action on a large scale to deal with the detrimental impacts of erosion, contamination, or other widely distributed pollutants. To circumvent the perceived inefficiencies in bureaucratic hierarchies, market-based and participatory structures were proposed as innovations for achieving better and more efficient environmental ends. In addition, new tools such as certification, tradable emissions permits, community right-to-know and pollution inventories, corporate reporting, and conservation easements, to name a few, were adopted as innovative management tools.

The movement toward decentralization can be seen as springing from the grassroots efforts that began in the 1960s, while being enhanced by the sweeping change in political philosophy that accompanied the Reagan and Thatcher revolutions in the 1980s. Delegation and devolution were the catchwords of "new federalism" as embodied in the Ronald Reagan and George H. W. Bush years, and these changes had great impact on environmental policy.[20] The federal government embarked on an explicit agenda to defund and decentralize federal environmental protection activities and place greater emphasis on state management and implementation of environmental and natural resource policy.[21] The ability of states to take on these responsibilities was uneven, but enhanced capacity at the state level paved the way for some states to capitalize on these newly delegated responsibilities.[22] Many states responded with innovative programs and initiatives.[23] While there is little empirical research about the trends in state-level environmental groups, other evidence suggests that as states were delegated greater authoritative power, interest group activity increased at the state level.[24]

The genesis for this shift in regulatory approach began when dominant agencies such as the EPA came under attack for using inefficient, heavy-handed, command-and-control management instruments for trying to accomplish even its point-source goals. When the EPA emerged in 1969 from piecemeal legislation to tackle pollution problems, the interconnections among air, water, and soil were not recognized in the agency's design. Additional mandates were added through an ad hoc political process, and insufficient resources coupled with political appointees that circumvented or undermined the agency's goals eroded the efficacy and the authority of the agency in the 1980s. As new regulatory territory was uncovered, such as the need to regulate non–point-source pollutants, traditional command-and-control instruments that provided adequate regulatory solutions to point-source problems fell out of favor as the appropriate regulatory tools.

The same agency misfit was apparent in public lands management. The USFS, NPS, BLM, and USFWS struggled with implementing new laws imposed on them in an effort to balance the many interests to whom they now were responsible. While many of the laws were passed in the 1960s and 1970s, their impacts were not made clear until the 1980s. Public land management institutions had been established, in most cases more than one hundred years before during a radically different time in the nation's history, to serve very different purposes than those found in the changing social context of the 1980s and 1990s. In some cases the public land management agencies adapted to the changes demanded of them, and in other cases they floun-dered.[25] For both the EPA and the public land management agencies, the brittleness of their organizations was brought into sharper relief, as was the fact that the institutions failed to regulate significant aspects related to environmental and natural resource management challenges. The very structure of the agencies was out of step with the function needed for society.

In addition to the actors who were present in the previous eras, the 1980s and 1990s saw the ascendance of grassroots' individual and community action.[26] On their own and building on the gains made by national groups, individual grassroots activists and communities began to play a more vocal role in natural resource and pollution management at the state and local level. For instance, the Citizen's Clearinghouse for Toxic Waste (established in 1981) is an umbrella organization connected to 7,000 grassroots community groups.[27] The land trust movement, which gained momentum beginning in the 1980s, was estimated in 2006 as having 1,667 land trusts in United States and accompanying territories with 1.5 million members and more than 90,000 active volunteers.[28] The watershed movement, which predominantly emerged in the 1980s and 1990s, has an estimated 400 to 3,500 groups nationwide.[29] The commu-nity forestry movement underwent the first inventory of groups in fall 2008. Current researchers estimate that some 2,000 groups exist throughout the United States.[30]

The heterogeneous values of environmental and natural resources that emerged in the 1960s and 1970s and then gained stature were institutionalized through laws passed by Congress and supported by national interest and advocacy groups. A fun-damental baseline of action and concern was established and codified in these laws.[31] These laws forced those with power to take into consideration the value preferences of underrepresented constituencies in decisions about environmental resources, as in the case of the Multiple Use and Sustained Yield Act, NEPA, and the National Forest Management Act. The passage of these laws served to raise the expectations that new constituencies would be able to influence policy, but for the most part they failed to deliver on these promises.[32] Many new constituencies continued to be disgruntled with those who possessed authority. Nonetheless, these actions paved the way for activists on more local and regional levels to effect change.

National environmental and conservation interest groups had acquired technical expertise, organizational know-how, and skillful strategies to challenge commodity and industrial interests. However, these skills were not as well developed in state and local advocates.[33] Rising education levels, increased availability of information about the environmental impacts of resource use, and expanding communication networks and policy commitments to allow the public to participate enabled new constituencies to challenge the power of those who traditionally held authority in environmental and natural resource management.[34] This expanding base of power combined with increasingly savvy protest techniques made the general public a more difficult entity to exclude from the decision-making processes that affected their lives, as evidenced in the "not in my backyard" (NIMBY) behavior that emerged in the 1980s.[35] When excluded from certain decision processes, protesting publics felt their only avenue of recourse was to block the policy outcome. Various groups and individuals mobilized to obstruct or prevent the implementation of certain policy decisions.[36] The resulting NIMBY behavior can be seen as an effort by those without power to exert power over the decisions made by those who traditionally held it.

In 1993, when Bill Clinton became president, environmental issues within the White House were given a higher level of attention. The Clinton administration used its powers of appointment, budgeting, reorganization, and oversight to reform environmental protection at the federal level.[37] As one of the thirty-two agencies targeted under the "reinventing government" agenda, the EPA was strengthened and refocused into a mission that placed greater emphasis on community-based environmental protection, collaborative decision making, public-private partnerships, and flexibility in rulemaking and enforcement. In many cases, the EPA was adopting innovations that had emerged out of the state and local levels.[38]

In the 1980s and 1990s, when innovations began to emerge, they did so within a complex of national, state, and local influences and constitutive, collective, and operational rule systems, as illustrated in figure 2.2. At the constitutive level, a variety of laws, executive orders, and proclamations were layered onto each other to

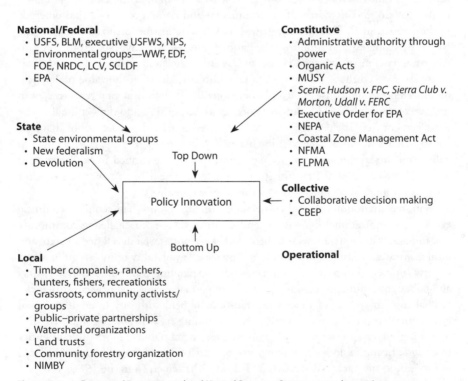

National/Federal
- USFS, BLM, executive USFWS, NPS,
- Environmental groups—WWF, EDF, FOE, NRDC, LCV, SCLDF
- EPA

State
- State environmental groups
- New federalism
- Devolution

Local
- Timber companies, ranchers, hunters, fishers, recreationists
- Grassroots, community activists/ groups
- Public–private partnerships
- Watershed organizations
- Land trusts
- Community forestry organization
- NIMBY

Constitutive
- Administrative authority through power
- Organic Acts
- MUSY
- *Scenic Hudson v. FPC, Sierra Club v. Morton, Udall v. FERC*
- Executive Order for EPA
- NEPA
- Coastal Zone Management Act
- NFMA
- FLPMA

Collective
- Collaborative decision making
- CBEP

Operational

Top Down

Policy Innovation

Bottom Up

Figure 2.2: Influences of Environmental and Natural Resource Governance on Innovations

effect change at the collective and operational levels. National, state, and local actors have fleshed out over time to include federal and state agencies, private companies, nonprofit actors, and local grassroots and community-based participants, all with increased knowledge, capacity, and tools to affect environmental and natural resource governance. The increased diversity of participants along with the multiple strata of laws, rules, regulations, and norms means that innovations have a host of historical, cultural, and administrative institutions with which they must contend. The potential for dissonance within this mix of influences is great. Some governance subsystems related to specific resource problems may be easier or more difficult to navigate depending on the type of innovation and how it is structured.

The following sections detail specific governance subsystems related to the cases I address in the following chapters. These more refined histories provide a context for understanding how the governance hierarchy diversified across local, state, and national levels and increasingly complex interactions among constitutive, collective, and operational decision making resulted in a nested web into which land protection, watershed remediation, and community forestry innovations must fit.

THE EVOLUTION OF THE LAND PROTECTION GOVERNANCE SYSTEM

Land use governance has played out in three dominant eras in the last one hundred years. The first era began in the 1920s with the rise of land use regulations at local levels. In the 1960s and 1970s the second era commenced with an emphasis on centralizing regulatory power at the state and federal levels. In the 1980s and 1990s a third era emerged with the focus shifting to new participants in the land protection arena.

Problems with land use governance did not emerge on a widespread basis in the United States until the 1920s when the first land use regulations in the United States were adopted. At that time, the U.S. Census reported that urban Americans outnumbered rural Americans for the first time in the nation's history.[39] Attracted to the economic opportunities in the growing cities, Americans were drawn to the promise of a better life. Until that time, the United States could be classified as a dominantly rural country with low population densities and vast reaches of open space. Concerns about the protection of land were given little attention due to the great expanses that existed across the country. Nonetheless, as the U.S. population grew and shifted from farms into the cities, land use problems came to the forefront of the U.S. policy agenda.

Accompanying the growing tide of urbanization was a variety of public health, safety, and welfare problems that affected the quality of life in America's emergent cities. Congestion in housing, crowded streets, structural fire issues, loss of open space, and change in neighborhoods provided the impetus for the nation to adopt land use regulations. Thus, the main problem in the earliest era of land use governance was a need to protect the health, safety, and welfare of growing, urban populations while also not constraining the promise of economic opportunity.

The dominant actors at this early stage in land use management were local municipal, city, town, village, and county governments, and the principal tool used by these local governments was land use zoning, or "Euclidean zoning." Named after the landmark U.S. Supreme Court case of *Village of Euclid v. Ambler Realty Company* in 1926 that gave constitutional approval to the use of zoning as a valid tool of land use governance, Euclidean zoning was the foremost institution in land use control until the 1970s.[40]

The power to zone is given to local governments by the state. Most of the metropolitan counties, and many rural counties, zone land in unincorporated areas within their borders. Zoning regulates three aspects of land use, including the use of private land, the density of structural development per unit of land, and the dimensions of buildings. The primary classes of land use for zoning purposes are residential, commercial, and industrial. In addition to zoning regulations, local governments possess other tools to regulate land use, including the power to regulate land subdivisions, the use of floodplains, wetland or seismic risk areas, and the ability to enforce building code requirements, designate historic districts, and control signs.[41]

The concept of zoning has been controversial since its inception and raises many issues about the values affecting land governance issues. Zoning is a powerful tool because of its use of public regulatory "police" power to stipulate how private land may be used. To exercise this police power, local governments must demonstrate that land use regulations serve to protect the public health, safety, and welfare of its citizens. No compensation is paid to owners of land that have their land uses curtailed when public regulatory police powers are used. Zoning gives power to the government to place the common good above individual uses of privately owned property. The use of the police power for land use purposes evokes concern under the Fifth Amendment of the U.S. Constitution, which stipulates, "nor shall private property be taken for public use without just compensation."

In contrast to the use of police power for regulatory purposes, the government can also exercise its right to "eminent domain" or "condemnation." With eminent domain private property is purchased for public use, such as the construction of a road, school, or park, and the government must pay the private owner "just compensation" for the land. While the exercise of eminent domain provides compensation to owners of private property, zoning or other land use regulations do not alter the ownership of the land, and the government does not compensate the landowner. Rather, the use of the property is restricted under the land use regulations to benefit the public health, safety, and welfare of the community as a whole. The use of the regulatory police power over the last ninety years has given rise to "takings" issues. Landowners claim that regulatory police power can reduce or nullify the value of a parcel of property through restrictions placed on the land use to the point that it constitutes an effective taking of the land, akin to a claim of eminent domain or condemnation. The landowner should be entitled to compensation from the government.

In conjunction with growing concern about environmental and natural resource issues, land use governance came under scrutiny again in the 1960s and 1970s. In this second era of land use governance, the problem definition shifted from the need for zoning to the unforeseen consequences associated with local zoning practices. Beginning in the 1960s, the use of zoning was coming under criticism for creating wasteful and unsightly land use patterns while also failing to protect important amenities. In short, the performance of local governments in protecting land left many unsatisfied.

In the 1970s a movement began to transfer power from local governments to state, regional, and federal authorities. Grounded in a belief that localities failed to consider the interjurisdictional dependencies that transcended their immediate boundaries, a "quiet revolution" was under way to place land use control in the hands of the states and/or federal authorities.[42] The perception at the time was that local governments were not protecting areas of critical national and regional concern, such as wetlands, coasts, watersheds, wildlife habitat, agricultural land, and recreation amenities. For the first time in the history of the United States, implementation of land use controls moved from its traditional place in local government into regional and state bodies.

Several states at the time, including California, Delaware, Florida, Hawaii, Minnesota, Massachusetts, Maine, New York, Oregon, Wisconsin, and Vermont, were at the forefront of this quiet revolution. Acting independently, these states recognized that local zoning laws were inadequate to cope with statewide or regional problems and adopted statewide or regional land use controls.[43] The types of land control policy adopted by the states varied considerably. Some states were concerned with protecting regional critical areas, such as coasts, wetlands, or forests. Other states required the review of construction projects of a certain size. Yet other states mandated planning and regulatory criteria for local governments. The desire to regulate land use at a regional or state level reflected awareness that states could and should play a role in solving interjurisdictional problems, such as critical areas, siting developments that could have regional impacts, and protecting areas that did not fall under regulatory jurisdictions.

In addition to the direct effect that states had on land policy, there was growing recognition that states had at their discretion a variety of indirect policies that influenced greatly the direction and intensity of development.[44] Highways, water and sewer facilities, hospitals, office buildings, prisons, universities, power-generating and transmission facilities, and state tax policy could easily have important indirect impacts on land use. Given the direct and indirect role of state government, land use was neither completely subjected to the whims of the market nor completely under the domain of local or state governments. Growing recognition of the nested levels of influence on land use reframed the problem to be one of regional and state concern, thereby providing the justification for centralizing power at a higher level within the governmental structure.

Concurrent with the efforts to centralize power at the statewide or regional level were efforts within Congress to pass the National Land Use Policy Act (1971), which provided federal assistance to states to develop programs dealing with land use issues of regional or state concern. While the National Land Use Policy Act passed the Senate in both 1972 and 1973, the House of Representatives rejected the bill in the Rules

Committee and in a floor vote, respectively.[45] The Ford and Carter administrations failed to show interest in federal land use policy, and the effort effectively faded with the end of the Nixon administration.

During the 1970s power over land use governance was extended to state and federal agencies, although with great variation across many states. Power continued to rest with economic interests at the local level, with national environmental interests playing an increasingly important role. Dissatisfaction with local government's use of zoning led to new tools at the state and federal levels to encourage greater care of interjurisdictional concerns.

And yet, centralization at the state and federal levels did not provide a stable solution for land use governance issues. A backlash against efforts to centralize power began in the late 1970s and early 1980s and continued into the 1990s. In the late 1970s the Sagebrush Rebellion epitomized the backlash against the growing role of the federal and state governments in land use governance. Beginning in Nye County, Nevada, the Sagebrush Rebellion embodied the concerns of many rural communities. Feeling a loss of control over their own land use decisions and fearing increased control over federal lands, rural residents in the West sought to take back power that was being given over to the states and federal authorities. Holding on to Lockean beliefs that asserted an individual's right to appropriate wealth from nature, the Sagebrush Rebels sought to retain control over what was perceived as their lands and foreshadowed the rise of the property rights, or Wise Use, movement in the 1980s and 1990s.

While the Sagebrush Rebellion was largely unorganized, the Wise Use movement was much more focused, with leadership, organization, and money. The Wise Use movement is centered on two principles—defending private property and the private use of public lands. Seeing federal rules governing wetlands, water rights, and endangered species as harmful to local economies and communities while also impinging on property rights, property owners, loggers, fishermen, off-road vehicle users, mining companies, ranchers, and others came together to become the Wise Use movement.[46] National, regional, and grassroots groups emerged, such as the Alliance for America, the Blue Ribbon Coalition, the National Wetlands Coalition, the Oregon Lands Coalition, Western States Public Lands Coalition/People for the West!, the National In-holders Association, and the Wise Use Coalition.[47]

In addition to concerns about the regulatory impact on private property rights, there also was increased attention to growing population pressures and disappearing land resources. Between 1960 and 1990 the percentage of people living in metropolitan areas rose from 65.9 percent to nearly 80 percent, or from 118 million to 197.7 million.[48] The Land Trust Alliance stated in 2005 that each year the United States lost two million acres of farms, forests, and open spaces.[49] Growing unease about the disappearance of land, agricultural landscapes, habitat, and cultural amenities gave rise to new approaches in addressing land issues. Since the early 1990s, there has been a rise in the number of nongovernmental organizations that have emerged or grown to take on a greater responsibility for protecting land, namely, nonprofit organizations such as land trusts.[50] Land trusts are private, nonprofit organizations that work with property owners to protect land through direct, voluntary land transactions.[51] Land trusts at every level of governance emerged or became more prevalent during the 1980s and 1990s. Making use of a variety of market-based mechanisms to purchase land with its entire bundle of rights (fee simple) or part of the bundle (conservation easement), land trusts provided acceptable solutions for both environmentalists and private property rights' enthusiasts and illustrate how new actors emerged to play a vital role in land protection.

In response to and in conjunction with the rise in concern about private property, a number of private land conservation organizations emerged or grew markedly in the 1980s, especially at the grassroots level.[52] In 1960 there were 130 land trusts in the United States, mostly in New England.[53] By 1980 the number grew to 430, in 1988 there were 741, in 1998 1,213, and in 2006 the Land Trust Alliance, a national organization of land trusts, identified 1,667 nonprofit national, state, and local land trusts operating throughout the United States, Puerto Rico, and the Virgin Islands with approximately 1.5 million members and more than 90,000 active volunteers.[54] In 1998 nearly five million acres of land were protected by local and regional land trusts, a 135 percent increase over the two million acres protected by the end of 1988.[55] Total acreage protected by local, state, and federal land trusts doubled between 2001 and 2006 to 37 million acres, an increase of 54 percent over the previous five years.[56] While the West was the fastest growing region in terms of the acres conserved and the number of land trusts, California, Maine, Colorado, Montana, Virginia, New York, Vermont, New Mexico, Pennsylvania, and Massachusetts were the states with the highest total acres conserved. Land trusts reported that they focused primarily on three areas of protection—natural areas and wildfire habitat, open space, and water resources.[57]

Land trusts vary in size from very large international organizations like The Nature Conservancy (TNC), to national nonprofits such as the Conservation Fund, the Rails-to-Trails Conservancy, the American Farmland Trust, the Trust for Public Land, and the Land Trust Alliance, to regional or statewide entities like the Colorado Cattleman's Agricultural Land Trust, the Conservation Trust for North Carolina, the Lancaster Farmland Trust, Vermont Land Trust, Pacific Forest Trust, Greater Yellowstone Coalition, the Piedmont Environmental Council, and the Chesapeake Bay Foundation, to the small, community-based land trust organizations that exist all over the nation. Even though national and regional land trusts have a wider scope and mission than the local land trusts, they also provide support for work at the local level. The missions of land trusts vary. Some land trusts protect parcels of land with an emphasis on biological diversity, like TNC, others protect forests, like the Pacific Forest Trust, while others focus on agricultural land, such as the American Farmland Trust.

In addition to increased interest from the nonprofit and grassroots private property and conservation sectors, many businesses also have increased cooperative efforts to work with communities and local governments to preserve open space and wildlife habitat and create recreational opportunities. DuPont, Tenneco, USX, and Weyerhaeuser began habitat protection programs in the 1980s.[58] The Wildlife Habitat Council was created in 1987 to encourage collaboration between conservationists and corporations.

The instruments or tools used to protect land by this expanding base of participants also have changed over time. Conservation easements—a voluntary, negotiated, legally binding set of restrictions that can be purchased or donated—are the dominant tool used by land trusts to protect land. In 1998 land trusts held more than 7,000 conservation easements protecting nearly 1.4 million acres of land.[59] In 2005 local and state land trusts increased the acres protected by conservation easements to 6.2 million from 2.5 million in 2000, an increase of 148 percent.[60]

In addition to the conservation easement, Congress and a growing number of states have adopted tax laws that encourage charitable donations of conservation easements. Two laws in particular are responsible for the popularity of the conservation easement as a land protection tool. In 1976 Congress passed the Historic Structures Tax Act that allowed conservation and historic preservation easements donations to be tax deductible. In 1997 a modified version of the American Farm and Ranch Protection Act was passed as part of the Taxpayer Relief Act and exempted land held under conservation easement from estate tax.[61]

The initiative process also has been used increasingly as a tool to protect land. From 1996 to 2004, voters authorized $27.3 billion in 1,071 ballot measures to be spent on state and local land protection.[62] These ballot measures passed 77 percent of the time with more than 60 percent voter support. These funds typically protected agricultural land, parks, habitat, and open space.

The largest percentage increase in the number of land trusts during the 1990s took place in the Rocky Mountains. In 1988 there were twenty land trusts throughout the Rocky Mountain states of Colorado, Idaho, Montana, Utah, and Wyoming. In 1998 there were fifty-two, a 160 percent increase.[63] In 2000 there were fifty-nine land trusts, and in 2005 there were seventy-six—a nearly 30 percent increase. In 2005 Colorado, with thirty-eight land trusts, ranked second in the country (behind Maine) with the most acreage held in conservation easements at 849,825 acres.[64]

This short history illustrates how the land use governance system evolved from the late 1920s to the 2000s. Primary control over land use governance rested at the local level until the 1920s, driven by Euclidean zoning at the collective and operational levels and supported constitutively by case law from the Supreme Court. Beginning in the 1970s, state and federal government began to assume a greater role in regulating land use. States established statewide or regional growth controls in the 1960s and 1970s leveraging their collective and constitutive decision-making authority. In the 1970s repeated attempts at national land use regulation fell short. In reaction to centralizing authority and the loss of control at the local level, the Sagebrush Rebellion and the Wise Use movements sprang up in the 1970s and 1980 at the local level. The land trust movement emerged in the 1980s and 1990s in part due to the challenges of protecting land within a context of private property rights enshrined in the Constitution. At the operational level, market-based tools such as conservation easements and fee simple land purchase were reasonable alternatives within an atmosphere that was not favorable to more centralized regulatory approaches at the state or federal level.

THE WATERSHED GOVERNANCE SYSTEM

Water resources long have been an organizing stimulus for society. Watershed management is not an innovative idea in itself, but its renewed application is. Watersheds are topographically defined areas that drain stream systems into lakes, rivers, or oceans. They include both surface and groundwater supplies and terrestrial and community resources.[65] In the late 1800s John Wesley Powell suggested watershed-level governance as a means to manage the western part of the United States.[66] Powell's vision was largely ignored until the late 1980s and the 1990s, when watershed initiatives proliferated rapidly.[67]

The failure to integrate water resource management at the watershed level in Powell's day led to an alternative path of governance organized administratively along state and county lines. These mostly linear political boundaries resulted in fragmentation of natural functions and the division of governing entities overseeing these functions. The very organization of the governing system made it easier to ignore the relationships between land and water, surface water and groundwater, and water quantity and quality.[68] Dividing natural resource management into a federated system with local, state, and national levels with responsibilities split among executive, legislative, and judicial branches further discouraged integration. The consequence of these governance decisions was management systems unable to address contemporary environmental challenges such as degraded habitats, disappearing water, and non–point-source pollution that face watersheds. Rising frustration with ineffective and inefficient solutions to these problems provided the incentive to seek new ways of managing water resources. Responding to these challenges, local residents, agencies, and others reinvigorated Powell's initial vision of watershed initiatives where "every man is interested in the conservation and management of the water supply" and "there is a body of interdependent and unified interests and values, all collected in one hydrographic basin."[69]

There are five dominant historical eras that relate to watershed governance.[70] These eras are not cleanly separated but partially overlap. Doug Kenney exhorts that this history must be taken into account because "reformers do not have the luxury of starting with a clean slate, but must instead adapt to and exploit the barriers and opportunities that have built up through decades of institutional inertia."[71] The following history conveys how the federal-state-local balance of power has shifted over time in response to a variety of conditioning factors, such as the rise in environmental activism, increases in fiscal conservatism, a decline in the status of federal water agencies, and a growing desire to incorporate a broader group of participants in decision making related to water resources.

Progressive Era

The first era covers the Progressive Era from 1890 to the 1920s. As has already been discussed, John Wesley Powell was strongly influenced during his tours of the West by the need to focus on the communal and cooperative management of water resources. He drew his inspiration from the Hispanic pueblo communities and the Mormons in Utah. Powell argued against the notion of the prior appropriation system of water rights. He presciently warned of the deleterious consequences that would follow when the land was separated from the value of water. While these sentiments were largely ignored, two vestiges of Powell's beliefs survived the Progressive Era and went on to influence water management activity. First, the idea of a hydrologically defined unit was married to the notion of multipurpose water projects, which formed the core of water project development for many years. Second, the idea of regionalism was applied to river basin development and management.[72] Arguably, these ideas were adopted at scales significantly larger than Powell envisioned, but they adhered to the notion of management along topographical and hydrological boundaries.

The federal government went on to play a major role in financing water development on a large scale during the Progressive Era. Eastern canal building had set a precedent for assisting the West. Consistent with Progressive Era ideals, irrigated agriculture became an important national goal, and federal funding for the efforts accomplished the dual objectives of assisting the family farmer and lessening the influence of monopolists. In 1902 the Reclamation Act was passed, thereby establishing the Bureau of Reclamation and providing the framework for the federal reclamation program. Another Progressive Era ideal that permeated water management was the belief that water development should serve many uses. Multiple-use projects, such as damming for water storage, irrigation, and hydroelectric use, embraced this vision.[73]

Depression Era

The second era in water management is typified by federal water projects and covers 1929 to 1942. National interest in water development projects ensured a strong federal role in these decades. In the East, interstate navigational needs instigated a variety of regional water studies that firmly established a legal and political role for the federal government. That perspective was transferred to the West by profederal constitutional interpretation of the commerce and property clauses, and the establishment of the federal water reclamation program.[74]

Federal water projects and development helped drive the country out of the Depression. The Public Works Administration, Works Progress Administration, and

Civilian Conservation Corps, among other agencies, provided the expertise and manpower for this intense era of development.[75] Formidable structures such as the Hoover, Shasta, Bonneville, and Grand Coulee dams were all products of this era. In addition to the water development projects, great efforts were made to create institutions for regional water development and management. Foremost among these was the TVA, established in 1933. TVA embodies regionalism and multipurpose water development within a highly autonomous and authoritative federal regional water agency.[76] Repeated attempts were made to create similar institutions in other river valleys, but they never gained traction as the crisis of the Depression receded.

Kenney claims that one of the lasting innovations from the Depression Era to have an impact on the current-day watershed movement is the U.S. Soil Conservation Service.[77] Established in 1933 as the Soil Erosion Service to combat the dust bowl, the agency has long been a proponent of federal, state, and local partnerships at regional scales. In 1935 with the Soil Conservation Act, the agency working in partnership with the states facilitated the establishment of conservation districts throughout the United States.[78] At one time, some three thousand conservation districts blanketed all the states.

Prewar and Postwar Era

The third era begins after World War II when additional projects undertaken by the Bureau of Reclamation and the U.S. Army Corps of Engineers (USACOE) resulted in massive interstate water development efforts.[79] Federal interagency river basin committees, on the rise between 1943 and 1960, were designed to coordinate regional water development activities. The basin interagency committees were in response to the turf wars between federal agencies, regional authorities such as the Tennessee Valley Authority (TVA), and the conservation districts. To overcome some of these divisions, they were to combine state and federal efforts. However, these were not participatory decision-making structures; rather, they became known as "iron triangles" for the strength of the bonds between agencies, interest groups, and congressional committees that authorized and implemented new projects. The interagency river basin committees were abolished and the Water Resources Council was established by the 1965 Water Resources Planning Act.[80] According to Kenney, these commissions were more responsive to the states, but they did a poor job in responding to the environmental movement in the late 1960s and 1970s. In 1981 the commissions were terminated by executive order, effectively ending the era of large water development projects and attempts at regional coordination. One of the big obstacles for the commissions was their inability to make enforceable decisions, since decision-making authority ultimately rested with Congress and the agencies.[81]

During this era we begin to see the beginning of the consolidation of regulatory power at the federal level in terms of pollution control. In 1948 the Federal Water Pollution Control Act was passed. This was the first major law to address water pollution. In its original form, the act authorized the surgeon general of the Public Health Service to carry out programs that would eliminate or reduce pollution in the interstate waters. The main focus was on public health and the need to reduce the flow of disease-carrying human wastes into rivers and streams.[82] The second focus in the law was to direct federal authorities to assist states and municipalities with sewage and waste treatment. Prior to this era, states and municipalities alone had been in charge of setting goals, implementing policy, and enforcing pollution control requirements.

Cooperative Federalism

The fourth overlapping era begins in the 1960s and extends through the 1970s. It is characterized by a more decentralized effort by the states and by cooperative federalism. The 1960s were the beginning of the end of the federal water development era. Environmentalists opposed these massive projects on the grounds of their effects on wildlife and resources. Greater attention was paid to how federal funds were spent, and there were fewer good dam sites left to pursue.

After the basin interagency committees were dismantled, efforts were made to develop an arrangement that featured "greater federal-state cooperation, a reduced policymaking role for federal water agencies, a greater respect for environmental values, and an attempt to limit the influence of the iron triangles."[83] It is during this era that emphasis begins to shift from regional water development to regional water management. The focus shifted to water quality planning and federal subsidies for wastewater treatment. Previously the states had been in charge of developing water quality standards. However, this approach was largely ineffective, and when Cleveland's Cuyahoga River literally caught fire in 1969 from the amount of industrial pollution choking the river, Congress decided to take another look at water policy. In 1972 and again in 1977, the Federal Water Pollution Control Act was amended and took the form that is better known today as the Clean Water Act. The 1977 amendments in particular ceded greater authority to the federal government and the EPA.[84] This included granting the EPA authority for establishing the basic structure for regulating point-source discharges into waterways, implementing pollution control programs such as setting wastewater standards, and funding the construction of sewage treatment plans under the construction grants program. This also meant that the federal government, in keeping with its new role as the central regulator for water quality, shared financial responsibility for the construction of municipal sewage treatments plans through significant cost-sharing programs with the states. The federal portion of each grant was up to 75 percent of the total capital cost of a wastewater facility. Likewise, the states were to assume the lead role in implementing and enforcing federally approved standards. This was done through the National Pollutant Discharge Elimination System (NPDES). Through the NPDES, the EPA authorized states to issue permits to discharging facilities.

New Federalism

As Kenney observes, "by the 1980s, Cooperative Federalism was giving way to the States-rights philosophy known as 'New Federalism,' which had become the battle cry of the incoming Reagan administration."[85] Under these new arrangements, the states were encouraged to take the lead on water management innovations.

Subsequent revisions to the Clean Water Act in 1981 and 1987 modified and then phased out the municipal construction grants program delegating greater responsibility to the states for the construction of treatment plants through a revolving loan fund. Also in 1987 Congress addressed the problem of non–point-source pollution as it pertained to storm water by incorporating industrial storm water dischargers and municipal storm sewer systems under the NPDES system. A non–point-source pollution demonstration grant program was extended to the states to address agricultural discharge issues, which remained unregulated.[86] In 1992 EPA published regulations establishing total maximum daily load (TMDL) procedures as a means to manage the maximum amount of pollutants a body of water could receive while still meeting water quality standards. This process incorporated both point and nonpoint sources of pollution in a watershed.

Regional water management was dismantled when the Water Resources Planning Act was phased out in 1981. However, the desire for regional management remained, and states began innovating with different forms of governance.[87] The Northwest Power Planning Council (NWPPC) emerged as one innovative organization. The Pacific Northwest Electric Power Planning and Conservation Act of 1980 authorized the creation of the NWPPC so that it could manage the future energy needs in the Columbia River basin while also protecting fisheries. The NWPPC is an interstate compact body with appointees from Washington, Oregon, Idaho, and Montana and is funded by revenues from the Bonneville Power Administration. The NWPPC was charged with developing fish, wildlife, and energy plans for the region. To do so, it solicits input from the relevant agencies, Indian tribes, industry interests, and other parties before engaging in broader public participation. The plans are then implemented by the relevant federal agencies—the Bonneville Power Administration, the USACOE, the Bureau of Reclamation, and the Federal Energy Regulatory Commission. According to Kenney, "few (if any) [regional organizations] exhibit the high level of regional focus and accountability, environmental consciousness, and formal management authority of the NWPPC."[88] Beyond the Pacific Northwest, there has been little innovation in river basin administration.

Beginning in the 1980s and into the 1990s, the real action in innovative watershed management occurred at the substate level with the rise of community-based and collaborative watershed efforts. During this era the watershed came to be viewed as place-based ecological, socioeconomic, political units that could be used for conservation and management planning.[89] Watershed management at this more localized scale was a means to complement more traditional, top-down methods of management that deemphasized hydrological boundaries and ecological and human interconnections.[90] Ineffective government solutions to water quality and quantity problems stimulated the search for new alternatives to address water issues. The rise of ecosystem management, the reauthorization of the Clean Water Act, and the Endangered Species Act (ESA) all provided incentives for innovation at the watershed scale. The trend was additionally supported by the movement toward federal devolution in which federal control and ownership of natural resources was pushed down the government hierarchy.[91]

Watershed management groups typically feature both governmental and nongovernmental participants to address stubborn water-related problems and utilize collaborative mechanisms to facilitate interaction across and among these various stakeholders. Collaboration is usually essential due to the maze of bureaucratic and intergovernmental institutions these groups must navigate to pursue their objectives. Sometimes watershed groups are granted rulemaking authority to assist state agencies.[92] However, this is more the exception than the rule. Often the groups work at the collective decision-making level to coordinate operational-level decisions to improve their watershed.

What was initially seen as a grassroots-driven movement has now been embraced by federal resource agencies and state governments. As the idea of more localized watershed management gained popularity, so did interest in spreading the idea. Federal and state agencies took up the charge of promoting watershed management, with the EPA leading the way.[93] Altogether, nine federal agencies have endorsed the Clean Water Action Plan, which called for watershed protection efforts.[94] Additionally, the USFS and the Department of the Interior have recognized the role of stakeholders in watershed assessments, monitoring, planning, and implementation. Many state legislatures have authorized or supported watershed efforts. Oregon's watershed councils are perhaps the best-structured and best-organized example, and others states have joined in, including California's CALFED program, Washington State's Watershed Planning Act of 1998, the Massachusetts Watershed Initiative, Montana, and West Virginia's Clean Streams program, among others. In these cases states provide technical assistance, staff, training, and financial support among other resources to support watershed groups in their objectives.[95]

While watershed efforts in the 1980s and 1990s were primarily focused at place-based scales, states and the federal government have important if not essential roles to play in these efforts. It would be a mistake to characterize watershed management as solely a local effort. Only about one-fifth of the four hundred-plus watershed initiatives investigated by the Natural Resources Law Center at the University of Colorado in 2000 were instigated without the encouragement of a local, state, or federal agency.[96] State governments have established approximately 40 percent of all these initiatives, while federal and local governments play a role in 20 percent each. In a nationwide survey of watershed groups, Brad Clark and others found that state agency personnel were active in 68 percent of the groups and federal agencies were present in 53 percent of the groups.[97]

As of 2008 the EPA listed more than 3,500 watershed groups in its voluntary database.[98] Because state law generally determines water allocation and priorities, there are differences between watershed groups in the East and West. The prior appropriation doctrine and issues related to water quantity are more prevalent in the West. According to Clark and others, states out West are more likely to be concerned with in-stream flows, endangered species—especially salmon and steelhead—and water supply. In the East, the riparian doctrine and water quality (industrial pollution, urban or agricultural runoff) concerns are more dominant. Concerns in the East have centered on past and present industrial pollution, especially coal mines, and urban and agricultural runoff. States in the East tend to have watershed groups that have been around longer on average than groups in the West. States in the West tend to have larger budgets and fewer members than watershed groups in the East.[99]

Case study and more aggregated work on watershed groups have occurred on organizations across the United States. Several regions have been featured in this research, including the Pacific Northwest and California, the intermountain West, the upper Midwest, the Atlantic coast, and the Northeast.

Watershed governance has a long history. Consequently any innovation finds itself within a nested web of actors, agencies, and laws that can potentially affect its success. The era of watershed development was dominated by federal actors and constitutive proclamations. These projects operated on massive scales and were partially responsible for pulling the nation through the Great Depression. In the post–World War II era, emphasis on watershed development declined and watershed management rose. Federal actors became more prominent in pollution reduction and control, where state and localities had previously controlled water treatment. The federal government, in the form of the newly formed EPA, assumed control for setting and enforcing water quality standards for the states with the passage of the Clean Water Act Amendments of 1972 and 1977. Efforts to govern river basins and watersheds at the regional level never gained much traction, mostly due to lack of constitutive decision-making power to support such efforts. The major agencies that had been in charge of water development and management were reluctant to give up control to regional decision-making authorities. In the 1980s states were given greater power to manage pollution. Cooperative federalism and new federalism characterized efforts to give states greater control over water quality management. The constitutive power for this shared authority makes clear that states are working on behalf of the EPA, which continues to set standards. In the 1980s local watershed councils and collaborative watershed groups emerged. These trends continued throughout the 1990s and into the twenty-first century. Watershed groups represent collective attempts to create norms for operational action at the local level. Sometimes watershed groups are granted rulemaking authority, but more often formal decision-making power is limited. State and federal officials, working in supportive roles, have provided resources in terms of staff, training, technical assistance, and funding to groups.

THE FOREST GOVERNANCE SYSTEM

Community-based forestry or community-based forest management emerged in the 1980s in response to the frustrations experienced by residents, workers, activists, and others who value forest resources. Community-based forestry has been characterized as emerging out of the sustainable communities movement because (much like the sustainable community movement) community-based forestry places emphasis on the interconnections between environmental quality, equity, and community well-being along with place-based solutions and the need for social engagement.[100]

Facing declining health in communities and forests, divergent groups sought alternatives to existing management practices that all too often had previously ended up in appeals, lawsuits, or other forms of obstruction that prevented work from being accomplished on the ground. Environmentalists, timber workers, government officials, and community residents joined together to engage in sound forest management that provided not only jobs but also, in the process, healthier and more sustainable ecosystems.

New tools, including stewardship contracts, voluntary working agreements, and multiparty monitoring, enabled communities to work with state and federal agencies to thin forests, thereby protecting and enhancing flagging ecosystems and communities. Stakeholder groups and outreach efforts gave new participants a greater degree of influence in decision making. As Mark Baker and Jonathan Kusel put it, "Community forestry is about encouraging bottom-up forms of development and forest management that are conceived, developed, implemented and monitored by communities themselves, often in partnership with supporting public and private institutions."[101] These new innovations took different forms in different communities, some of which were more successful than others.

Community forestry can be divided into four eras that have shaped its evolution. First, the Progressive Era and emergence of the USFS is important to illustrate the agency's pervasive influence on communities and why communities sought alternatives in forest management. Second, the environmental movement ushered in a host of new constitutive rules that allowed greater participation by those who had historically been excluded from agency decision making. While the agency continued to be the primary decision maker, new perspectives needed to be taken into account. Third, there are historical precedents for community forestry that do not fit cleanly into the historical time line. There is a history of communal resource management in New Mexico that is particularly relevant for this book. This history helps contextualize the case study of the Camino Real Ranger District. Finally, the current community forestry movement emerged in the 1980s in response to the failures of traditional forest management.

The Progressive Era and Growth of the USFS

Community-based forestry appeared against a backdrop in which the USFS played a leading role. The roots of the USFS and the national forest system emerged during the late 1800s amid growing concerns about the conservation and efficient use of forest resources. The impetus for establishing the forest reserves—precursors to today's national forests—arose after a century of intense settlement and development left many previously forested areas barren. Prior to the establishment of the forest reserves, the federal government had had little role in forest management. Decision-making authority rested with the existing timber industry and with new entrepreneurs who were eager to capitalize on the low prices of forested land. At the time there was considerable scandal attached to the disposal of timberlands in the public domain to private interests. With easy entry into the timber market, opportunistic businessmen cut and abandoned many areas. The increase in competition posed a threat to the existing timber industry, which complained that waste and unsound practices used by the emergent lumbermen threatened the health and long-term supply of the country's timber.[102] Subsequent flooding, fires, erosion, and potential timber shortages raised awareness of the need for managed forests and forestry practices.[103] After a century of public lands disposal, the federal government reversed its policy direction and gave the president the authority to set aside lands in what were then called "forest reserves." The Creative Act of 1891, also known as the General Revision Act, allowed the president to "set apart and reserve . . . public lands wholly or in part covered with timber or undergrowth . . . as forest reserves."[104]

By 1893 presidents Benjamin Harrison and Grover Cleveland had created reserves totaling 17.5 million acres.[105] While the General Revision Act authorized the establishment of forest reserves, no provisions were made to manage or administer the lands, and President Cleveland was hesitant to add additional acreage until provisions were made for the reserves to be managed. In 1897 Congress passed the Forest Management Act, otherwise known as the Organic Act, which established custodial management direction for the forests. In 1898 Gifford Pinchot took over what was then known as the Division of Forestry. As Glen Robinson has remarked, "Pinchot was a man for the times" and capitalized on the country's progressive fervor and his own considerable bureaucratic skills to build his agency.[106] The genesis of the USFS must be viewed in the context of the Progressive conservation movement, whose "essence was rational planning to promote efficient development and use of all natural resources."[107] The vital players in the Progressive movement, among them President Theodore Roosevelt and Pinchot, sought to transform a "decentralized, nontechnical, loosely organized society, where waste and inefficiency ran rampant, into a highly organized, technical and centrally planned and directed social organization which could meet a complex world with efficiency and purpose."[108] The goal was to create a cadre of professionally trained foresters to oversee the management of what was to become the national forests, thereby removing the influence of corrupt locals, who often exerted control over the resources. In the process, the Progressive Era reforms effectively separated community well-being from forest health—a lasting influence that eventually gave rise to the community forestry movement.[109]

The Progressive prescription for providing order to society rested with employing scientifically trained, expert personnel who were not politically beholden to the controlling influences that had permeated government since the Jacksonian era. These independent experts were mandated to assert their authority to use economic and silvicultural planning to provide ample prosperity and material abundance for the growing nation. To counter what was believed to be the corruptive power of local political influence, the conservation movement vested decision-making power in centralized authorities. As Hays observed, "Their entire program emphasized a flow of authority from the top down and minimized the political importance of institutions which reflected the organized sentiment of local communities."[110]

A competing vision for the organization of the nation's forests resources, based on community management of locally owned lands, also emerged in the late 1800s. Advocated by Bernard Fernow, Samuel T. Dana, and Theodore Zon, all foresters and contemporaries of Pinchot, the idea was modeled after German examples of communal forest management that yielded steady income and employment opportunities to locals.[111] Pinchot did not support the idea; instead he devoted his energies to the establishment of scientific forest management on national lands. The idea for a more locally embedded forestry, this time on public lands, again was raised in the early 1900s by Benton Mackaye.[112] Mackaye placed emphasis on community-based development, participation, equity, and cooperation that would integrate social and environmental concerns on the national forests. MacKaye was especially troubled by the federal government's concentration of power over labor and resources, which he feared would fail to provide social equity and environmental stewardship at the local level.[113] Pinchot also rejected this idea, for he believed that communities did not possess sufficient skills to manage forests. The goal was to insulate public forests and "consolidate power and authority away from local communities within centralized public agencies."[114]

In keeping with this vision, the responsibilities of the USFS grew throughout the early and mid-1900s. Several major pieces of legislation expanded its scope of activities and size. Twenty million acres of land in the East were added between 1911 and 1950. Cooperative forestry programs with the states were started in 1924. Experimental forests and a research program were initiated in 1928. Land conservation and replanting programs were established in the 1930s. Grasslands were added to the national forest system in 1937.

As of 2009 the USFS employed thirty thousand people and oversaw 191 million acres of land on a total of 155 national forests and twenty national grasslands. Organizationally the agency is divided into three parts—the national forest system, forestry research, and state and private forestry. The national forest system, which makes up the largest and best-known part of the agency, holds the greatest share of total USFS staff and funding. There are four levels of administration within the national forest system hierarchy: the national office in Washington, D.C., nine regional offices, 155 national forests, and approximately six hundred ranger districts. The chief forester is the USFS's top administrator. Regional foresters possess responsibility for all activities within their nine respective regions. Forest supervisors are in charge of the individual national forests, and district rangers provide direction at the local level.

In the early years, the USFS was widely admired, and Pinchot cultivated a work-force of experts that were shown to be trustworthy stewards and worthy of respect.[115] The national forests were protected from "fire, insects, disease, and rapacious develop-ers," and the Forest Service performed a great public service.[116] Forestry proved to be a reliable science that provided an endless supply of resources for an ever-growing nation. However, as the demand for timber increased in the 1950s with the demands of the suburban housing market, the perception of the agency and its management practices began to change.

Environmental Era

In the 1960s and 1970s observers asserted that the USFS no longer protected the forests but had been "captured" by timber industry interests.[117] Timber production, they accused, was the agency's main concern. The multiple-use doctrine and the "greatest good for the greatest number in the long run" philosophy had consistently been interpreted to mean that timber was the primary focus and would be harvested in a manner that was beneficial to wildlife, watersheds, and other forest uses. In fact, it was this consistency, or unwillingness to change, that led the agency to find itself "out of step" with the times and increasingly facing challenges from those who were asserting control over the nation's forests.[118]

When the USFS discovered that it was being portrayed as "the enem[y] of the environment and the people," it came as a great shock to many employees.[119] For the first fifty years of its existence, the USFS had gained its authority through consistency and professionalism. Throughout the early decades, the agency fought off numerous challenges to its authority while enjoying popular support for its actions.[120] Therefore, as the agency entered the 1960s, it had survived many challenges to its authority, and the tenets of professional forestry provided sufficient and defensible policy for the agency. However, as the national culture began to change in the 1960s, the USFS failed to change with it. Diverse groups became interested in the way forests were managed, especially for recreation and aesthetic values. But the agency remained rooted in commodity production. Other disciplines such as ecology, botany, and zoology challenged the primacy of forestry as a management option. As David Clary asserted, forestry no longer represented the collective national wisdom on forests.[121]

Rising environmental awareness manifested itself in many constitutive changes, and Congress enacted numerous pieces of legislation giving weight to environmen-tal values (e.g., Wilderness Act, NEPA, Clean Air Act, Clean Water Act, and ESA). Armed with these new laws, emergent environmental interests began to challenge the USFS's power and ability to protect noncommodity resources. These new laws threatened to reduce not only timber harvests but also the authority of the agency.[122]

Perhaps the most revolutionary aspect of the new laws was that the public was given an expanded role in decision making. In contrast to the earlier values of economy and efficiency, a premium had been placed on representativeness and responsiveness.[123] National environmental groups were instrumental in seeking and securing the passage of these new rules.

The relationship between the USFS, Congress, and the public also had taken on a fundamentally new character. Prior to the 1960s the USFS had written most of its own forestry legislation.[124] Working in an "iron triangle" mode with the timber industry lobby and congressional committees, the USFS had controlled its own legislative destiny for decades. But with the advent of the Multiple Use and Sustained Yield Act of 1960, NEPA of 1969, the Resources Planning Act of 1974, and the National Forest Management Act of 1976, Congress was crafting legislation with significantly less input from the USFS and the timber industry. The agency faced a higher authority that imposed on it a whole new set of unfamiliar policies; in addition, numerous watchdog groups were overseeing the policies' implementation. Indicating the growing power of groups that challenged the USFS, memberships in the forty-four largest environmental groups with forest-related interests doubled during the 1980s.[125] Moreover, interest groups had become technically sophisticated and knowledgeable, thereby breaking the information monopoly once held by the agencies.

While social values have changed greatly to appreciate noncommodity resources, it has been difficult for the USFS to overcome its deeply entrenched commitment to commodity resources, such as timber and rangeland. The organizational structure was founded on the primacy of commodity management, and many of the professional norms and incentive structures within the agency evolved to reflect this bias. These factors have contributed to the USFS's reputation as unresponsive to changing societal preferences and have compounded the agency's inability to be more responsive to the new social context in which it finds itself. The erosion of authority within the USFS and the rise of power among interest groups have led to increased polarization and divisiveness as the battle between commodity and noncommodity values plays out in the courts and in Congress. Forest management in recent decades has been derided as an inefficient process that leads to obstruction and legal paralysis. Controversies over red-cockaded woodpeckers in the South, spotted owls and old-growth forests in the Pacific Northwest and Southwest, and persistent threats of forest fires to communities throughout the United States have focused national attention on the failings of forest management.

Beginning in the 1970s, and throughout the 1980s and 1990s, timber harvests on public lands began to fall drastically, as did the jobs associated with them. Environmental lawsuits, consolidation and automation within the timber industry, and increased global competition all contributed to the decline. Starting in the 1980s, gridlock, conflict, and frustration provided the incentive for communities to seek alternative solutions for their forest management problems. As related above, communities dependent on forestry had become disenfranchised from the management of the forests on which they were reliant. The closure of small mills, loss of jobs, and deteriorating forest conditions instigated a call for greater emphasis on improved community and forest health.[126]

Historical Precedents in Community Forestry

There are two noteworthy historical precedents in community forestry that predate the current era. One example takes place in New England and the other in the Southwest. Because the case study addressed in this book deals with the Southwest, more attention is given to this historical background. However, it is worth mentioning that some of the earliest examples of community forestry practiced in the United States (outside of indigenous communities) occurred in New England in the 1900s. "Tree wardens" appointed by town authorities coordinated such forest management and stewardship activities as timber auctions, rental agreements for land leasing, and overseeing reforestation.[127] Proceeds from these agreements and sales became important revenue sources for some towns. These community forests have persisted into 2009 and make up a large portion of town and municipal forests now managed by local public agencies.

Likewise, community forestry has a long history in the Southwest. A centuries-old tradition of communal ownership and management of water, livestock, and forests exists among Southwest Hispano people. These traditions followed the settlers of the Southwest from their home countries of Spain and Mexico and have persisted in spite of hundreds of years of competing institutions that favor private property management and the isolation of community from resource management.

From 1598 until Mexico achieved independence in 1821, the Spanish government ruled the lands throughout the Southwest. During the colonial period Spain bestowed land use and ownership through grants to the settlers. These land grants took two dominant forms—individual and communal ownership. Individual ownership was awarded for building a house and cultivating small agricultural plots. Communal ownership of larger land parcels was conferred to the village for pasture for sheep, goats, cattle and horses, hunting, firewood, and harvesting building materials. Local subsistence use typified the economy. Mexico achieved independence from Spain in 1821 and adhered to Spanish law by recognizing and extending land grants to encourage settlement in unoccupied areas.[128]

Landownership in the region entered a new era following the end of the Mexican War with the 1848 Treaty of Guadalupe Hidalgo. While the United States agreed to honor the Spanish and Mexican land grants of the Hispano settlers, great portions of the land were lost through chicanery, legal process, theft, or ignorance, depending on whom you ask.[129] Congressional survey and adjudication processes were established to determine the validity of land grant claims. To retain title to their land, residents had to hire an attorney, file a claim, and gather the necessary supporting documents and testimony. The ensuing processes were fraught with problems. Land boundaries were unclear, titles to land had been lost, U.S. conceptions of private property fit poorly with traditions of common property management, and transactions conducted in English prevented many Spanish-speaking owners from fully comprehending their circumstances or participating in the events.[130] As a result, great portions of the land grants made to individuals and communities were lost. Much of the contested land now resides within the Carson and Santa Fe national forests in New Mexico. Among the lands that were confirmed, U.S. property tax systems foreign to the Hispano villagers resulted in additional forfeitures of land. While many of the processes under which lands were acquired may be considered legal technically, they were perceived widely to be unfair by the people who inhabited the region and abided by different customs. The perception of many in the area to this day is that the lands were taken unjustly from the owners.

In 1948 the federal government established the Vallecitos Federal Sustained Yield Unit on the Carson National Forest. One of five federal sustained yield units established throughout the country with the Federal Sustained Yield Unit Act of 1944, the Vallecitos unit was intended to provide communities with stable employment and forest products. It largely failed. Large operators and multinational corporations from outside the community were hired to manage the unit. The cutting and milling wage-labor jobs never trickled down to the local community. Local Hispano-owned businesses, too small to achieve the scale envisioned by the USFS, were turned down by the agency when they requested to be designated as operators on the unit. An absence of skilled workers in the region made hiring local help difficult. For decades the unit sat idle or failed to accomplish its objectives of providing stability to the community.[131]

Civil disobedience, protest, and, some would claim, outright insurrection typified northern New Mexico communities in the 1960s. Fed by the lingering perception that their land had been taken from them unfairly, exacerbated by the USFS inattention to local needs while servicing industrial corporations, and inflamed by a groundswell of national activism, some residents took matters into their own hands. Local activists took over USFS property in an attempt to seize back what was "their" land, and according to some accounts, USFS employees were held hostage. Additional USFS property was burned and bombed. The local uprising led to national attention and the development of a policy for the management of the forests in northern New Mexico in 1972.[132]

In 1967 William Hurst, then USFS regional forester, recognized the need for a distinct policy for the people of northern New Mexico. Milo Jean Hassell took Hurst's idea and detailed ninety-nine policy recommendations for the region in a report issued in 1972. This became known as the "The Northern New Mexico Policy" and was circulated to the forest supervisors and district rangers in the Carson, Cibola, and Santa Fe national forests, areas with the greatest concentration of land grant peoples. The Northern New Mexico Policy called for the three forests to recognize the unique cultural connection of the Hispano descendants to the land and to include changes in (a) timber sales to make them more compatible with the needs of local communities, (b) grazing policy to accommodate small permit numbers to better fit the needs of the Hispano communities, (c) firewood and building materials policy to provide communities with deadwood and small-diameter trees for poles, posts, and vigas, (d) attention to Indian ceremonial areas and religious shrines, and (e) attitudes of the USFS employees to acknowledge the uniqueness of northern New Mexico.[133]

The Northern New Mexico Policy was successful in its first years, but relationships and management practices returned to their previous level of antagonism. Power or decision-making authority never moved outside the USFS. By 1980 free-use permits for milk cows and draft horses, mostly for community residents, were abolished by the USFS. Permits were required for people cutting personal-use timber. Goats and sheep were banned from the forests. And large commercial timber sales typified USFS activity. In retrospect, the failure of the Northern New Mexico Policy was less of vision than of poor implementation. Much like the Vallecitos Federal Sustained Yield Unit, the policy was sound, but means to achieve and sustain it were faulty.[134]

Emergence of Community Forestry

Working from the grassroots since the late 1990s, the community forest movement has been a vocal and active participant in fostering change in local opportunities, and this often meant the need to change national forest policy.[135] Community forestry practitioners and activists advocate a vision of community-based ecosystem management. For them, healthy forests mean managing and restoring ecosystems, and this is best done with input from the communities most dependent on the resources in question. Recognizing their close relationship with the USFS, community-based forestry practitioners realized that to effect change they would need to alter the constitutive processes that shaped decision making at their most local level. From the start of the twenty-first century, the community forestry movement has devised a set of foundational principles and has advocated for legislative change to support their vision.[136]

The evolution of the community forestry agenda can be traced to a series of organizational meetings that began in 1995 and proceeded through 2001.[137] These meetings helped consolidate regional interests and then networked these regional interests with national advocacy groups. Beginning in the late 1980s, there was a simultaneous and uncoordinated emergence of a variety of groups throughout the United States interested in a more community-based vision of forest management. Broadening the social network to connect pockets of activists throughout the country and strengthening the collective vision of the movement, the alliances between grassroots practitioners and Washington policy advocates led to strategies to initiate and implement a coherent vision. The initial meetings began with the Roundtable on Communities of Place, Partnerships, and Forest Health that met in October 1995 in Blairsden, California. Organized by the Lead Partnership Group, the meeting sought to work with national interest groups such as American Forests to demonstrate that community forestry did not mean local control.[138] Less than a year after the Blairsden meeting, in February 1996, the Seventh American Forest Congress met in Washington, DC. The objective of the meeting was to bring together a diverse group of government, business, nonprofit, and other interests to discuss the status and future of the nation's forests. Meetings in preparation for the Congress in Washington had concluded that current forestry practices were in a state of dysfunction and that new ideas were needed.[139] The goal was to work toward "a shared vision, a set of principles and recommendations that will ultimately result in policies for our nation's forest that reflect the American people's vision and are ecologically sound, economically viable and socially responsible."[140] One of the most important outcomes of the Forest Congress was the creation of the Communities Committee, which has become the leading voice for communities' ideas about forestry.[141]

In June 1998 American Forests, a bridge group that linked local communities with policymakers in Washington, DC, organized a workshop on community-based forestry in Bend, Oregon. An active steering committee crafted draft papers on topics of concern, and out of these papers and subsequent discussions four topics emerged as the cornerstones of community forestry.[142] These foundational goals were process, stewardship, monitoring, and investment. Process addresses open, democratic processes and the empowerment of communities. This entailed the involvement "of communities through inclusive resource planning and decision making processes that actively engage diverse interests, including forest workers and under-represented groups, and that promote collaboration between public and private organizations by restructuring relationships." Stewardship meant a commitment to the health of land. Ecological health was understood to be linked to the economic, social, and cultural health of the community, and so stewardship activities emphasize ecosystem health while also working toward the social and economic well-being of the community. Monitoring involved gathering and sharing "information in ways that build trust, promote learning, and ensure accountability, including taking immediate corrective measures to inform future actions."[143] The community forestry movement advocated multiparty monitoring in particular. Multiparty monitoring meant involving diverse stakeholders who have an interest in the project to periodically assess the project. Active monitoring encouraged adaptive innovation and the ongoing incorporation of practical and scientific knowledge. Multiparty monitoring recognized that "there are many ways to know and understand a landscape beyond the more conceptually based and formalized knowledge generated by agencies and academia."[144] Investment addressed the real resource needs of communities to enable them to "restore and maintain healthy ecosystems and develop lasting stewardship between ecosystem and communities."[145] Increasing funding for ecosystem restoration and maintenance and developing investment mechanisms that link ecosystem restoration and maintenance activities to the economic vitality of communities were the biggest challenges facing community forestry.

An additional organizational meeting took place in December 2001 in Portland, Oregon, and helped link regional organizations and practitioners to the national community forestry movement. At this meeting the movement laid out a plan of action that included twelve policy issues of greatest concern that then were boiled down to four priority action items. These were (a) adequate appropriations and funding;

(b) contracting and procurement practices; (c) collaboration with communities; and (d) NEPA and ESA.[146] The strategy for appropriations and funding was to focus on budget and appropriation processes, advocating for USFS and BLM programs that provided resources to communities, such as the USDA Economic Action Program and the National Fire Plan funding and other legislation. Contracting and procurement practices were seen as obstacles to good stewardship since the practices were designed to serve industrial forestry as opposed to the restoration and maintenance of ecosystems. The strategy pursued and supported new contracting authorities, such as stewardship contracting. Collaborative processes were emphasized due to the inconsistency of federal agencies, namely, the USFS and BLM, in working with communities and external interests. Multiparty monitoring was one recommended solution for encouraging productive collaboration and using performance measures to track collaborative efforts. Concern with NEPA and ESA had to do with ensuring that laws promoted stewardship rather than prevented it. Litigation, delays, and problems with NEPA implementation often hindered restoration projects from moving forward. The strategy was to improve NEPA and ESA decision making.

Different pieces of legislation have incorporated the goals of the movement, including USFS Economic Action Programs and stewardship contracting. The USFS Economic Action Programs targeted rural communities to create natural resource-based businesses, especially those related to forest health and resource stewardship.[147] For instance, grants could be used for the development of forest products technologies, to increase commercial use of smaller trees and woody biomass, or to meet the challenges of unplanned growth and wildland/community interface. Stewardship contracting provides new contracting tools more amenable to the needs of communities. Most contracting regulations were created to allow large-scale timber sales. But communities needed contracting mechanisms that facilitated smaller sales and the ability to restore or maintain healthy ecosystems through the removal of small trees and vegetation from trimming trees. In 1999 legislation was passed to enable some of the changes to contracting laws. An initial pilot program of twenty-eight projects then was expanded in 2001 and 2002 to a total of eighty-four pilot projects using the novel contracting tools. The pilot projects required project-level multiparty monitoring to encourage collaboration among agency officials, environmental interests, business interests, community interests, and others. By working together through monitoring, the projects might experience fewer roadblocks, appeals, and delays. Additional influence of the community-based forestry movement is manifest in the National Fire Plan and the Healthy Forests Restoration Act.

NOTES

1. Lawrence MacDonnell and Sarah Bates, eds., *Natural Resources Policy and Law: Trends and Directions* (Covelo, CA: Island, 1993).

2. USFS was established in 1905 when Gifford Pinchot effectively lobbied Theodore Roosevelt to transfer lands in the forest reserves within the Department of the Interior to

Pinchot's management in the Department of Agriculture. Congress had established the forest reserves in 1891. However, Pinchot believed that the forests could not be managed effectively within the Department of the Interior due to scandals remaining from the General Land Office. The creation of the USFS in the Department of Agriculture signified the movement to a more professionalized discipline of forestry in line with the Progressive movement's philosophies; see Robert H. Nelson, "The Federal Land Management Agencies," 37–60, in *A New Century for Natural Resources Management*, ed. Richard L. Knight and Sarah F. Bates (Washington, DC: Island Press, 1995), 40, 44–45; BLM was established in 1934 when the public domain was closed. Many lands were removed from availability under the Taylor Act and placed under active federal management. The predecessor agency to the BLM was the General Land Office, which was established in 1812 to oversee the disposal of the federal lands (Nelson, "The Federal Land Management Agencies," 40, 52–53); USFWS was established in 1940 within the Department of the Interior from two agencies that had been located in the Department of Commerce and Department of Agriculture, respectively. The first national wildlife refuge was established in 1903 on Pelican Island in Florida, and additional national refugees were added throughout the early 1900s (Nelson, "The Federal Land Management Agencies," 41, 50–51). NPS was established in 1916 by bringing together many separate parks that had been managed individually, including the first national park, Yellowstone, established in 1872 (Nelson, "The Federal Land Management Agencies," 40).

3. Margaret A. Shannon and Alexios R. Antypas, "Open Institutions: Uncertainty and Ambiguity in 21st Century Forestry," in *Creating a Forestry for the 21st Century*, ed. Kathryn Kohm and Jerry F. Franklin (Washington, DC: Island Press, 1997); Herbert Kaufman, *The Forest Ranger: A Study in Administrative Behavior* (Baltimore: Johns Hopkins Press, 1960); and Samuel P. Hays, *Conservation and the Gospel of Efficiency: The Progressive Conservation Movement 1890–1920* (Cambridge, MA: Harvard University Press, 1959).

4. Hans Gerth and C. Wright Mills, *From Max Weber* (Oxford: Oxford University Press, 1958); and Herbert Simon, *Administrative Behavior: A Study of Decision Making Processes in Administrative Organizations*, 3rd ed. (New York: Free Press, 1976).

5. Errol Meidinger, "Organization and Legal Challenges for Ecosystem Management," in *Creating a Forestry for the 21st Century*, ed. K. Kohm and J. Franklin (Covelo, CA: Island, 1997).

6. Hays, *Conservation and the Gospel of Efficiency*.

7. Hanna Cortner and Margaret Moote, *The Politics of Ecosystem Management* (Covelo, CA: Island, 1999); and Jeanne Nienaber Clarke and Daniel C. McCool, *Staking Out the Terrain: Power and Performance among Natural Resource Agencies*, 2nd ed. (Albany: SUNY Press, 1996).

8. Sierra Club was established in 1892, Audubon in 1905, National Parks and Conservation Association in 1919, Izaak Walton League 1922, Wilderness Society in 1935, National Wildlife Federation in 1936, and Defenders of Wildlife in 1947.

9. MacDonnell and Bates, *Natural Resources Policy and Law*; and Robert M. Cutler, "Old Players with New Power: The Non-governmental Organizations," in *A New Century for Natural Resources Management*, ed. Richard L. Knight and Sarah F. Bates (Washington, DC: Island Press, 1995).

10. Hays, *Conservation and the Gospel of Efficiency*; and Robert Gottlieb, *Forcing the Spring: The Transformation of the American Environmental Movement* (Washington, DC: Island Press, 1993).

11. Robert Cameron Mitchell, Angela G. Mertig, and Riley E. Dunlap, "Twenty Years of Environmental Mobilization: Trends among National Environmental Organizations," in

American Environmentalism: The U.S. Environmental Movement, 1970–1990, ed. Riley E. Dunlap and Angela G. Mertig, 11–18 (Washington, DC: Taylor and Francis, 1992); and Cutler "Old Players with New Power."

12. Nicholas Freudenberg and Carol Steinsapir, "Not in Our Backyards: The Grassroots Environmental Movement," in *American Environmentalism*, ed. Riley E. Dunlap and Angela G. Mertig (Washington, DC: Taylor and Francis, 1992).

13. Willet Kempton, James S. Boster, and Jennifer A. Hartley, *Environmental Values in American Culture* (Boston: MIT Press, 1995); and Dunlap and Mertig, *American Environmentalism*.

14. Neil Gunningham and Peter Grabosky, with Peter Sinclair, *Smart Regulation: Designing Environmental Policy* (Oxford: Clarendon Press, 1998), 40.

15. Shannon and Antypas, "Open Institutions"; and S. T. A. Pickett and Richard S. Ostfeld, "The Shifting Paradigm of Ecology," in *A New Century for Natural Resources Management*, ed. Richard L. Knight and Sarah F. Bates (Washington, DC: Island Press, 1995).

16. Meidinger, "Organization and Legal Challenges"; and Shannon and Antypas, "Open Institutions."

17. Meidinger, "Organization and Legal Challenges"; and Jeff DeBonis, "Natural Resource Agencies: Questioning the Paradigm," in Knight and Bates.

18. Vawter Parker, "Natural Resources Management by Litigation," in Knight and Bates; and A. Dan Tarlock, "Environmental Law, But Not Environmental Protection," in *Natural Resources Policy and Law: Trends and Directions*, ed. Lawrence J. MacDonnell and Sarah F. Bates (Covelo, CA: Island, 1993), 162–92.

19. Julia Wondolleck and Steve L. Yaffee, *Making Collaboration Work: Lessons from Innovation in Natural Resource Management* (Covelo, CA: Island, 2000); DeWitt John, *Civic Environmentalism: Alternatives to Regulation in States and Communities* (Washington, DC: Congressional Quarterly Press, 1994); DeWitt John and M. Mlay, "Community-Based Environmental Protection: How Federal and State Agencies Can Encourage Civic Environmentalism," working paper (Washington, DC: National Academy of Public Administration, 1998); Doug S. Kenney, "Resource Management at the Watershed Level: An Assessment of the Changing Federal Role in the Emerging Era of Community-Based Watershed Management" (University of Colorado Law School, March 15, 1997); Steve Selin and Deborah Chavez, "Developing a Collaborative Model for Environmental Planning and Management," *Environmental Management* 19, no. 2 (1995): 189–219; Steve L. Yaffee and Julia M. Wondolleck, "Building Bridges Across Agency Boundaries," in *Creating a Forestry for the 21st Century*, ed. Kathryn Kohm and Jeffy F. Franklin (Washington, DC: Island Press, 1997); and Steve L. Yaffee, Ali F. Phillips, Irene C. Frantz, Paul W. Hardy, Sussanne M. Maleki, and Barber Thorpe, *Ecosystem Management in the United States: An Assessment of Current Experience* (Washington, DC: Island Press, 1996).

20. The legislative groundwork for the Reagan devolution revolution was laid in 1972 with the State and Local Fiscal Assistance Act, which mandates an expanded role for state and local governments. However, the meaningful implementation of this law did not gain full effect until the 1980s (Laurence O'Toole, *American Intergovernmental Relations* [Washington, DC: Congressional Quarterly Press], 1985).

21. James Lester, "Introduction," in *Environmental Politics and Policy: Theories and Evidence*, 2nd ed., ed. James P. Lester (Durham, NC: Duke University Press, 1995), 1–14.

22. For instance, states such as Oregon, Maine, Vermont, California, Minnesota, and Massachusetts have been identified as most committed to the environment, while states like Texas,

Mississippi, Arkansas, Louisiana, and Alabama are the least committed (Bob Hall and Mary Lee Kerr, *1991–1992 Green Index: A State-by-State Guide to the Nation's Environmental Health* [Washington, DC: Island Press], 1991); and Lester, "Introduction." In the 1980s many states revised their constitutions, professionalized their legislatures, modernized and strengthened their governor's office, reorganized their executive branches, reformed their courts, changed their tax structure to increase revenues, and increased opportunities for citizen involvement (Ann O. Bowman and Richard Kearney, *The Resurgence of the States* [Englewood Cliffs, NJ: Prentice Hall, 1986]); Hall and Kerr, 1991; Lester, "Introduction"; and Bowman and Kearney, *Resurgence of the States.*

23. Barry Rabe, "Federalism and Entrepreneurship: Explaining American and Canadian Innovation in Pollution prevention and Regulatory Integration," *Policy Studies Journal* 27, no. 2 (2000): 288–306; and Phillip Shabecoff, "The Environment as Local Jurisdiction," *New York Times*, January 22, 1989, E9.

24. Robert S. Erikson, Gerald C. Wright, and John P. McIver, *Statehouse Democracy: Public Opinion and Policy in the American States* (New York: Cambridge University Press, 1993); and James P. Lester, "Federalism and State Environmental Policy," in Lester, 39–60.

25. Clarke and McCool, *Staking Out the Terrain.*

26. Freudenberg and Steinsapir, "Not in Our Backyards"; and Chris J. Bosso, "After the Movement: Environmental Activism in the 1990s," in *Environmental Policy in the 1990s*, 2nd ed., ed. Norman J. Vig and Michael E. Kraft (Washington, DC: Congressional Quarterly Press, 1994).

27. Fruedenberg and Steinsapir, "Not in Our Backyards."

28. Hocker, "Patience, Problem Solving, and Private Initiative"; Land Trust Alliance Land Trust Alliance, "National Land Trust Census," 1998, www.lta.org/aboutlta/census.shtml (accessed March 30, 2001); and Land Trust Alliance, "National Land Trust Census," 2005, www.lta.org/aboutus/census.shtml (accessed August 22, 2007).

29. Doug S. Kenney, S. T. McAllister, W. H. Caile, and J. S. Peckham, *The New Watershed Source Book: A Directory and Review of Watershed Initiatives in the Western United States* (Boulder, CO: University of Colorado School of Law Natural Resources Law Center, 2000); and Michael V. McGinnis, "Making the Watershed Connection," *Policy Studies Journal* 27, no. 3 (1999): 497–501. EPA lists 3,500 watershed groups in its voluntary data base, www.epa.gov/adopt/network.html (accessed April 2, 2008).

30. Personal communication with Barbara Wycoff; see also www.conservationalmanac.org/forests/map.html (accessed February 2, 2009).

31. Parker, "Natural Resources Management by Litigation."

32. Helen Ingram and Scott J. Ullery, "Public Participation in Environmental Decisionmaking: Substance or Illusion?" in *Public Participation in Planning*, ed. W. R. Derrick Sewell and J. T. Coppock (London: John Wiley & Sons, 1997), 123–39.

33. Deborah J. Salazar, "The Mainstream-Grassroots Divide in the Environmental Movement: Environmental Groups in Washington State," *Social Science Quarterly* 77, no. 3 (1996): 626–43.

34. Terry F. Yosie and Timothy D. Hebst, *Using Stakeholder Processes in Environmental Decisionmaking: An Evaluation of Lessons Learned, Key Issues, and Future Challenges* (Ruder Finn Washington and ICF Incorporated, September 1998).

35. Freudenberg and Steinsapir, "Not in Our Backyards."

36. Frank J. Popper, "The Environmentalist and the LULU," *Environment* 27, no. 2 (1985): 7–40; and Daniel A. Mazmanian and David Morell, "The NIMBY Syndrome: Facility

Siting and the Failure of Democratic Discourse," in *Environmental Policy in the 1990s: Toward a New Agenda*, ed. Norman Vig and Michael Kraft (Washington, DC: Congressional Quarterly Press, 1990).

37. Norman J. Vig, "Presidential Leadership and the Environment; From Reagan to Clinton," in *Environmental Policy*, 4th ed., ed. Norman J. Vig and Michael E. Kraft (Washington, DC: Congressional Quarterly, 2000).

38. Rabe, "Federalism and Entrepreneurship."

39. Richard H. Platt, *Land Use and Society: Geography, Law and Public Policy* (Washington, DC: Island Press, 1996), 215.

40. Ibid.

41. Ibid., 295, 235.

42. Fred Bosselman and David Callies, *The Quiet Revolution in Land Use Control* (Washington, DC: President's Council on Environmental Quality, 1970); and Robert G. Healy and John S. Rosenberg, *Land Use and the States*, 2nd ed. (Washington, DC: Resources for the Future, 1979).

43. Ibid.

44. Healy and Rosenberg, *Land Use and the States*, 12–13.

45. Ibid.

46. Henry L. Diamond and Peter F. Noonan, "New Interests Awaken, New Strategies Emerge, New Problems Arise," in *Land Use in America*, ed. H. L. Diamond and P. F. Noonan (Washington, DC: Island Press, 1996), 79; and Jon Roush, "Freedom and Responsibility: What Can We Learn from the Wise Use Movement," in *Let the People Judge: Wise Use and the Property Rights Movement*, ed. John Echeverria and Raymond Booth Eby (Washington, DC: Island Press, 1995), 1–12.

47. Margaret Kriz, "Land Mine," in *Let the People Judge: Wise Use and the Property Rights Movement*, ed. John Echeverria and Raymond Booth Eby (Washington, DC: Island Press, 1994), 27–35.

48. Platt, *Land Use and Society*, 305.

49. Land Trust Alliance, "National Land Trust Census" (2005), www.lta.org/aboutus/census.shtml (accessed August 22, 2007).

50. Land trusts originated in Massachusetts in 1891. See Jean Hocker, "Patience, Problem Solving, and Private Initiative: Local Groups Chart a New Course for Land Conservation," in *Land Use in America*, ed. H. L. Diamond and P. F. Noonan (Washington, DC: Island Press, 1996), 245–59.

51. Ibid., 246.

52. Diamond and Noonan, "New Interests Awaken," 43.

53. Hocker, "Patience."

54. Ibid.; and Land Trust Alliance, "National Land Trust Census" (1998), www.lta.org/aboutlta/census.shtml (accessed March 30, 2001); Land Trust Alliance, "National Land Trust Census" (2005).

55. Land Trust Alliance, "National Land Trust Census" (1998).

56. Land Trust Alliance, "National Land Trust Census" (2005).

57. Ibid.

58. Diamond and Noonan, "New Interests Awaken," 44.

59. Land Trust Alliance, "National Land Trust Census" (1998); and J. A. Gustanski, "Protecting the Land: Conservation Easements, Voluntary Actions, and Private Land," in *Protecting the Land: Conservation Easements Past, Present and Future*, ed. J. A. Gustanski and R. H. Squires

(Washington, DC: Island Press, 2000), 9–25. For comparative purposes, Gustanski asserts that 828,000 acres of land were protected through fee title ownership in 1998 compared to 1.4 million acres in conservation easement.

60. Land Trust Alliance, "National Land Trust Census" (2005).

61. S. J. Small, "An Obscure Tax Code Provision Takes Private Land Protection into the Twenty-first Century," in Gustanski and Squires, 55–66.

62. Peter S. Szabo, "Noah at the Ballot Box: Status and Challenges," *BioScience* 57, no. 5 (2007): 424–27.

63. Land Trust Alliance, "Summary Data from the National Land Trust Census" (1998), www.lta.org/aboutlt/censum.htm (accessed March 30, 2001).

64. Land Trust Alliance, "National Land Trust Census" (2005).

65. B. T. Clark, N. Burkardt, and M. D. King, "Watershed Management and Organizational Dynamics: Nationwide Findings and Regional Variation," *Environmental Management* 36, no. 2 (2005): 297–310.

66. John W. Powell, "Institutions for Arid Lands," *The Century* 40 (1890): 111–16; and W. Stegner, *Beyond the Hundredth Meridian* (Lincoln: University of Nebraska Press, 1953).

67. Donald Worster, "Watershed Democracy: Recovering the Lost Vision of John Wesley Powell," *Journal of Land, Resources and Environmental Law* 23, no. 1 (2005): 57–65.

68. Doug S. Kenney, "Historical and Sociopolitical Context of the Western Watershed Movement," *Journal of the American Water Resources Association* 35, no. 3 (1999): 493–502.

69. Powell, "Institutions for Arid Lands," 113–14.

70. Doug Kenney, *Resource Management at the Watershed Level: An Assessment of the Changing Federal Role in the Emerging Era of Community-Based Watershed Management* (Boulder, CO: Natural Resources Law Center, 1997). Kenney identifies six eras, but these are consolidated here.

71. Ibid., 87.

72. Ibid.

73. Hays, *Conservation and the Gospel of Efficiency*.

74. Kenney, *Resource Management at the Watershed Level*.

75. Marc Reisner, *Cadillac Desert: The American West and Its Disappearing Water* (New York: Viking Penguin, 1986).

76. Phillip Selznick, *TVA and the Grassroots* (New York: Harper and Row, 1966).

77. Kenney, *Resource Management at the Watershed Level*.

78. Clarke and McCool, *Staking Out the Terrain*.

79. Kenney, *Resource Management at the Watershed Level*.

80. C. B. Griffin, "Watershed Councils: An Emerging Form of Public Participation in Natural Resource Management," *Journal of the American Water Resources Association* 35, no. 3 (1999): 505–18.

81. Kenney, *Resource Management at the Watershed Level*.

82. A. Myrick Freeman, "Water Pollution Policy," in *Public Policies for Environmental Protection*, ed. Paul Portney and Robert Stavins (Washington, DC: Resources for the Future, 2000), 169–214.

83. Kenney, *Resource Management at the Watershed Level*, 105.

84. Walter A. Rosenbaum, *Environmental Politics and Policy*, 7th ed. (Washington, DC: Congressional Quarterly Press, 2007), especially chapter 6.

85. Kenney, *Resource Management at the Watershed Level*, 112–13.

86. Freeman, "Water Pollution Policy."

87. Kenney, *Resource Management at the Watershed Level*, 112–13.

88. Ibid., 115.

89. Clark et al., "Watershed Management and Organizational Dynamics."

90. William D. Leach, and Neal W. Pelkey, "Making Watershed Partnerships Work: A Review of Empirical Literature," *Journal of Water Resources Planning and Management*, (Nov./Dec. 2001): 378–85.

91. Kenney, *Resource Management at the Watershed Level*.

92. Toddi Steelman and JoAnn Carmin, "Community-Based Watershed Remediation: Connecting Organizational Resources to Social and Substantive Outcomes," in *Toxic Waste and Environmental Policy in the 21st Century United States*, ed. Dianne Rahm (Jefferson, NC: McFarland, 2002), 145–78; Koontz et al., *Collaborative Environmental Management*. See chapter 6 on the Animas River Stakeholder Group for an example of a group that was given rulemaking authority.

93. Environmental Protection Agency, *Watershed Approach Framework*, 840-S-96–001 (Washington, DC: Environmental Protection Agency, Office of Water, 1996).

94. William D. Leach, Neal W. Pelkey, and Paul A. Sabatier, "Stakeholder Partnerships as Collaborative Policymaking: Evaluation Criteria Applied to Watershed Management in California and Washington," *Journal of Policy Analysis and Management* 21, no. 4 (2002): 645–70.

95. Steelman and Carmin, "Community-Based Watershed Remediation."

96. Kenney et al., *New Watershed Source Book*.

97. Clark et al., "Watershed Management and Organizational Dynamics." East and West in this context are divided roughly along the 100th meridian.

98. U.S. Environmental Protection Agency, "Catalog of Watershed Groups," July 2, 2007, www.epa.gov/adopt/network.html (accessed April 2, 2008).

99. Clark et al., "Watershed Management and Organizational Dynamics."

100. Mark Baker and Jonathan Kusel, *Community Forestry in the United States: Learning from the Past, Crafting the Future* (Covelo, CA: Island, 2003), 6.

101. Ibid., 66.

102. Hays, *Conservation and the Gospel of Efficiency*, 29.

103. Glen O. Robinson, *The Forest Service: A Study in Public Land Management* (Baltimore: Johns Hopkins University Press, 1975), 4–5.

104. Section 24.

105. Robinson, *Forest Service*, 6.

106. Ibid., 8.

107. Hays, *Conservation and the Gospel of Efficiency*, 2.

108. Ibid., 265.

109. Baker and Kusel, *Community Forestry in the United States*.

110. Hays, *Conservation and the Gospel of Efficiency*, 266, 272.

111. Baker and Kusel, *Community Forestry in the United States*, 24–25.

112. Ibid., 27.

113. Ibid., 30.

114. Ibid., 36–38.

115. Gifford Pinchot, *Breaking New Ground* (New York: Harcourt, Brace, 1947), 31.

116. Arnold Bolle, "Foreword," in *Land and Resource Planning in the National Forests*, ed. Charles F. Wilkinson and H. Michael Anderson (Covelo, CA: Island, 1987), 1–5.

117. Gordon L. Bultena and John C. Hendee, "Foresters' Views of Interest Group Positions on Forest Policy," *Journal of Forestry* 70, no. 6 (1972): 337–42.

118. Bolle, "Foreword," 3.

119. Ibid.

120. David A. Clary, *Timber and the Forest Service* (Lawrence: University Press of Kansas, 1986), 196.

121. Ibid., 196–97.

122. Bolle, "Foreword," 3.

123. Terence J. Tipple and J. Douglas Wellman, "Herbert Kaufman's Forest Ranger Thirty Years Later: From Simplicity and Homogeneity to Complexity and Diversity," *Public Administration Review* 51, no. 5 (1991): 421–28.

124. Bolle, "Foreword," 3.

125. Robert G. Healy and William E. Shands, "A Conversation with Marion Clawson: How Times (and Foresters) Have Changed," *Journal of Forestry* 87, no. 1 (May 1989): 18–19.

126. Baker and Kusel, *Community Forestry in the United States*, 1–2.

127. Ibid., 24.

128. S. Clark, "Causes of Land Loss among the Spanish Americans in Northern New Mexico," *Rocky Mountain Social Science Journal* 1 (1963): 201–11.

129. Clyde Eastman, "Community Land Grants: The Legacy," *Social Science Journal* 28, no. 1 (1991): 101–17.

130. Ibid.; and Clark Knowlton, "Reies L. Tijerina and the Alianza Federal de Mercedes: Seekers of Justice," *Wisconsin Sociologist* 2, no. 4 (1985): 133–44.

131. Ernest Atencio, *La Vida Floresta: Environmental Justice Meet Traditional Forestry in Northern New Mexico* (Santa Fe Chapter of Sierra Club, 2001); Carl Wilmsen, "Fighting for the Forest: Sustainability and Social Justice in Vallecitos, New Mexico," PhD diss., Clark University, 1997.

132. William Hurst, "Evolution of Forest Service Policy for Managing the National Forest Land in Northern New Mexico," paper presented before R-3 Forest Officers at a Northern New Mexico Policy Discussion Forum (March 28, 2001); William Hurst, "Region 3 Policy on Managing National Forest Land in Northern New Mexico," memo (March 6, 1972); Patricia Bell Blawis, *Tijerina and the Land Grants: Mexican Americans in Struggle for their Heritage* (New York: International, 1971); and Knowlton, "Reies L. Tijerina and the Alianza Federal."

133. Hurst, "Region 3 Policy."

134. Ernest Atencio, *Of Land and Culture: Environmental Justice and Public Lands Ranching in Northern New Mexico* (Report by the Quivera Coalition and the Santa Fe Group of the Sierra Club, 2001).

135. Jonathan Kusel, "Introduction" in *Forest Communities, Community-based Forestry*, ed. Jonathan Kusel and Elisa Adler (Boulder, CO: Rowman & Littlefield, 2003), xv–xxi.

136. Gerald J. Gray, Maia J. Enzer, and Jonathan Kusel, "Understanding Community-based Forestry Ecosystem Management: An Editorial Synthesis," in *Understanding Community-based Forestry Ecosystem Management*, ed. Gerald J. Gray, Maia J. Enzer, and Jonathan Kusel (New York: Food Products, 2001), 1–25; and Christina Cromley, "Community-based Forestry Goes to Washington," in *Adaptive Governance: Integrating Science, Policy and Decision Making*, ed. Ronald D. Brunner, Toddi Steelman, Lindy Coe-Juell, Christina M. Cromley, Christine M. Edwards, and Donna W. Tucker (New York: Columbia University Press, 2005).

137. Cromley, "Community-based Forestry."

138. The Lead Partnership Group is a consortium of ten groups from northern California and southern Oregon who met to discuss with President Clinton in 1993 the strategies they had found successful in improving forest management in their own backyards.

139. Kusel, "Introduction" in Kusel and Adler.

140. Ibid., xvi.

141. Cromley, "Community-based Forestry Goes to Washington."

142. Ibid.

143. Gray et al., "Understanding Community-based Forestry Ecosystem Management," 19–22.

144. Ibid.

145. Ibid., 22.

146. Cromley, "Community-based Forestry Goes to Washington."

147. The George W. Bush administration canceled the EAP.

CHAPTER 3

Aligning Institutional Characteristics

Implementing Innovation in Land Protection

THE INNOVATION OF GREAT OUTDOORS COLORADO (GOCO) is nestled into the influence of land use governance as detailed in chapter 2 and as depicted in figure 3.1. GOCO represents a statewide innovation that works at the collective and constitutive decision-making level. As an initiative, it leverages the power of constitutive change while specifying the collective decision-making rule. GOCO works with state and regional actors using conservation easements and fee simple ownership to accomplish its goals. GOCO is classified as an innovation because it represented a new way of protecting and conserving land that previously did not exist within Colorado.

INNOVATION IN LAND PROTECTION: INITIATED REGULATION WITH GREAT OUTDOORS COLORADO

People long have been drawn to Colorado for its scenic beauty. The attraction of living and working in a metropolitan setting coupled with easy access to world-class recreational and aesthetic amenities has made the Front Range, especially, a magnet for people seeking a better quality of life. A consequence of this attraction and subsequent growth in population has been the loss of open space, farmland, and wildlife habitat, and the encroachment of people and development into the places that make Colorado special. For instance, even before the large population booms of the 1990s, more than four hundred thousand acres of agricultural lands on the Front Range were developed from 1975 to 1985—the equivalent of seventy-five football fields every day—and approximately one hundred thousand acres of wildlife habitat were

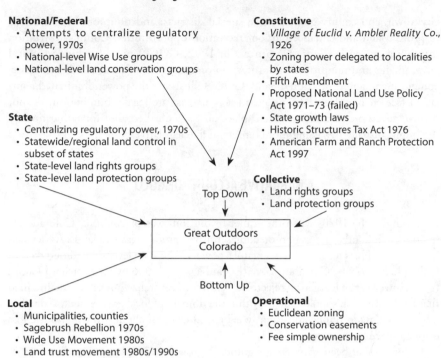

National/Federal
- Attempts to centralize regulatory power, 1970s
- National-level Wise Use groups
- National-level land conservation groups

Constitutive
- *Village of Euclid v. Ambler Reality Co.,* 1926
- Zoning power delegated to localities by states
- Fifth Amendment
- Proposed National Land Use Policy Act 1971–73 (failed)
- State growth laws
- Historic Structures Tax Act 1976
- American Farm and Ranch Protection Act 1997

State
- Centralizing regulatory power, 1970s
- Statewide/regional land control in subset of states
- State-level land rights groups
- State-level land protection groups

Top Down

Collective
- Land rights groups
- Land protection groups

Great Outdoors Colorado

Bottom Up

Local
- Municipalities, counties
- Sagebrush Rebellion 1970s
- Wide Use Movement 1980s
- Land trust movement 1980s/1990s

Operational
- Euclidean zoning
- Conservation easements
- Fee simple ownership

Figure 3.1: Influences on Land Use Governance

lost each year to land use changes.[1] In addition to the loss of open space, agricultural lands, and wildlife habitat, more people placed pressure on existing parks and open spaces. From 1980 to 1990 annual visits to state parks increased nearly 50 percent, to more than eight million with more than two-thirds of Coloradoans visiting a park at least once a year.[2] During the economic and population boom throughout the 1990s, these trends intensified.

Typical of the West, Colorado's lands are under 35 percent federal ownership and protection.[3] Colorado places a premium on residents' concerns about maintaining private property rights, preserving "home rule," and preventing the overregulation of land use at the state and local level.[4] Consequently, like the majority of states, Colorado lacks enabling legislation to support state or regional planning. In a setting dominated by an antiregulatory state legislature influenced heavily by Colorado's rural constituencies, local county and municipal governments are granted the authority to plan for and regulate the use of land without any state-level guidelines or goals.[5]

With increasing pressure on natural resources, robust growth in population, and a political culture that favored local action on land issues, Colorado provided an innovative solution to its land protection challenges in the form of GOCO—a quasi-governmental agency with dedicated funding to provide competitive grants to city, town, and county governments; special districts; and nonprofit organizations to protect land and enhance outdoor recreation opportunities. Coming to fruition through a citizen-led initiative process in 1992, GOCO provided funds to local governments and nonprofit land protection organizations to facilitate the purchase, enhancement, and protection of land. GOCO illustrates the power of initiated regulation (see chapter 1), which results in actions that are legally binding but do not involve government. Rather, citizens place an issue on the ballot for ratification by the public, usually bypassing more representative legislative bodies.

A NARRATIVE ACCOUNT OF GOCO

Beginning in the 1970s when the "quiet revolution" was playing out, Colorado attempted to join other states in protecting sensitive natural areas and lands. As detailed in table 3.1, efforts to centralize regulatory power at the state level were undertaken in Colorado in 1972 by Gov. John Love (D) and again in 1976 by Gov. Richard Lamm (D).[6] However, the legislature rejected all efforts to centralize power and maintained that land protection should remain within the domain of local government. Nonetheless, the Colorado public consistently expressed concern about growth and the loss of open space in their state.

Colorado had been witnessing significant growth in its population. From 1970 to 1980 the population grew approximately 25 percent, and from 1980 to 1990 the population grew an additional 12 percent.[7] In 1988 a poll by The Nature Conservancy (TNC) revealed that only 30 percent of Coloradoans felt the state was doing enough to facilitate land acquisition.[8] In 1990 another poll indicated that 87 percent of the Coloradoan public felt that it was important to devote additional public and private resources to acquire and promote open space, outdoor recreation, and wildlife in their state.[9]

To address open space concerns, the General Assembly of Colorado used the referendum process to submit a constitutional amendment to voters to allow a statewide lottery in 1980. Article XVIII of the Colorado Constitution stated that proceeds from the lottery would be "allocated to the conservation trust fund of the state for distribution to municipalities and counties for park, recreation and open-space purposes."[10] Enabling legislation adopted in 1982 required that the net lottery proceeds were allocated with 50 percent dedicated to capital construction, 10 percent to state parks, and the remaining 40 percent to the Conservation Trust Fund, which made per capita payments to local governments for expenditures on local parks, open space, and recreation projects.[11] After passage, however, the legislature interpreted a clause in the amendment to enable legislators to spend a larger portion of the money on capital construction. In 1988 under great pressure to build more prisons, lawmakers amended lottery statutes to permit the game of Lotto and altered the funding formula to direct lottery proceeds to the construction of correctional facilities. Beginning in

Table 3.1: Chronological Developments in Great Outdoors Colorado

Year	Significant Chronological Events
1970s	Efforts were made by Governors John Love and Richard Lamm to protect sensitive natural areas and lands.
1970s and 1980s	Increased population growth occurred in Colorado.
1980	The General Assembly of Colorado used referendum process to amend the constitution to allow statewide lottery. Proceeds intended to go to parks, recreation, and open space.
1982	Enabling legislation stated that net lottery proceeds would be allocated 50% to capital construction, 10% to state parks, and 40% to local parks, open space, and recreation projects.
1980s and early 1990s	Increased population growth and development of open spaces occurred throughout Colorado.
1990	Gov. Roy Romer calls together the GOCO Citizen's Committee and charges them to figure out a way to sustain and enhance Colorado's outdoor resources. GOCO Citizens' Committee recommends creation of a GOCO trust fund.
1991	The General Assembly of Colorado declines to put GOCO trust fund on ballot as part of referendum.
1991	Citizens for GOCO decides to undertake a campaign to place GOCO initiative on the ballot in 1992. Lottery funds would be redirected to open space protection.
1992	Colorado voters approve GOCO initiative by a 58% margin. Half the lottery funds would go to the Trust Fund, 40% would go to Conservation Trust Fund, and 10% to the Colorado Division of Parks and Outdoor Recreation.
1994	GOCO hires Will Shafroth as first GOCO executive director. First grants disbursed in January 1994.
1997	Colorado House Education Committee proposes bill to siphon money from GOCO to fund school construction. Bill is defeated.
1998	Voters reauthorize lottery. Lottery will sunset in 2024.
2000	John Hereford replaces Shafroth as executive director.
2001	Colorado voters give GOCO authorization to sell $115 million in bonds.
2003	John Swarthout replaces Hereford as executive director.
2005	The General Assembly of Colorado members propose to divert GOCO funds to other programs. Proposal is defeated.
2007	The General Assembly of Colorado members propose to privatize the lottery with the state receiving lump sum payment. Proposal is put on hold.
2009	GOGO has invested more than $575 million in more than 2,800 projects that have protected 850,000 acres of open space throughout Colorado.

1989 the relative shares of lottery revenues going to the Division of Parks and Outdoor Recreation and the Conservation Trust Fund began to decrease.[12] While the original intent of the 1980 referendum had been to fund localities' park, recreation, and open space needs, many of these needs still were going unmet in the early 1990s.

Growing concern over disappearing agricultural land and wildlife habitat; increased pressure on parks, trails, and recreation areas; and the desire to preserve remaining opens spaces in Colorado led Democratic Gov. Roy Romer in April 1990 to call together the GOCO Citizen's Committee, a cross section of business, conservation, and political leaders from across Colorado.[13] The GOCO Citizens' Committee was charged to figure out a way to sustain and enhance Colorado's outdoor resources. Meeting over a nine-month period, the GOCO Citizens' Committee gathered information, held twelve public meetings throughout the state, and heard from more than five hundred citizens. The GOCO Citizens' Committee recommended the adoption of a nine-point program that entailed protection and enhancement of trails and rivers, rivers and reservoirs, state parks, wildlife habitat, nongame and rare species, local parks, open space, and natural areas of statewide importance. To accomplish these land protection goals, the GOCO Citizens' Committee suggested the establishment of a GOCO Trust that would generate interest income to fund a land protection and enhancement program. The cost for the program was estimated at $30 million per year and would be funded through a dedicated mechanism in the form of an increase in state sales tax. Independent of legislative oversight, a board of trustees would oversee the GOCO Trust.

The GOCO Citizens' Committee suggested that the state legislature place the GOCO Trust on the ballot though the referendum process. However, the Senate Banking Committee was unsupportive of increasing the sales tax, making the proposal unlikely to emerge from the committee for a vote. Republican Bill Owens, later elected as Colorado's governor in 1998, served on the Senate Finance Committee and led the effort against placing the GOCO Trust on the ballot.[14] Moreover, general support for the GOCO Trust in the legislature was questionable. As recalled by Gov. Roy Romer, "The legislature was generally very conservative on environmental matters. . . . It was not a legislature that was necessarily thinking of environmental matters, particularly ones that were at the cutting edge."[15] The geographical political dynamics in Colorado meant that rural constituencies dominated in the General Assembly, and land protection issues were not as important in rural areas as they were along the urbanized and urbanizing Front Range. When the proposal was killed, no one was surprised. But time was running out if action was to take place in 1992, and so the Citizens' Committee regrouped, deciding to take the proposal directly to the Colorado public through the initiative process. Land protection's time had not come in the General Assembly. An alternative means was necessary to achieve the benefits of land protection in Colorado.

Believing that the GOCO Trust concept was sound and supported by the Colorado public, a new group formed to undertake a campaign to place a GOCO initiative on the ballot in 1992.[16] Citizens for GOCO emerged out of the GOCO Citizens' Committee along with others to promote the GOCO Trust through the initiative process. Two lawyers in Denver, Richard W. Daily and David Harrison, played active roles in moving the initiative forward. The group conducted polls to determine what the Colorado public would support in terms of a dedicated funding mechanism to bring the GOCO vision to reality. A sales tax increase seemed unlikely to garner the needed votes. Real estate transfers also did not appeal to the public. But the lottery moneys struck a responsive chord. Polls indicated that the public remained aware that money had been set aside for open space in 1980 but was less aware that the legislature had diverted these funds away from open space protection to capital construction projects.

A key theme in the public campaign for the initiative process capitalized on pervasive feelings of resentment toward government. The lottery issue was key to this message. According to Harrison, "Most Coloradoans thought this problem had been fixed in 1980 with the passage of the lottery. But they were told that the problem had not gotten fixed and that most of the money was being spent on prisons. They were outraged. That was the time bomb."[17] Floyd Ciruli, the pollster for the GOCO initiative, summarized, "Coloradoans don't like centralized government; they hold it at a distance with a lot of skepticism. In general they don't trust government. What we argued was that state government distorted the will of the people in terms of their use of lottery dollars."[18] Recalled Harrison, "We tripped upon a feeling among Coloradoans that they had been lied to about the lottery moneys." This sentiment gave Citizens for GOCO emotional leverage to see their idea to fruition. The success of the GOCO initiative "was as much an anti-government reaction as much as a pro-environment action. If we hadn't tripped upon that issue, I am not sure we would have gotten anything done."[19]

Three dominant arguments were put forth in support of the proposal. First, the GOCO amendment would ensure that the lottery funds were spent on Colorado's outdoor infrastructure. The original intent of the lottery in 1980 was for proceeds to fund parks, outdoor recreation, and open space. With the authorization of Lotto, in conjunction with the lottery finance reconfiguration, the majority of gaming proceeds were going to capital construction, which was not the original intent of the people.[20] As recalled by Sydney Macy, head of The Nature Conservancy and one of the drivers behind the GOCO initiative, "We were fortunate that the lottery was there and had been mishandled. That made for a very strong campaign."[21] Second, Colorado had pressing needs in terms of its outdoor infrastructure. The Division of Parks and Outdoor Recreation needed funding for capital improvements, maintenance, and renovation, and the Division of Wildlife needed funding for nongame wildlife programs. Third, increased investment in Colorado outdoor infrastructure would return great economic benefits through the tourism industry.[22]

To place the GOCO initiative on the ballot, supporters needed to collect nearly fifty thousand signatures. To accomplish this goal, the GOCO campaign used paid petition circulators as well as volunteers to collect signatures.[23] "We needed to pay the money and buy the signatures and buy the TV time. That is how the initiative process runs," remembered Harrison. Between eighty thousand and ninety thousand signatures were collected with approximately twenty thousand collected through volunteers.[24] Andrew Purkey, the GOCO campaign coordinator, recalled how he and Laurie Mathews, director of Colorado State Parks, would collect signatures on the weekends: "The State Parks people were really behind the effort."[25]

Money was raised from the Colorado business community, which saw quality of life as an important aspect of the overall business environment—$400,000 was raised to support administration, advertising, and signature collection. Democrat Ken Salazar, director of the Colorado Department of Natural Resources (and later the state attorney general, U.S. senator, and head of the U.S. Department of Interior) and a principal supporter of the GOCO initiative, recalled how they promoted the effort: "We got the mayor, Wellington Webb had just been elected, to come to fund raisers, and we raised money from the business community. . . . My pitch to them for raising money for the campaign was that for Colorado to continue to have a thriving economy, we would have to protect our natural heritage. If we weren't careful our quality of life would be compromised."[26]

There was very little organized resistance against the GOCO initiative, and reaction to the initiative in the legislature was mixed. "There was never a significant opposition campaign. They never organized themselves, but there were some members of the legislature that were very opposed and actively outspoken. They didn't feel this was good for Colorado," recalled Salazar.[27] Arguments against the GOCO amendment took two dominant forms. First, passing the GOCO amendment would negatively affect the state's capital construction fund. The lottery provided the majority of the funds for capital construction during the 1980s, and removing the lottery as a dedicated stream of revenue would hinder the state's ability to engage in lease/purchase agreements, thereby affecting the state's ability to engage in longer-term capital construction projects.[28] If the initiative passed, money would be taken from the capital construction fund and dedicated to open space protection, which was seen as a challenge to the authority of the legislature, especially to those overseeing the capital construction committee. The legislature looked at the "lottery money as being the legislature's money" and removing the legislature's ability to control the money was not well received by the legislature.[29] While the proposed GOCO initiative would succeed in insulating the GOCO Trust from the vagaries of the annual legislative appropriations process, legislators involved in longer-term planning of capital investments were very unhappy.

The second argument against the initiative focused on the policy implications of establishing GOCO. As a constitutional amendment, the GOCO initiative would give the protection of open space special priority at the expense of other state programs. As part of the constitution, GOCO would be difficult to change, and budgetary discretion would be removed from the legislature. Likewise, GOCO, as a constitutionally insulated entity, would be unaccountable to the governor, General Assembly, and electorate.[30] One of the challenges remaining for the Citizens for GOCO was how to counter the opposition's arguments. Citizens for GOCO was worried about a backlash if prisons and schools could not be built. In the end, "we didn't want to be irresponsible. . . . We tried to address these types of concerns by stating that we would meet any current commitments."[31]

To counter these arguments, the shift in lottery funds away from capital construction and to GOCO would be phased in over a five-year period to honor the state's existing capital construction commitments through 1998. Local governments would continue to get their money for parks, open space, and recreation projects through the Conservation Trust Fund. After 1998 a new formula for distributing the net lottery proceeds would take effect. Forty percent would continue to go to the state's Conservation Trust Fund for redistribution for local parks and open space spending on a per capita basis, 10 percent would go to the state Division of Parks and Outdoor Recreation, and the remaining money, up to $35 million in constant 1992 dollars, would go to the GOCO Trust Fund. Any remaining net proceeds from lottery sales over $35 million would go to the general fund. Until 1998, and the reallocation of funds away from capital construction, GOCO was anticipated to receive $7 million to $10 million per year, depending on the volume of lottery sales. An independent board appointed by the governor and confirmed by the state senate would oversee how GOCO funds were distributed.

Despite those opposed to the GOCO initiative, Colorado voters approved Article XXVII of the state constitution by a 58 percent margin (876,424 to 629,490), thereby creating GOCO in November 1992. The GOCO initiative confirmed the original intent of providing funds for parks and open space as approved by voters in 1980 with the lottery. The GOCO initiative stipulated that half the proceeds from the lottery would be split four ways in the Trust Fund—25 percent for matching funds for local parks and open space, 25 percent for statewide open space acquisitions, 25 percent for state parks, local trails, and water recreation, and 25 percent for wildlife and wildlife habitat programs. Forty percent of the remaining half of lottery proceeds would go the Conservation Trust Fund and 10 percent to the Colorado Division of Parks and Outdoor Recreation.

GOCO's funding is capped at $35 million per year and is adjusted for inflation. So, for instance in 2002, GOCO received $46.5 million and in 2003 GOCO received $55.9 million.[32] In 2006 the lottery took in $120 million, and GOCO received $50.2 million of this total.[33] If GOCO's share of lottery funds exceeds the capped amount, the remainder goes to the state Public School Fund. Since 2002 more than $16 million has gone to the capital construction fund for schools. Article XXVII of the Colorado Constitution required GOCO to allocate its lottery proceeds to four areas in roughly equal portions over time. These four areas were investments in (a) wildlife resources through the Colorado Division of Wildlife; (b) outdoor recreation resources through the Colorado Division of Parks and Outdoor Recreation; (c) competitive grants to the Colorado Divisions of Parks and Outdoor Recreation and Wildlife and to counties, municipalities, or other political subdivisions of the state, or nonprofit land conservation organization to identify, protect, and acquire open space of statewide significance;

and (d) competitive matching grants to local government or other entities eligible for distribution from the Conservation Trust Fund to acquire, develop, or manage open lands and parks. From these four funding areas, GOCO developed seven grant programs: the Legacy Initiative, Open Space Land Conservation Grant Program, Local Government Park, Outdoor Recreation and Environmental Education Facilities Grant Program, Outdoor Recreation Grants through Colorado Divisions of Parks and Outdoor Recreation, Wildlife Grants through the Colorado Division of Wildlife, Trail Grant Program, and the Planning and Capacity Building Grant Program.

Once the initiative was passed, additional work remained to get the actual organizational structure up and running. The grants programs had to be clarified. A board had to be appointed. And an agency had to be formed. Ken Salazar became the first chairman of the board of directors. Salazar and Daily began working on hiring someone to be the executive director. As recalled by Salazar, "After it passed, I remember working with the governor to put together a board. I think that was the most stellar board of directors that I have ever seen that has been affiliated with government."[34] Rick Daily had been the legal counsel for the campaign and served as interim director, and they launched a national search for a permanent director. They ended up hiring Will Shafroth in 1994. Shafroth, a Colorado native who had been working in California, was a good fit for the job given his ability to work with a variety of governmental and nongovernmental agencies. He had been associated with the American Farmland Trust, the California Department of Natural Resources, and the California Coastal Commission. Once Shafroth was on board, the discussions about how to set up the grant programs began in earnest.

GOCO used two dominant techniques to accomplish land conservation through these programs—conservation easements and acquisitions of fee title. The competitive grants process encourages various partnerships to work together to protect or enhance land. GOCO's flexible organizational structure did not try to overorchestrate how the various partners should work together, but it did encourage the collaboration among various stakeholders explicitly as part of its application guidelines. This quasi-bureaucratic, market-based approach fit well the culture and political climate of Colorado.

The grants program was not formed when Shafroth came on board as executive director. Creating the grants process and developing the organization of GOCO was an evolutionary process. As recalled by Shafroth, "We didn't expect money to flow until 1994 and the first money came in August 1993, so there was urgency to get some money out the door." The GOCO board had to have discussions with the Parks and Wildlife divisions to figure out what could be done. "My first day on the job was a board meeting in January 1994, and they made a $1 million commitment to State Trails through a yet-to-be-defined process and $1.5 million to State Parks. In February they made a grant to Wildlife for $1.5 million."[35]

Grants are selected through a combination effort by GOCO staff, who screen eligible projects, and the GOCO board of directors, a seventeen-member board appointed by the governor and subject to confirmation by the state senate.[36] Two board members from each of Colorado's seven congressional districts are required, and no two board members from one congressional district can be from the same political party.[37] The grants are disbursed by GOCO staff once the successful applicants are selected and other requirements fulfilled.

The small but growing GOCO staff had to figure out the grant application process. They collected information from other states and foundations: "We did an extensive amount of staff work and then put it before the board at committee meetings, and we also actively engaged stakeholders—people who were involved and were potential recipients of the grants—Parks, Wildlife, local government and nonprofit organizations."[38] In June 1994 the GOCO board met in Alamosa to discuss application requirements for the planning and capacity-building grant cycle and the open space cycle. Later that summer GOCO issued the first request for proposals, which were due in the fall of 1994. The first competitive grants were awarded in November 1994. Since the initial grants programs were created, they have continued to evolve over time. In response to changing demand from the Coloradoan public, grant programs have been changed or added. As recalled by Shafroth, "We had to develop different applications and criteria and programs as the organization evolved. We started out with the trails program, but over the course [of the program] the trails program criteria have changed dramatically." For instance, GOCO now requires that impacts on wildlife be considered. In 1995 the Legacy grants came into being. GOCO held a retreat after its 1994 strategic planning process. Lottery proceeds were higher than expected, and GOCO staff and the board did not want to increase funding to the four traditional programmatic areas: "We wanted to rethink what we might do with these funds. We came up with the idea of Legacy projects."[39] The vision for Legacy grants was to provide funding to protect the remaining crown jewels Colorado had to offer. All four programmatic areas would have to work together to compete for Legacy Grant money.

GOCO grants require applicants to meet several funding criteria. These include partnership, leveraging and matching fund requirement, integration, planning, environmental education, project sustainability, impact, and stewardship. For instance, in each programmatic area, GOCO encourages collaboration among and between partner agencies and organizations to leverage scarce resources.[40] The criteria are the means to encourage local agencies and organizations to think strategically about land protection and how to utilize resources from potential partner entities. GOCO requires matching funds from grant applicants in all of its programs. This stipulation also encourages the search for and formation of partnerships. GOCO program managers estimate that the lottery money has leveraged more than an additional $1 billion in cash and in-kind services from project sponsors and partners.[41] These partners include local governments, state and federal agencies, special districts, private businesses, nonprofit organizations, landowners, school districts, community groups, foundations, individuals, and volunteers. Integration of these interests is encouraged on both large and small scales, depending on the scope of the project. For instance, in Idalia, a small community in northeastern Colorado, GOCO funds helped spur a partnership between the town of Idalia, Yuma County, and the Idalia Vision Foundation to secure $111,260 in GOCO grants to construct an outdoor recreational facility and environmental education center.

In addition to the local agencies and organizations targeted for GOCO programs, the GOCO money also encouraged larger state bureaucratic agencies to broaden their traditional mission and involve participants that otherwise might be excluded. The money created an incentive to apply, but the criteria for award acceptance provided inducements for the agencies to alter their behavior and expand into nongame wildlife conservation. For instance, GOCO funds helped support efforts to reintroduce threatened and endangered species such as the boreal toad and Canada lynx through a multiagency program. The program included maintenance of existing populations and habitats, and restoration and protection of habitats.[42] In this manner, Harrison said, "GOCO helps pull together resources for Division of Wildlife, Parks and nonprofit organizations around the state."[43]

Legacy grants are the most explicit in terms of encouraging large-scale collaboration among agencies and organizations to achieve land protection objectives. Legacy projects are of regional or statewide significance. They are large-scale, multiyear projects that integrate and coordinate across the categories of outdoor recreation, wildlife, open space, and local government. For instance, GOCO provided $5.48 million to the Gunnison Ranchland Conservation Legacy Project, which has preserved seventeen family ranches through conservation easements in Gunnison County. A diverse group of ranchers, environmentalists, local governments, and businesses formed a partnership with the Colorado Cattlemen's Agricultural Land Trust, The Nature Conservancy, and other partners to protect 6,650 acres of open space. Likewise, GOCO has provided $13.30 million to the I-25 Conservation Corridor Project, which has protected 30,000 acres along the rapidly developing throughway between Denver and Colorado Springs via the purchase of fee title and permanent conservation easements. The City of Castle Rock, El Paso County, Douglas County, the Conservation Fund, Greenland Ranch, and others worked together to realize the vision of protecting this cross-county, interjurisdictional area from development.[44]

Since the passage of the initiative in 1992, and the awarding of the first grants in 1994, GOCO has committed $575 million to more than 2,800 projects throughout the state. Projects have included the protection of 850,000 acres of open space in perpetuity, including 299,221 acres of agricultural land, 218,254 acres to protect habitat and create new state wildlife areas, and 21,947 acres as new state parks.[45] Additionally, GOCO has created or enhanced 944 community park and outdoor recreation areas and involved more than 5,500 young people in the Colorado Youth Corps Association. Working in conjunction with the Colorado Division of Wildlife, GOCO has funded projects to assist in the conservation of federal threatened and endangered species including the boreal toad, Gunnison Sage Grouse, black-footed ferret, Colorado River cutthroat trout, and the lynx. GOCO has assisted Colorado State Parks to improve or expand campgrounds and add new visitor centers at state parks throughout the state.[46]

GOCO survived turnovers in its leadership in its first fourteen years of existence. And different executive directors placed different emphasis in areas of land protection and enhancement. Shafroth left GOCO in 2000, two years after the Democratic Roy Romer administration was replaced by Republican Bill Owens. John Hereford, a GOCO board member, took his place until 2003, when John Swarthout, a senior policy adviser to Gov. Bill Owens and Sen. Wayne Allard, assumed the executive directorship. "GOCO has managed to stay in the center," said Hereford. "We've focused on doing deals, on acquiring land and protecting species. We've been through cycles of Republican and Democratic administration without becoming a political football."[47] However, different trends under different administrations are apparent. GOCO spent less than half the average amount of money annually on long-term land acquisition ($12.2 million) during the Owens administration than under the Romer administration ($27.2 million). The Division of Wildlife doubled the percentage of GOCO money used for operational costs, rather than capital expenditures, under the Owens administration.[48] Romer was an advocate for preserving open space and appointed board members who shared his views. When Owens was elected to office in 1998, the original board was replaced with people with different perspectives about land purchases. For instance, Greg Walcher, Natural Resources director, used to run Club 20, a group of developers, ranchers, farmers, miners, and energy executives opposed to public ownership of land. Walcher, Hereford, and others felt the new approach was better. They pointed to the 2002 Legacy Grant of nearly $12 million to the St. Vrain River and Trails Legacy Project, a joint project between the city of Longmont and Colorado State Parks that added land and trails to the Barbour Ponds State Park. The $12 million purchased 287 acres of land and was to expand warm-water ponds for recreational fishing. Critics decried the expensive price tag and pointed to the 21,000 acre Greenland Ranch purchase for an equal amount of funding. Overall, less money was being spent on acquiring state park lands—an annual average of $414,000 under Owens versus $1.2 million under Romer. And the Division of Wildlife spent 30 percent less on land protection than under the Romer administration.[49]

GOCO survived in spite of threats from the legislature. The General Assembly's Capital Development Committee continued to resent the use of lottery dollars beyond their reach, while other groups within the General Assembly tried to lay claim to GOCO dollars. In 1997 the House Education Committee proposed H.B. 1007. The proposal would have helped fund local school construction by siphoning off money from GOCO. Nonetheless, H.B. 1007 was defeated. While some members in the General Assembly challenged GOCO in 1997, ultimately they supported the reauthorization of the lottery, and thus ongoing financial support for GOCO, in 1998. In 2001 Colorado voters gave GOCO authorization to sell $115 million in bonds to maintain cash flow and to accelerate purchase of open space and wildlife habitat while interest rates were low. The referendum was supported by Republicans and Democrats alike.[50] In 2005 two Republican legislators proposed to divert GOCO funds to other programs, including ongoing operational expenses in the parks and wildlife agencies. This proposal did not make much headway.[51] In 2007 there were efforts to privatize the lottery through a proposed constitutional amendment. This would have created a concession contract for the lottery with the state receiving a lump sum payment in exchange for future proceeds. Backers of the bill estimated that $1.5 billion could be gained from the sale. Interest from the trust fund would be divided among local governments, state parks, GOCO, and local schools.[52] This proposal was placed on hold in 2008 with no plans to revive it, according to the sponsor of the proposed amendment.[53] According to Chris Leding, who had been communications director for GOCO for nearly a decade, the people who had been "most aggravated about GOCO are gone now. A lot of the hostility that initially existed has dissipated."[54] She attributed this to term limits in the General Assembly. In other cases, former opponents have been won over by GOCO's mission. For instance, a former state senator, Norma Anderson, led the charge against GOCO in the 1997 effort to poach GOCO money for schools. She is now the chair of the GOCO board. Moreover, GOCO made a concerted effort to keep its finger on the pulse of the legislature. According to Leding, "We are always diligent about what is going on. We have two contract lobbyists who work in the General Assembly. We send up an annual report to let the General Assembly know what we have been doing. In addition they each get an individual report about what projects have been funded in the counties in their district."[55]

As early as 1995 state auditors identified the need to improve grant monitoring procedures and administrative oversight policies. The GOCO board was criticized for not having an effective postaward grant-monitoring process and administrative policies. Staff made many efforts to develop and improve postaward grant-monitoring processes, but the procedures were identified as not being systematic. GOCO had trouble identifying projects that had not met their completion dates or over expended resources.[56] Recommendations included a "grant monitoring system . . . to ensure that projects receiving funds are appropriate and that resources allocated to grantees are used effectively."[57] In response to these concerns, GOCO put in place a grant-tracking system in the early 2000s. The board also endorsed a "deauthorization policy" to provide incentives for project completion. There had been a tendency for some projects to languish. Now the staff and board have some leverage if a project is not completed within a specified time period. If a grantee misses a deadline, staff can give an extension. However, if the grantee misses the staff-approved deadline, the grantee must then come before the board and request an extension. According to Leding, "We don't want money sitting around." As such, the deauthorization policy has been "very effective for getting grantees moving and staying on track."[58]

While the organizational structure and mission have been successful, others have criticized how GOCO is going about fulfilling its mission. Speaking in 2002 Susan

Kirkpatrick, a member of the original GOCO board, feared that GOCO was suffering from mission creep: "GOCO has moved away from its vision of large-scale permanent land protection and toward a smattering of smaller-scale investments."[59] Some environmental groups, such as the Sierra Club, were critical of the $3.35 million that went toward the Division of Wildlife's operating budgets for monitoring of threatened and endangered species. Their vision was for the money to be spent on the preservation of land. They also did not like GOCO's decision to consider temporary conservation easements, instead of permanent conservation easements.[60] Some also were frustrated with GOCO's lack of use of the $115 million in bonding authority to save land threatened by development. Three full years after receiving approval from the voters, GOCO had yet to issue any open space preservation bonds.[61] As of 2009 GOCO had not exercised its bonding authority. Leding explained that GOCO sought bonding authority because revenues from the lottery had been down. However, right about the same time bonding authority was granted, PowerBall came into existence, which ended up boosting lottery revenues. The increase in revenues with PowerBall allowed GOCO to "meet bonding intent without having to incur debt service."[62] Bonding authority, Leding said, is still available to GOCO if it chooses to use it: "The tool is not off the table. If need arises, we still have it available to us."[63]

In spite of these criticisms, most agree that GOCO is a unique and beneficial program for the state. Speaking in 2002, John Hereford, executive director of GOCO exclaimed, "We are the absolute envy of the land trust world. . . . People still can't believe that Colorado has an institutionalized funding source dedicated to these programs."[64] The permanent source of funding is a continuous boon for local and state agencies and organizations that want to protect or enhance land. According to state director of the Trust for Public Land, Doug Robotham, "It's the goose that keeps laying the golden egg."[65] GOCO clearly has made a difference in "creating an institutional culture of preservation and conservation across Colorado."[66] GOCO pulls together groups that previously kept each other at arm's length. The money created a whole new generation of land trusts that have in turn raised funding for their own projects. The matching requirements have created incentives for voters in Douglas, Adams, Larimer, Routt, and Gunnison counties to pass their own open space funding mechanisms. Will Shafroth reflected that "it's been a catalyst for action at all levels."[67] According to Salazar,

> I think Great Outdoors Colorado is the single most important [program for] protecting the natural heritage in this state in the last fifty years. Without it you would have some efforts at the local level, like in Jefferson County, but nothing statewide. It is the best thing for the environment that has happened in the last fifty years. You have concrete examples in every part of the state where things have happened because of GOCO. You'll never have Castle Rock and Colorado Springs growing together because of GOCO and the purchase of the Greenland Ranch. You would never have seen the river conservation and river corridor efforts that have taken place in about ten different places in the state from the Yampa to the Arkansas.[68]

GOCO still enjoys widespread support among the Colorado public in 2009. Small, flexible, and facilitative, the agency remains in touch with its constituencies through surveys, polls, focus groups, and stakeholder groups to take the public's pulse. As the product of an initiative process, the agency has a mandate to be responsive to the people, and it knows all too well from its own genesis what can happen if it betrays that trust. Initiated regulation in this case has fulfilled the dream of Teddy Roosevelt, who once proclaimed, "I believe in the Initiative and Referendum, which should be used not to destroy representative government, but to correct it whenever it becomes misrepresentative."

The lottery will sunset in 2024, and the legislature will decide at that time whether to continue the programs funded, including GOCO. For the time being, GOCO's continued implementation looks fairly secure. In the early 2000s there were worries that lottery revenues would decline because of decreasing interest in lottery games.[69] However, PowerBall has continued to pull people in, and revenues have been fairly stable. If revenues were to fall, the bonding authority would provide GOCO some measure of protection to regroup to continue to accomplish its goals.

APPLYING THE ANALYTICAL FRAMEWORK

The analytical framework laid out in chapter 1 is applied here to the GOCO case study. The three macro categories of culture (shocks, framing, and legitimacy), structure (rules and communication, incentives, opening, and resistance), and individuals (motivation, norms and harmony, and congruence) are laid over the details of the case to illustrate how these factors were or were not accounted for in the implementation of this innovation.

Culture

Shocks In the absence of shocks to the system, opportunities for learning may be constrained, and alternative courses of action may be limited to existing practices, thereby restricting the potential for innovation.[70] In the case of GOCO, no clear shock was present. And yet the innovation still took place.

The problem of population growth, disappearing open space, and development is characterized best as a gradually occurring threat rather than an abrupt or sudden shock or disaster. Population grew by 25 percent from 1970 to 1980 and another 12 percent from 1980 to 1990.[71] Developed land throughout the state covered 1.3 million acres in 1970, and by 2000 it covered 2.5 million acres.[72] Agricultural land and wildlife habitat were being consumed in suburban and rural areas. These open spaces were disappearing more quickly along the I-25 corridor along the Front Range than in other places, but these changes were still best characterized as gradual trends: "You didn't have concerned citizens and leaders coming together addressing the situation as a crisis. . . . It was remarkable that something happened."[73] Overall, no shocks were present and cannot account for fostering the innovation associated with GOCO.

Legitimacy Legitimacy is important because organizations are concerned with their own status and how they will be perceived. GOCO was a legitimate organizational alternative to the land protection problem because it was not threatening within the broader social and political context in which Colorado is situated. Efforts by Governor Love and Governor Lamm in the 1970s and 1980s to centralize power at the statewide level failed due to the political culture of the state that placed a primacy on home rule. Consequently, the solution to Colorado's land protection problems rested in finding a way to bridge the gap between localities' needs and a state culture that resisted centralizing power in the hands of the state. Working through the market to create incentives for action, GOCO encouraged local and regional grant applicants to explore and work within their own governance structures to achieve their land protection goals. The program was respectful of property rights. It did not create another layer of government. Importantly for Colorado, GOCO built on solid values supported by the independent-minded residents of the West. Summarized by Ken Salazar, a key figure in the creation of GOCO,

> If you look at the Republican platform about private property rights, one of the issues in terms of protection of open space has always been whether you do it via regulatory fiat or whether you let the market address the issue. My own view as to why GOCO works is that it has created a pot of money that has incentivized those who own the land to protect the land through a market approach. Without the money you can't get the work done, and then you have to use the regulatory authority or the land use power of the local government, and when that happens you established a huge conflict between the land owners and the government. What GOCO does is avoid that debate. We say we want to protect the land, and we have the money to do it.[74]

Consequently, GOCO can be interpreted as a socially legitimate solution given the cultural proclivities of Colorado.

Framing Framing processes are important because they can condition people's response to a given problem. Framing processes were a key factor not only in getting GOCO on the ballot but also in continuing to make GOCO's mission relevant to the Coloradoan public. Three framing narratives were created and directed at key constituencies. The distortion of the original 1980 intent for the lottery funds created an opportunity for the first narrative frame that involved righting the injustice of the General Assembly diverting funds away from open space protection. This narrative was aimed at the voting public. The second narrative capitalized on open space protection as an economic strategy for the state. This narrative was aimed at the Colorado business community. The final narrative was aimed at the existing bureaucratic agencies in the state that had been charged with protecting the state's outdoor amenities—the

Division of Parks and Outdoor Recreation and the Division of Wildlife. This narrative focused on filling gaps in funding for much needed programs.

The narratives were evident in the media campaign undertaken by Citizens for GOCO. As recalled by Sydney Macy, "We had positive ads and negative ads. Positive ads were focused on protecting open space and Colorado's heritage. The negative ads were focusing on 'big blue' . . . building prisons and asking the public if they knew their lottery dollars were going for this. There were some full-page ads on the prisons that ran in the newspapers."[75]

Skillful framing of the issues conditioned people's perception that they were aggrieved and that by acting collectively they could improve open space protection in the state. Harrison and Ciruli intentionally capitalized on the public's feeling of resentment toward government to frame the GOCO initiative: "We argued . . . that state government distorted the will of the people in terms of their use of lottery dollars."[76] "If we hadn't tripped upon that issue, I am not sure we would have gotten anything done."[77] Framing the issue along these lines facilitated getting the signatures needed for putting the GOCO initiative on the ballot and in getting the Coloradoan public to support the initiative at the ballot box.

Polls consistently indicated that the Coloradoan public supported open space, outdoor recreation, and wildlife and that these amenities were underserved. Additional polls conducted by Ciruli found that the Coloradoan public would support the redirection of lottery funds over new taxes and that the public was unaware of how the legislature had diverted funds to capital construction projects from their originally intended purpose.

Without the support of the business community, however, it is unlikely that the initiative would have made its way on the ballot. The business community responded well to the economic development arguments put forth by the GOCO supporters. Without world-class recreation and outdoor amenities, Colorado would not be an attractive business or tourism location. To make sure the golden goose was not killed, the business community put up funding for the initiative effort. As recalled by Ken Salazar, "I approached many of the organizations affiliated with Colorado ski country, Aspen, Vail, U.S. West, etc. . . . My pitch to them for raising money for the campaign was for Colorado to continue to have a thriving economy we would have to protect our natural heritage. If we weren't careful our quality of life would be compromised. We would find ourselves on the path of another California or Florida. Quality of life was very much a strong theme in our campaign."[78] Without this financial support, the GOCO campaign organizers could not have paid their petition circulators to collect signatures or would not have had a public relations budget to push their message out to the Coloradoan public.

Finally, an additional framing strategy appealed to the Division of Parks and Recreation and Division of Wildlife. Both of these agencies were short on funds for their capital construction and maintenance needs and nongame wildlife programs, respectively. Framing the issue to intentionally aid or assist these agencies created opportunities for these agencies to see the GOCO initiative not as a threat but as a windfall.

Structures

Opening The political structure and vested interests can block innovation. Without a clear opening in the political structure, change is unlikely. GOCO's architects were quite skilled in prying open the political structure through which change occurred. The General Assembly had effectively cut off any opportunity of a legislative solution or referendum. Lawmakers were opposed to any new taxes and committed to their current capital expenditures that reallocated funding from the first referendum in 1980 that dedicated funding to land protection. Political opening occurred because Gov. Roy Romer was committed to change and a group of skilled political elites knew how to use the initiative process to alter the state constitution, which effectively bypassed the General Assembly. Citizens for GOCO were committed to a constitutional amendment because they were "convinced that . . . if we didn't there was a very high likelihood that the legislature would come back in another year and repeal the law."[79] For a constitutional amendment, they needed signatures to get the initiative on the ballot. To get the signatures they needed to raise money. To make sure the initiative passed, they needed an effective media campaign that would get out the vote on their issue. Every step in the process was calculated to lead to change to counter the prevailing power in the General Assembly. Because Colorado allows for initiative, those outside the General Assembly have access to a tool that can be used to open the political structure to innovative solutions that otherwise might be blocked by the status quo.

Incentives Organizations can provide incentives to encourage compliance with new practices. Incentives helped tip the cost-benefit calculus for individuals and organizations to support and sustain GOCO. Citizens for GOCO had a dual vision in mind for the new trust fund. According to pollster Ciruli, the intent was to "change the culture within Parks and Wildlife while also incentivizing local areas to think about their open space."[80] The primary resource to accomplish these twin goals was money and the use of funding guidelines to modify behavior. To change traditional bureaucratic attitudes and practices within existing agencies, they would need to provide incentives for altering behavior. They also understood that to change practices at the most local level, incentives could encourage local coalitions to take action and coalesce if they were interested in land protection.

First, Citizens for GOCO wished to change how the traditional bureaucratic agencies worked in relation to land protection. GOCO founders felt that change was needed, especially within the Division of Wildlife. The feeling by Citizens for GOCO was that "their culture needed to be shifted if they [were] going to survive and be more than the Division of Hunting."[81] The challenge was to figure out effective structural incentives. Prior to the availability of GOCO grant dollars, the Division of Parks and the Division of Wildlife both were grappling with different types of initiatives that they wanted to undertake, but could not fund. David Harrison remembered that "the Division of Parks was looking at a number of opportunities that they couldn't pursue.

The Division of Wildlife was grappling with habitat conservation issues that called for capital investments. There was a tight situation fiscally in Colorado. . . . Wildlife has been this embattled agency that has trouble getting moneys for the projects that they have laid out."[82] This opened the way for GOCO to entice change in behavior through the strategic use of funding. What the organization wanted to do was encourage "the state through the Division of Parks and Division of Wildlife to think a little less in terms of their narrow management perspective. . . . The initiative process was used in this case to affect big state bureaucracies that were at that point largely into very traditional modes of behavior because of their constituencies and culture and funding. . . . Changing that culture has been a very interesting aspect of GOCO."[83]

Citizens for GOCO explicitly did not want to create a new bureaucracy to complete with the existing agencies. Rather, they wanted to preserve existing institutions but alter their behavior to work more effectively on the issue of land protection: "Either GOCO was going to evolve in a parallel, dual bureaucracy or you would turn the money over to the agencies and let them spend it. It would be less of a grant process and more of an entitlement. That was not acceptable. We thought the money would get absorbed into the general fund of the agency."[84] Harrison described a vision to create a financial incentive through GOCO that would not disturb the existing structures of the Parks and Wildlife agencies but would provide a strong financial incentive to encourage them to work in a different way: "GOCO is basically a quasi-public endowment with broad powers to empower existing institutions. There is a special place for a fiduciary board to govern long-term capital assets and these types of agencies or structures can partner with existing government at the state and federal levels. This all fits within a good representative democratic structure and helps avoid the conspiracy of the annual fiscal emergency, which is a reality within our existing governing structures. This is a way of complementing the process."[85] According to Harrison, they needed to be "innovative with agencies we have, instead of the agency structure itself."[86] In the end they decided the best way to proceed was through a small agency, GOCO, which could offer a dedicated source of funding that no longer was subjected to the vagaries of the annual appropriations process while also providing an incentive for the Parks and Wildlife agencies to work cooperatively and think more broadly about land and habitat protection.

Second, they wanted to encourage greater land protection at the local level. GOCO provided money as an incentive for local, state, and federal agencies and organizations to work together to address local land protection issues. Once the lottery funding was available it was up to the GOCO staff and board to create a process that would provide incentives for agencies and organizations within Colorado to protect land voluntarily. Money was the grease that encouraged local governments, park and recreation districts, Colorado Division of State Parks and Recreation, Colorado Division of Wildlife, and nonprofit land protection organizations to work together. The pools of funding, through the competitive grants process, provided incentives to cities, towns, counties, nonprofits, special districts, and statewide organizations to respond to the pressing land protection issues they identified. Grant criteria rewarded applicants that engaged in collaborative arrangements and leveraged funding from additional resources, among other requirements. Collectively, the grant guidelines encouraged applicants to think strategically about what they wanted to accomplish. It is difficult to imagine that the same level of collaboration for land protection would have taken place in the absence of GOCO. Recall Ken Salazar's earlier statement as indicative of GOCO's success: "I think Great Outdoors Colorado is the single most important program to protect the natural heritage in this state in the last fifty years. Without it you would have some efforts at the local level, but nothing statewide. . . . With GOCO, especially with the lands of statewide significance or the legacy projects, you have a catalyst and incentive for the protection of open space."[87]

Resistance When a new institution, like GOCO, is created, some institutional theorists predict resistance to new practices, especially from competing, well-established and preexisting institutions. The challenge for Citizens for GOCO was to create a new agency and processes that would change how land protection was carried out in the state while overcoming political resistance from the institutions that could block their attempt. This meant thinking how to avoid opposition and devising strategies to deal with the General Assembly, the Division of Parks, and the Division of Wildlife.

The legislature resisted the GOCO initiative because it threatened its authority. GOCO had the potential to create problems in ongoing capital expenditures by removing the lottery as a dedicated stream of revenue for capital construction projects. To alleviate these concerns, GOCO proposed a phased plan that would honor the current capital commitments through 1998 and then transition in 1998 to a formula that would distribute a greater portion of lottery funds to the GOCO program. Additionally, GOCO founders agreed to cap the amount of money that would go to GOCO. Any lottery funds above $35 million (in 1992 constant dollars) would revert back to the General Assembly general fund. Opposition within the legislature was not great to begin with, but GOCO proponents did not want to create opportunities for opposition to grow. Consequently, they allayed the initial concerns that the lawmakers raised about the new program.

Over the life of the program, GOCO officials continued to be effective in dealing with the General Assembly when periodic threats arose to the lottery or how its proceeds were allocated. GOCO actively anticipated resistance to its goal and countered with specific strategic activities. GOCO was attentive to what was happening in the General Assembly, employed lobbyists to make legislators aware of GOCO's accomplishments, and actively promoted how GOCO helps individual legislators in their home counties. They successfully recruited legislators into their ranks who initially were opposed to their mission. GOCO officials got nervous when they saw an economic downturn and foresaw legislators' needs to go looking for new revenue sources. However, they were quite skilled in neutralizing potential opposition and mitigating any attempts to change the agency's mission.

In the early years of GOCO, the Division of Parks and Recreation was much more amenable to GOCO's mission than the Division of Wildlife. Relatively little opposition occurred from Parks and Recreation. In fact, the director of Parks and Recreation, Laurie Mathews, participated actively in the design and establishment of GOCO in the mid-1990s. However, in recent years, Parks and Recreation has experienced changes in leadership, and those new leaders have been more resistant to the GOCO mission. According to Chris Leding, "Parks has been in a bad revenue place for years with a backlog of projects. They wanted to build event centers, but that is not part of the GOCO's mission. Our money can't go for that, so we put the brakes on. This has been the ongoing tension between Parks and the GOCO mission."[88] Another big challenge has been in trying to create transparent accounting practices so GOCO officials could be confident their funds were going to agreed-upon Parks and Recreation projects. As political and administrative leaders changed, staff within GOCO remained optimistic that Parks and Recreation will once again become less resistant to GOCO's mission: "We are hopeful that new leadership within the Division of Parks and Recreation will begin to change this dynamic."[89]

Change in administrative leadership has been constructive for the relationships between GOCO and the Division of Wildlife. As of 2008, GOCO had a very cordial working relationship with Wildlife. Early on Wildlife did not outright oppose GOCO, but rather was unsupportive of the visions GOCO had for Wildlife. The original vision of altering the behavior of Wildlife to focus on habitat protection was met with resistance by Wildlife because they wanted to channel funding according to their own vision of agency mission. "There has been a pretty good battle with [Division of Wildlife] on how the money should be spent," observed Ciruli, one of the founders of GOCO.[90] After an initial focus on habitat and land protection, the Division of Wildlife increased the amount of GOCO money devoted to operational costs, rather than land expenditures from 2000 to 2003. This caused several people, including State Attorney General Ken Salazar, to bring attention to the practice. Salazar stated that his reading of the state's constitution indicated that the practice of substituting funds should be forbidden. He asked the Division of Wildlife to change its practices.[91] At that time, not much changed. For a while, the Division of Wildlife successfully resisted using all the funds for land purchases. During that time, the Division of Wildlife expanded its threatened and endangered species program with GOCO assistance. Some within the division state that putting funding toward operations enables them to hire people that otherwise would not be supported to work on threatened and endangered species issues. Over time, as leadership within the Division of Wildlife changed, so did the relationship with GOCO. Observes Leding, "We are in a much better position with the Division of Wildlife these days. There is a cap on the full-time employees we will fund. They are diligent about tracking operational expenses. When we have extra money to give, it goes to habitat protection . . . They increased their real estate division. Their new director has a real commitment to habitat. . . . The culture is starting to change."[92]

The tensions between GOCO and the Division of Wildlife and Division of Parks and Recreation are testimony to the inertia that existing institutions carry with them to perpetuate old practices. Even with incentives to change behavior, the Division of Wildlife and Division of Parks have used their power at different times to fund positions and operational expenses rather than use all the money for land protection.

Rules and Communication Minimizing communication distortions and creating clear rules of operation can facilitate structures that foster effective implementation. From a rules and communication standpoint, GOCO appears to be effective because of its size and its clear sense of mission. Applicants in the GOCO process felt that the agency had well-defined boundaries and goals that were communicated to them. In-person interviews with a representative sample of twenty-nine more and less successful GOCO grant applicants in 1998 indicated that 76 percent of the interviewees thought that GOCO was a good fit for the problems they faced in land protection.[93]

As a small agency, there were few layers of bureaucracy through which program managers had to work.[94] Since its inception, GOCO had ranged from twelve to eighteen employees, with fourteen employed in 2007.[95] GOCO's mission aimed at land protection has been clear and direct. "We run lean and mean so we get as much money on the ground as possible," explained Leding about the desire to stay small and focused on their mission.[96] As a small program, GOCO is also flexible. As observed by a GOCO employee, "GOCO is a small agency, and it is easier to be flexible and adapt programs to the needs of the constituencies because of its size."[97]

Administrative rules, communication, and information exchange between the GOCO board, staff, and grant applicants supported compliance with the overall goals of GOCO. The newly hired GOCO staff, working in conjunction with the GOCO board of directors, developed grant guidelines and specific programmatic areas to fit diverse needs throughout Colorado. Simplicity in the grant guidelines helped facilitate clear expectations and communication. According to Shafroth, "When you get down to it, there were basically three fundamental elements of criteria: (1) significance of resource, (2) need and impact, (3) leverage and partnership. These same fundamental criteria end up being important for all of GOCO's grant categories."[98] Staff aimed to make the application process direct and uncomplicated. Regular technical assistance workshops were held around the state annually to explain the grant selection process and help applicants prepare their grants. One-on-one planning assistance was also available from staff. To maintain consistency in rules and communication between staff and those who apply for grants, GOCO regularly sought input from its grantees and citizens about whether the grant program, as offered, met the state's needs. In 1994 GOCO went through a strategic planning process that included broad public involvement. Meetings were held all over Colorado to solicit input. In 2001 GOCO repeated the exercise and received input from participants in meetings conducted in thirteen cities around the state and from a six hundred–person public opinion survey. In April 2002 the GOCO board adopted a revised strategic plan to guide its spending.

These exercises helped the agency keep in contact with the public it serves by periodically adapting its guidelines so that land protection goals throughout Colorado were met. A public opinion survey took place in June 2008, and a customer satisfaction audit followed in August 2008.[99]

Individuals

Motivation The impetus for innovation rests on discontented individuals who are free to devise alternative possible solutions. Several people worked together to get GOCO on the political agenda and see it through implementation. Gov. Roy Romer, Sydney Macy (director of TNC), Ken Salazar (head of the Colorado Department of Natural Resources), David Harrison (attorney and TNC board member), Laurie Mathews (head of Colorado Division of Parks and Recreation), and Floyd Ciruli (Democratic pollster and media consultant) were the key individuals behind the effort. All were fearful of how growth could affect the state's quality of life and were highly motivated to find a permanent source of funding for land protection. The legislature was not motivated to change the situation, and this created an opportunity for others to take action.

At the time this group of individuals was very clear about their own motivations as well as what would motivate the broader public. As Ciruli put it: "What we had in the early 1990s was Colorado's continuing concern about the environment. But keep in mind in 1990–1992 we were not in a growth surge. Colorado has a great population interested in outdoor recreation, but the concerns about growth were nowhere near as high as they are right now. Back in 1990, the elite were motivated by their own environmental values to address the growth issues. But that was not going to motivate the voters."[100] Consequently, there was recognition that different strategies would apply not only to get GOCO on the political agenda but also in getting it passed and then implemented in its final form.

As recalled by Ken Salazar, "Those of us who were involved in GOCO from the beginning were looking ahead in Colorado at what was happening with growth, and I think we were interested in looking for alternatives for Colorado to invest in our natural legacy long term. The premise for me in that campaign was that protecting the environment went hand-in-hand with economic development."[101] At that time, there were no other land protection organizations outside of TNC, and "finding permanent funding was a key objective for us," recalled Sydney Macy, a key participant in the campaign for GOCO.[102] Laurie Mathews, head of the Division of Parks, "was looking at a number of opportunities that they couldn't pursue." Likewise, the Division of Wildlife was "grappling with habitat conservation issues that called for capital investments." Universally, these individuals were frustrated with the General Assembly and its inability to take action on the issue of land protection. Recalled Harrison, "You could not go to the legislature and get resources for these types of projects."[103]

An attempt was made to work through the General Assembly at first. As head of the Colorado Department of Natural Resources, Ken Salazar established land protection as a top priority within his agency. But the General Assembly was not cooperative. Salazar said, "I went to work at the Department of Natural Resources in 1990, and I had five priorities. One of the five was the creation of a program that would invest in the outdoors and open space. I still remember being home late one night about twelve in the morning and working on the draft of the legislation for GOCO. . . . We introduced the legislation with some fanfare. However, it was not something that was high on the agenda of the legislature. The consequence was that it was killed immediately."

The General Assembly's inaction provided motivation for Salazar and his partners to find an alternative for getting the issue on the agenda: "We regrouped and decided we weren't going to get it through the legislature, and so we would have a poll done to see how Coloradoans felt about the issue and what kinds of funding streams they would be willing to support."[104]

Roy Romer's leadership on the issue was crucial because he appointed the Citizens Committee that ultimately provided the basis for the initiative. Ciruli recalled, "Essentially, Romer as a moderate liberal activist governor came to the conclusion that these things simply cannot pass the state legislature. . . . There was no constituency in the state legislature that was interested. It was out in left field."[105] This sentiment is backed up by Romer: "The legislature was generally very conservative on environmental matters, and they did not value them nearly as highly as I did. We knew very clearly that if you wanted to do something about it you would have to go to the public"[106]

Reflecting on why the initiative process was successful, David Harrison commented that it was a combination of opportunity, effective action, and leadership. "When you have inaction on one level you can create an incentive for action on another level," he observed. "If there was a failure to act or a vacuum, there is a condition that gives rise to the possibility of movement. But there must also be leadership. The vacuum makes leadership possible to actualize."[107]

After the 1992 election these individuals continued to be motivated to see the idea put into action. Governor Romer, Salazar, and the others began putting together a board of directors. Salazar became the first chairman of the board of directors. Rick Daily, legal counsel to the campaign, served as interim director of the agency while Salazar and Daily launched a national search for the executive director. Will Shafroth was hired as executive director in 1994.

Individuals associated with GOCO were highly motivated to see the organization succeed. Chris Leding asserted, "Morale here is great. We are actually having an effect and doing things on the ground." She said her sense of satisfaction came from seeing so many places around the state where GOCO has made a difference: "There is land in the Gunnison Valley, Saguache and Routt counties that will be protected for the next generation. That feels good."[108]

Norms and Harmony Maintaining social norms and harmony in the workplace is important for facilitating change. Individuals who feel that they are asked to work outside the bounds of their traditional culture or expectations may resist change. As a new agency, GOCO did not have to consider how previous social norms would coexist with new norms or how new practices would harmonize with old practices. GOCO was creating its own norms from scratch. Likewise, harmony in the workplace was less a matter of how to harmonize old practice with new than devising practices that would work from the outset.

Congruence If there is incongruence between the dominant values within an agency or organization and lower levels where individuals must execute decisions, then problems may arise in implementing innovative practices. In the case of GOCO, the agency was not very stratified, so congruence was not that challenging. The board of directors, GOCO staff, and grant applicants typified the active participants within the hierarchy of the program. As a new program, GOCO did not have to consider congruence within a dominant culture. Rather, it was creating its own new culture or capitalizing on the prevailing culture under which the initiative was passed. GOCO was a market-based solution that respected private property rights and worked predominantly through local governments to protect land and in conjunction with other agencies to assist in accomplishing their missions. As Harrison observed, "GOCO can help counter the corrosive impact of cynicism in bureaucracy since it can empower professionals to realize their potential."[109] Democrats and Republicans both could embrace the solution. Democrats and Republicans were equally appointed to the board. Staff get to "help people accomplish what is important them and come up with creative solutions to achieve their goals."[110] Staff was eager and energetic to carry out the mission.

SUMMARY

The framework presented in table 3.2 categorizes how we can understand the success of GOCO both initially and over time. The culture, structure, and individual characteristics align in mutually supportive ways to foster the emergence and persistence of the innovation. No formidable barriers emerged from the analysis.

From a cultural standpoint, framing and legitimacy were the most important factors. Shocks did not apply to this case study. Issue framing appealed to the Colorado voting public to create a sense of deprivation. This instigated the voting public to act to correct the situation with an alternative that was perceived as legitimate within the Coloradoan culture. There were no obvious external shocks to the system. Rather, Colorado faced a gradually changing land use situation. Innovation often is seen as arising out of crises or shocks.[111] In this case, no shocks were present. Rather, a group of concerned citizens mobilized in response to a steady threat to open lands and valued resources.

Structurally, skillful policy entrepreneurs associated with the Citizens for GOCO understood how the existing political organization, namely the legislature, would

Table 3.2: Summary of Cultural, Structural, and Individual Characteristics Related to GOCO

Culture	Structures	Individuals
Shocks: Not relevant. Growth was a gradual trend. *Legitimacy:* GOCO viewed as a culturally legitimate market-based alternative to top-down, command-and-control forms of land protection. *Framing:* Strategic issue framing was essential in getting the GOCO passed and implemented. The GOCO initiative was framed to appeal to the voting public by "righting a wrong" by the legislature. It was framed for the business community as essential for economic development. It was framed for key bureaucratic agencies as a financial boon. Marketing efforts capitalized on all three frames to appeal to key constituencies.	*Opening:* The initiative process allowed GOCO's organizers to pry open the political structure that had been closed off by the legislature. *Incentives:* Key incentives motivated change at the individual and agency level. Funding induced individuals and agencies to collaborate and think about land protection more broadly. *Resistance:* Resistance was most likely from the General Assembly, the Division of Parks and Recreation, and the Division of Wildlife. GOCO effectively mitigated resistance from the General Assembly and Parks and Recreation. State Parks and Recreation continues to resist after implementation but not to completely disrupt the program. *Rules and Communication:* Minimal bureaucratic stratification facilitates clear communication among board, staff, and grant applicants. Rules are unambiguous and supportive of agency objectives.	*Motivation:* Discontented individuals, namely the Citizens for GOCO, devised an alternative for land protection. They were highly motivated to act and had the resources and skill to act effectively. *Norms and Harmony:* GOCO was a new agency and did not have to take into consideration how previous social norms would coexist with new norms or how new practices should harmonize with old practices. *Congruence:* As a new agency, GOCO did not have to take into consideration dominant values within a preexisting culture. It embraced a relatively new approach of a market-based solution. The organization was not overly stratified so maintaining congruence among the board, staff, and applicants was straightforward.

block efforts to establish a new alternative for land protection. Notably, there was not one policy entrepreneur pushing for change but a group of individuals with specialized function advocating not only for change but also a resilient agency that could support a long-term program. The individualist model of policy entrepreneur does not hold up here.[112] These entrepreneurs opened the political structure through the initiative process. They addressed the concerns of legislators to provide incentives so the cost-benefit calculus for those opposing GOCO would be mitigated. Resistance was limited to the divisions of Wildlife and Parks and Recreation, each of which had resisted at different times GOCO's direction on the use of funds. This opposition did not threaten the overall existence of GOCO. Other than the Division of Wildlife and Parks and Recreation, there was little resistance from other vested interests. Individuals, both the political advocates behind the GOCO effort and the Coloradoan public, were discontented with the status quo in land protection in their state and highly motivated to challenge the status quo. Communication and information exchange clearly supported the creation of the new organization. There were not multiple layers of governance structures that needed to be negotiated. The administrative rules aligned well with the policy intent.

From an individual perspective, the new practices that were proposed—the GOCO program—did not threaten existing norms or harmony among staff because it was a new organization made of whole cloth. Congruence with dominant values and new values was not a problem because it was a new organization.

Because it was a new organization, GOCO avoided many of the problems that can plague the implementation of innovation. The hypothesis posited in chapter 1 suggested that when the individual, structural, and cultural categories are aligned and sustained within a mutually supportive hierarchy, then the probability that innovation will be implemented increases. The cultural, structural, and individual categories indicate a great deal of mutual support in the case of GOCO. Individuals were highly motivated and not impeded by incongruent norms or disharmony. Structures were opened, incentives were consistent with mission accomplishment, rules were clear, communication was open, and resistance was mitigated. The broader culture was supportive of the issues and approach, which was seen as legitimate, and it was framed to continue to be seen as legitimate to key constituencies and the public at large. In almost every case, with the exception of the continued resistance at different times of the Division of Wildlife and the Division of Parks and Recreation to GOCO's vision for land protection, GOCO dealt constructively with the potential factors suggested by the analytical framework.

NOTES

1. Great Outdoors Citizens Committee, "GO Colorado: Great Outdoors Colorado—Final Report," December 1990, 9–10.
2. Ibid., 7.

3. Colorado has a total of 66.7 million acres. Thirty-five percent is under federal control with 22 percent (14.5 million acres) in national forests or grasslands, 12 percent (8.3 million acres) in Bureau of Land Management, and 1 percent (600,000 acres) in national parks and monuments. A remaining 5.3 percent is under state control with 0.3 percent (180,000) in state parks and recreation areas, 0.5 percent (450,000) in state wildlife areas, and 4.5 percent (3 million) under the state land board ("GO Colorado," 13).

4. "Home rule" is the legal autonomy or self-government granted by a central or regional government to its dependent political units. Marshall Kaplan, Toddi A. Steelman, and Allan Wallis, "Sprawl and Growth Management: Problems, Experience and Opportunity" (Denver: Institute for Policy Implementation, University of Colorado at Denver, 1999).

5. Ibid.

6. Center for Regional and Neighborhood Action, "Building Consensus for Growth Management: Addressing Land Use Dilemmas in a Low-Regulatory Environment," working paper, 1997; and Allan Wallis, "Colorado Growth Management: Is the Third Time the Charm?" (Denver: Graduate School of Public Affairs, University of Colorado at Denver, 1996).

7. U.S. Census, 1984, "Intercensal Estimates of the Total Resident Population of States: 1970 to 1980," www.census.gov/populations/estimates/state/stts/st7080ts.txt (accessed March 20, 2001); and U.S. Census, 2001, "USA Statistics in Brief—Census 2000 Resident Population of States and DC," www.census.gov/statab/www/part6.html (accessed March 20, 2001).

8. "GO Colorado," 30.

9. Ibid., 31.

10. Colorado Public Expenditure Council, "Payoff for Parks: Amendment 8 Would Dedicate Lottery Fund to Great Outdoors," *Rocky Mountain News*, October 18, 1992.

11. John Fryar, "Great Outdoors Colorado Backers Gather Signatures for Ballot Initiative," *Canon City Daily Record*, June 11, 1992.

12. "Payoff for Parks."

13. "GO Colorado."

14. Susan Greene, "State Shifts Land Preservation Funds' Focus under Owens, GOCO buying Fewer Sites," *Denver Post*, November 10, 2003, A1.

15. Roy Romer, telephone interview, April 20, 2001.

16. An initiative is a proposed law or resolution placed on the ballot as the result of a petition drive among registered voters. The electorate then votes on it.

17. David Harrison, in-person interview, Boulder, CO, April 24, 2001.

18. Floyd Ciruli, in-person interview, Denver, CO, May 17, 2001.

19. Harrison, in-person interview.

20. Legislative Hearing, "GOCO Ballot Initiative—Amendment No. 8," transcript, August 31, 1992, 2. On file with author.

21. S. Macy, telephone interview, April 26, 2001.

22. "GOCO Ballot Initiative."

23. Fryar, "Great Outdoors Colorado Backers."

24. Andrew Purkey, telephone interview, May 9, 2001.

25. Ibid.

26. Ken Salazar, in-person interview, Denver, CO, June 7, 2001.

27. Ibid.

28. "GOCO Ballot Initiative," 2–3.

29. Ciruli, in-person interview.

30. "GOCO Ballot Initiative," 3.

31. Ciruli, in-person interview.

32. Great Outdoors Colorado, "Achieving Results," www.goco.org/overview/achieve.html. (accessed March 5, 2003); and Great Outdoors Colorado, "Annual Report," www.goco.org/annualreport (accessed July 7, 2004).

33. Mark Couch, "Lotto Holds Schools Ticket? Privatizing State Lottery Could Yield Billions Say Authors of Proposed Amendment Two," *Denver Post*, April 18, 2007.

34. Salazar, in-person interview.

35. Will Shafroth, in-person interview, April 5, 2001.

36. Three program officers and three support staff are responsible for the different grant cycles that run throughout the year.

37. One member of the board must represent agricultural interests, and two members must live west of the Continental Divide. In addition, the executive director of the Colorado Department of Natural Resources and one representative each from the Colorado State Parks Board and the Wildlife Commission are members of the board.

38. Shafroth, in-person interview.

39. Ibid.

40. Great Outdoors Colorado, "Great Outdoors Colorado Grant Criteria," www.goco.org/aboutGOCO.html (accessed March 7, 2001).

41. Great Outdoors Colorado, "Achieving Results" (accessed July 6, 2004).

42. Great Outdoors Colorado, "Wildlife Grants," www.goco.org/overview/wildlife.html (accessed March 5, 2003).

43. Harrison, in-person interview.

44. Great Outdoors Colorado, "Legacy Grants," www.goco.org/overview/legacy.html (accessed March 5, 2003).

45. GOCO, "Accomplishments," www.goco.org/Results/Accomplishments/tabid/115/Default.aspx (accessed February 22, 2009).

46. Ibid.

47. Jerd Smith, "GOCO's Funding Record in 10 Years, Agency Has Put $295 Million toward the Outdoors," *Rocky Mountain News*, November 2, 2002, A23.

48. Susan Greene, *Denver Post*, A1.

49. Ibid.

50. Julia Martinez, "Vote to Decide Land Purchase Funding," *Denver Post*, October 28, 2001.

51. Joanne Ditmer, "Protecting, Preserving Colorado's Open Space," *Denver Post*, September 16, 2005.

52. Couch, "Lotto Holds Schools Ticket?"

53. Chris Romer, telephone interview, December 13, 2007.

54. Chris Leding, telephone interview, April 24, 2008.

55. Ibid.

56. Colorado State Auditor, "State Board of the Great Outdoors Colorado Trust Fund Financial Compliance Audit. Fiscal Year Ended June 30 1995," www.state.co.us/auditor/96fin/23305.html (accessed February 23, 2001).

57. Ibid.

58. Leding, telephone interview.

59. Theo Stein, "Great Outdoors Colorado Gets High Marks. But Shift from Land Purchases Is Drawing Fire," *Denver Post*, November 7, 2002, A29.

60. Smith, "GOCO's Funding Record."

61. Jerd Smith, "GOCO's 'Go Slow' Pace Irks Backers: 2 Years after Voters OK, No Bonds Issued for Land Preservation," *Rocky Mountain News*, October 20, 2003, A4.

62. Leding, telephone interview.

63. Ibid.

64. Stein, "Great Outdoors Colorado Get High Marks."

65. Ibid.

66. Ibid.

67. Smith, "GOCO's Funding Record."

68. Salazar, in-person interview.

69. Smith, "GOCO's Funding Record."

70. Ronald L. Jepperson, "Institutions, Institutional Effects, and Institutionalism," in *The New Institutionalism in Organizational Analysis*, ed. Walter W. Powell and Paul J. DiMaggio (Chicago: University of Chicago Press, 1991), 143–63.

71. "GO Colorado," 9–10.

72. Ditmer, "Protecting, Preserving Colorado's Open Space."

73. Harrison, in-person interview.

74. Salazar, interview.

75. Macy, interview.

76. Ciruli, interview.

77. Harrison, interview.

78. Salazar, interview.

79. Ibid.

80. Ciruli, interview.

81. Ibid.

82. Harrison, interview.

83. Ciruli, interview.

84. Ibid.

85. Harrison, interview.

86. Ibid.

87. Salazar, interview.

88. Leding, interview.

89. Ibid.

90. Ciruli, interview.

91. Trent Seibert, "GOCO Urged to Revise Its Funding Policy," *Denver Post*, February 5, 2003.

92. Leding, interview.

93. Toddi Steelman, "Innovation in Local Land Protection: The Case of Great Outdoors Colorado," *American Behavioral Scientist* 44, no. 4 (2000): 579–97.

94. Harrison, interview.

95. GOCO, "About," www.goco.org/About/GOCOOrganization/tabid/105/Default.aspx (accessed November 28, 2007).

96. Leding, interview.

97. Janis Wisman, in-person interview, April 10, 2001.

98. Shafroth, interview.

99. Leding, interview.

100. Ciruli, interview.

101. Salazar, interview.

102. Macy, interview.

103. Harrison, interview.

104. Salazar, interview.

105. Ciruli, interview.

106. Roy Romer, interview.

107. Harrison, interview.

108. Leding, interview.

109. Harrison, interview.

110. Wisman, interview.

111. James Q. Wilson, "Innovation in Organization: Notes toward a Theory," in *Approaches to Organization Design*, ed. James D. Thompson (Pittsburgh: University of Pittsburgh Press, 1966); and Martin A. Levin and Mary B. Sanger, *Making Government Work: How Entrepreneurial Executives Turn Bright Ideas into Real Results* (San Francisco: Jossey-Bass, 1994).

112. Nancy C. Roberts and Paula J. King, "Policy Entrepreneurs: Their Activity Structure and Function in the Policy Process," *Journal of Public Administration Research and Theory* 1, no. 2 (1991); David Osborne and Ted Gaebler, *Reinventing Government: How the Entrepreneurial Spirit Is Transforming the Public Sector* (Reading, PA: Addison-Wesley, 1992); and Francis Berry, "Innovation in Public Management: The Adoption of Strategic Planning," *Public Administration Review* 67, no. 3 (1994): 322–30.

CHAPTER 4

Intermittent Alignment of Institutional Characteristics

Implementing Innovation in Watershed Management

FRIENDS OF THE CHEAT IS NESTED within various hierarchical influences as documented in chapter 2 and detailed in figure 4.1. Friends of the Cheat uses voluntary and self-regulatory approaches to mitigate acid mine drainage (AMD) and non–point-source pollution from numerous polluters throughout its watershed. The group works collaboratively to pull together the many actors from the federal, state, and local level that are essential for making progress in addressing water quality problems in its watershed. At various times in its history, the group has experienced problems with executive leadership and federal and state collaborators that have effectively stymied its efforts. Working intermittently over the years, the group has realized significant improvements in water quality that would have been unimaginable only twenty years prior. Friends of the Cheat and their working agreement called "The River of Promise" represent an innovation because together they address water quality problems associated with acid mine drainage that had been neglected by West Virginia state agencies.

INNOVATION IN WATERSHED MANAGEMENT: VOLUNTARILY REGULATION WITH FRIENDS OF THE CHEAT

West Virginia's history is enmeshed with the practice of coal mining. Coal from West Virginia significantly fuels the nation's energy needs and provides important jobs in what is an otherwise underdeveloped economic region. Extraction of coal has also taken a toll on the natural resources in the region. Beginning around the mid-1800s, coal was extensively mined in the fields throughout northern West Virginia.

Particular to this region, and other coal seams in Pennsylvania, Maryland, Ohio, Illinois, eastern Tennessee, and Kentucky, is a water quality problem known as acid mine drainage (AMD).

AMD is created when the mining process exposes pyrite in sulfur-rich rocks to air and water causing oxidation and then acidification of the water flowing through the mine.[1] As the acidification of the water increases, heavy metal concentrations also can increase, becoming toxic to fish and other water-dwelling plants and animals.[2] If the water is buffered farther downstream, then the metals will precipitate out of solution and cover rocks and the bottom of streams with a thick, bright orange or white sludge that also is toxic to aquatic flora and fauna. The federal Office of Surface Mining Reclamation and Enforcement (USOSM) is the federal agency that oversees the nationwide regulation of coal mining and reclamation. USOSM estimates that in West Virginia a total of 1,900 stream miles are polluted by AMD, making AMD the major source of pollution to West Virginia waterways. AMD is responsible for 50 percent of the streams in West Virginia not meeting water quality standards.[3]

National/Federal
- Federal water development projects
- PWA, WPA, CCC
- TVA, SCS/NRCS, USACOE
- Federal government granted power for pollution control
- EPA
- Federal support for watershed programs (CA, OR, MA, MT, WV, etc.)

State
- States in charge of water pollution until 1948
- States gain greater control of sewage treatment/wastewater facilities
- New federalism 1980s
- NWPPC 1981

Constitutive
- Reclamation Act, 1902
- Commerce and property constitutional clauses
- Prior appropriation/riparian rights
- Federal Water Pollution Control Act, 1948
- Water Resources Planning Act, 1965
- CWA amendments 1972, 1977
- Pacific NW Electric Power and Planning Act, 1980
- Surface Mine Control and Reclamation Act, 1977

Collective
- Regional river basin development
- Interagency river basin committees
- Water Resources Council
- State program support for watershed groups

Top Down

Friends of the Cheat

Bottom Up

Local
- Soil and water conservation districts
- Watershed groups

Operational

Figure 4.1: Hierarchical Influences on Watershed Governance

Friends of the Cheat formed in 1994 to address the persistent water quality problems associated with AMD. Two core principles guided the organization. The first was to "restore, preserve and promote the outstanding natural qualities of the Cheat watershed." The second was to "foster a cooperative effort by state and federal agencies, private industry, academics, grassroots organizations and local landowners to address the severe AMD in the Cheat Canyon." Friends of the Cheat's first principle—to restore, protect, and promote the qualities of the Cheat watershed—was embodied in many types of activities undertaken by the group throughout the watershed. These included watershed education and outreach, land protection, fisheries enhancement, advocating for a recreation-based tourism economy, and remediation of AMD. The second principle focused exclusively on the AMD challenge. To foster a cooperative effort focused on AMD, the group coordinated what is known as "The River of Promise: A Shared Commitment for the Restoration of the Cheat River, West Virginia" (River of Promise)—a document and signed agreement to remediate the watershed from the damaging effects of AMD. The River of Promise took one aspect of the vision that Friends of the Cheat had for the watershed—the remediation of AMD—and worked on prescriptive elements to make that vision a reality. River of Promise took two dominant forms, a diverse working group that included members of Friends of the Cheat as well as others, and a written agreement that articulated the vision for the river and how that vision would be implemented. Signed by twenty public, private, and nonprofit members that commit staff, funding, technical assistance, and other resources, the River of Promise agreement is a formal, yet voluntary, collective commitment to the restoration of the watershed.

Friends of the Cheat has had its ups and downs over the years. The organization and the River of Promise thrived from 1995 to 2000. At that point, it lost its executive director, and it took eighteen months to replace him. During that period, Friends of the Cheat and the River of Promise struggled. With the appointment of a new executive director in 2001, the group was reenergized with fresh direction. At various points throughout its history, the group had faced challenges in working with key participants. Working strategically with these less cooperative entities allowed Friends of the Cheat and the River of Promise to continue implementing their vision, but not as easily or smoothly as if they had the full cooperation of all stakeholders.

In spite of these challenges, Friends of the Cheat is thriving in 2009. From the original 32 members, the current membership of Friends of the Cheat has swelled to nearly 400, with more than forty-five businesses, fourteen agencies and organizations, and 325 individuals that support the organization financially.[4] In 1994 Friends of the Cheat had $28 in its budget. In 2007 the budget was nearly $350,000, most of which was directed into reclamation projects to remediate the Cheat River.[5] Total income to the group from 1995 to 2007 was just at $2.4 million, with an average annual income of approximately $180,000. The group has completed ten reclamation projects in the watershed. Water quality improvements are evident in terms of changes to water chemistry and anecdotal sightings of fish, fish-eating birds, otter, and beaver—all of which have been absent from the river for decades. True to its local roots, memberships, combined with other local fund-raising activities, make up 34 percent of the Friends of the Cheat operating income.[6]

In terms of the types of innovations categorized in chapter 1, Friends of the Cheat and the River of Promise agreement fall into the category of volunteerism. Friends of the Cheat is considered voluntary regulation because the multiple members of the group undertake cleanup efforts without any coercive action from state or federal agencies. Friends of the Cheat brings together diverse stakeholders that are interested in supporting positive change in their region. The actions decided upon by Friends of the Cheat are not legally binding; the group members implement of their own free will. The River of Promise agreement also is considered voluntary. The River of Promise agreement effectively integrates the actions and strategies of the multiple participants involved in AMD mitigation throughout the region. Public, private, non-profit, academic, and research-oriented participants from the local, regional, state, and national levels work together through the River of Promise agreement coordinating their joint action. Government agencies are actively part of the agreement, but they do not control the group or unilaterally determine the actions that need to take place. The agreement is not binding legally, but it does establish a framework for action. The conditions of "communities of shared fate" are useful to understand the effectiveness of the River of Promise agreement.[7] The questionable behavior or poor performance of one member has ramifications for the other participants. Peer pressure has been an effective mechanism to reengage errant participants or instigate constructive actions to address watershed problems. Through meetings and various activities in the watershed, participants reconcile each other's behavior to detect noncompliance with actions stated in the agreement. People in the immediate community value highly the efforts made on behalf of the various participants in the Friends of the Cheat and River of Promise activities. Every year the accomplishments of the group are celebrated at a Cheat River Festival that draws thousands from the area and beyond.

A Narrative Account of Friends of the Cheat and the River of Promise

In 1994 Randy Robinson, a videographer for a local raft company, was returning home after a day of paddling his kayak in the spring floods that filled the free-flowing rivers and creeks that are interwoven throughout Preston County, West Virginia (see table 4.1 for a table of significant chronological events). As he came around a turn in the road, a flash of orange caught his eye. Bereft of foliage, the trees along the road could not hide what was usually obscured from the eye, a gaping hole in the side of the mountain that was pouring hundreds of thousands of gallons of reddish orange water into the nearest waterway—Muddy Creek, a tributary of the Cheat River. Robinson parked his car, removed a video camera that he used for taping whitewater raft trips, and shot footage of the fissure in the mountainside and the impact that it

Table 4.1: Chronological Developments in Friends of the Cheat/River of Promise

Date	Significant Chronological Events
1991	West Virginia Rivers Coalition is established.
1994	U.S. Office of Surface Mining establishes Appalachian Clean Streams Initiative. ASCI funds cooperative agreements between USOSM and nonprofit groups for acid mine drainage remediation.
1994	Randy Robinson captures on video the blowout of the T&T coal mine and the acid mine drainage it poured into the Muddy Creek, a tributary of the Cheat River.
1994	Friends of the Cheat formed.
1995	Dave Bassage volunteers as first executive director of Friends of the Cheat.
1995	First Friends of the Cheat Festival held.
1995	River of Promise Document signed. Document articulates the shared commitment among signatories to clean up the watershed.
1995	Cheat River is named to American Rivers most endangered rivers.
1997	New gubernatorial leadership in West Virginia creates difficulty for some River of Promise signatories to continue participating in remediation work.
1997	John Faltis, owner of Anker Energy and River of Promise signatory, is killed in a helicopter crash.
2000	Dave Bassage, original executive director, leaves Friends of the Cheat.
2001	New gubernatorial leadership in West Virginia creates new opportunities for some River of Promise signatories to participate in remediation work.
2001	Keith Pitzer takes over as executive director of Friends of the Cheat.
2005	Friends of the Cheat receives EPA targeted watershed initiative grant.
2007	Abandoned Mine Land Program is reauthorized by Congress.
2009	FOC has nearly 400 members and $350,000 in its budget—most of it devoted to reclamation projects. Water quality is improving according to routine sampling and anecdotal evidence from local observers.

was having on the stream. In an attempt to trace the source of the flow, he scrambled up the hill about 200 yards to the site of T&T Coal Operations. While the water was not pouring out of the mine site directly, something was amiss, and Robinson intended to get to the bottom of it.[8]

T&T Coal Operations had shut down its last mine on the site in 1992.[9] In an effort to avoid costly treatment of the water flowing from its mine, T&T diverted its water illegally into a nearby abandoned mine and constructed a twelve-foot concrete seal to deter great amounts of water flowing out of the T&T mine entrance.[10] With no place to go, water pressure inside the mine built up following heavy spring rains and literally blew out the side of the mountain. The T&T mine eventually spewed millions of gallons of untreated acid mine drainage into Muddy Creek.[11] This massive pulse of AMD entered the Cheat at the confluence with Muddy Creek. The resulting discharge not only affected the Cheat River section but also killed fish sixteen miles downstream.[12] A second blowout in 1995 from the same mine further accentuated the problem and caused American Rivers Inc., a national river conservation organization, to name the Cheat to its top-ten list of the nation's most endangered rivers.[13]

For years whitewater paddlers and community members had seen the Cheat River degraded increasingly by AMD. Rocks in the river were stained a bright orange color, and the discoloration seeped farther into the canyon every year. People who came from nearby states to raft and kayak complained of stinging eyes, nosebleeds, and other ailments after having spent time in the Cheat's waters. Upon capturing the blowout on videotape, Robinson took the film to others outraged by the evidence of yet another environmental insult to the river. In doing so, Robinson instigated the formation of a stakeholder group to address the many issues plaguing the Cheat River.[14]

Authority for overseeing problems associated with AMD in West Virginia is fragmented among several agencies established when Congress passed the Surface Mining Control and Reclamation Act (SMCRA) on August 3, 1977. Signed into law by President Jimmy Carter, the SMCRA gives federal authorities the ability to regulate states' mining programs but then grants "primacy," or regulating authority, back to them. Consequently, the SMCRA allows the feds to oversee coal mining regulation while giving states discretion to deal with their individual circumstances.

There are two key provisions in SMCRA. Title IV established the Abandoned Mine Land Program, which is responsible for reclaiming lands that were mined prior to August 3, 1977, and abandoned without reclamation. Title V oversees existing coal mining programs and their operation and enforcement. After mining is completed, states must ensure that the disturbed area is revegetated, AMD is prevented, subsided lands are restored, hydrological disturbance and erosion control are minimized, and the land is generally restored to its approximate original contour prior to strip mining. Just as the federal legislation separates different aspects of mining regulatory responsibility, so are the responsibilities separated at the state level within West Virginia. The West Virginia Division of Mining and Reclamation (WVDMR) has authority for overseeing the permitting and inspecting of active mine sites, including those that discharge acid mine drainage. WVDMR is also responsible for bond-forfeited sites—those sites that had inadequate bonds to cover the damages inflicted by mining companies that went bankrupt and mined after the passage of the SMCRA. The West Virginia Abandoned Mine Lands (WVAML) program oversees mines that were abandoned prior to 1977. Together the WVDMR and the WVAML program are responsible for addressing the acid mine drainage issue in the state, among their many other duties. In West Virginia approximately 10 percent of AMD is caused by bond forfeitures and mine bankruptcies after 1977 when the SMCRA was passed, while 90 percent of the AMD is estimated to come from mines abandoned prior to 1977.[15]

The sheer scope and scale of the AMD problem in the Cheat River watershed was overwhelming for the regulatory agencies, and there was no feasible way to undertake a comprehensive cleanup. The polluted tributaries on the Cheat deliver an estimated 22,556 tons of acid every year to the main stem of the river.[16] In a study conducted in the 1970s, the EPA estimated that there were 457 mines on various tributaries of the Cheat. The same study estimated that approximately 188 of those mines contributed AMD to the Cheat.[17] Approximately 60 of these mines were abandoned before the SMCRA was passed in 1977, meaning that the state ultimately was responsible financially for their cleanup.[18]

WVAML and WVDMR coordinate loosely, and the fragmented responsibility makes the task of addressing AMD complicated. The AMD problem in the Cheat watershed stems primarily from sites abandoned prior to 1977, thereby falling under the jurisdiction of the WVAML program. WVAML traditionally has been resistant to addressing AMD and has interpreted its role to deal with highwalls, open portals, and vegetative reclamation processes, all of which can be defined as "protecting human health and safety," which the law prioritizes. AMD, in contrast, occupies a more uncertain area in the law and is given less legislative guidance or precedence. Moreover, the treatment methods for AMD are much less clear-cut than closing a dangerous mine portal or revegetating a spoiled landscape. AMD treatment can require elaborate chemical systems to neutralize acidity or engineered trenches through which acidified water travels to increase its alkalinity or the construction of artificial wetlands that leach metals from water. In contrast to closing a mine portal or revegetating a strip mine site, the criteria for judging success are more ambiguous. As a public agency charged with fiscally responsible management of the state's dollars, WVAML has tended to give priority to other problem areas, since cleaning up AMD is such a widespread, complicated problem with indefinite outcomes.

In 1982 the WVAML program first began working on the Cheat River AMD problem. The planner with the WVAML program, Marshall Leo, commented, "For a long time, various agencies and organizations have been concerned about the bad water that's still coming out of the many old deep mines in the lower Cheat River. While there had been some work done on the problem, it really was too big for any one entity to really tackle alone, much less solve."[19] Consequently, the WVAML program spent most of its money on reclaiming refuse piles and sealing mine entries and did not concentrate on water quality problems.

In 1994 when Randy Robinson captured the T&T mine blowout on video, the lack of focus on water quality issues in the watershed created an incentive to take action. Downstream Alliance, a watershed organization from neighboring Monongalia County, called a meeting to assemble people concerned about the problems arising from the blowout and the subsequent damage to Muddy Creek and the Cheat River. At that meeting, someone suggested the need for a local organization. Dave Bassage, a Cheat watershed resident, was inspired to take action.[20]

Bassage, a whitewater enthusiast in his mid-thirties, had "retired" from his life as math teacher in the mid-1980s to be closer to the outdoors. He moved to West Virginia and began to work as a guide, then manager, for a whitewater company that worked on the Cheat River. When the T&T blowout occurred, Bassage had been contemplating how to transition into a new career, and Friends of the Cheat provided an opportunity to combine his love of nature with a role in protecting it. Bassage agreed to call a meeting of people in the Cheat watershed to see if there was interest in forming a local group. The first meeting was attended by twenty to thirty people and included what would become the core membership of Friends of the Cheat. Community members, landowners, and other whitewater enthusiasts relished the thought of a cleaner river. Some remembered when you could fish in the Cheat's waters, and the prospect of making the river fishable again was very appealing. Whitewater boaters were among the most vocal and unhappy with the state of the river. The river increasingly was degraded, thereby infringing on one of their favored recreation spots. The Cheat is one of the few free-flowing rivers remaining in the East and had been a draw to kayakers, canoeists, rafters, and other whitewater enthusiasts from throughout the Eastern United States and beyond. The owners and operators of whitewater rafting companies had seen the numbers of people coming to the Cheat decline at a time when whitewater recreation throughout the nation was a growing sport.[21] The poor water quality was seen as one of the main reasons for the decline in customer interest. Without any effort to clean up the watershed, individual boaters and commercial whitewater outfitters could expect to see more of the same.

In preparation for a second meeting, Bassage put notices in the local paper and ran announcements on the local radio station. Approximately forty people from throughout the watershed attended the second meeting. A wide-ranging discussion took place. Out of the meeting Bassage forged what was to become the mission statement for Friends of the Cheat. Bassage and the members realized that even if the problems associated with the T&T mine were fixed, there would still be major problems in the watershed. As recalled by Bassage, "We needed to fix the problem *throughout* the watershed."[22] The group cast a wide net around the many issues faced in the watershed rather than focus only on the T&T blowout and the issues with AMD. From that point on, Friends of the Cheat became a membership organization with an active board of directors. While Friends of the Cheat did not hold membership meetings, it did hold regular board meetings, and the board charted the course for the group.

Since Friends of the Cheat focused on solving watershed scale problems broadly defined, this meant working with the coal industry, a controversial prospect. Many environmental groups in West Virginia had demonized the coal industry, and there was a long history of acrimony and conflict between environmentalists and the coal industry. Bassage understood that the Friends of the Cheat effort was one in which no one would be demonized, but all would be given the opportunity to work toward a more economically and ecologically sound watershed. "We needed to focus on problem solving, not on finger pointing," he recalled.[23] The mission that brought together these disparate participants was the opportunity to "restore, protect, and promote the outstanding natural qualities of the Cheat watershed." Within this mission statement, no one participant was made to be the scapegoat. Rather, the whole focus was on the end goal—a common interest solution to improve on the watershed—and what each member of the group could do to work toward that goal. "Righteous indignation is very destructive in the long run, and just because you are right doesn't mean you are doing the right thing. Our philosophy was one of looking beyond the immediate problem to the bigger problem," observed Bassage.[24] The massive pulse of AMD from the T&T blowout was an immediate problem that needed to be addressed but in the end was only one more part of a broader set of issues confronting the watershed.

To make Friends of the Cheat work, Bassage and others recognized the need to create a balanced board of directors that reflected the diverse interests in the watershed. As a consequence, the board members are a varied lot, representing the coal industry, local landowners, the whitewater industry, environmental activists, teachers, other local businesses, and community interests. This diverse base broadened the appeal of Friends of the Cheat beyond the whitewater community and gave the group legitimacy and credibility throughout the county and region. Tolerance, reliable information, and discussion were the ground rules that allowed the group to maintain its focus.

Bassage voluntarily ran Friends of the Cheat out of an extra room in his house with the help of the board of directors. During the time of the initial formation of the group, he commented, "we made phone calls, requested documents, and set about educating ourselves about the reasons our streams were dead and what could be done about it."[25] In addition to learning about the AMD problem facing the watershed, Bassage and the board learned of other issues that needed to be addressed. The USACOE had a plan to dam part of the Cheat River, members of another watershed group sought Friends of the Cheat's support in dealing with the siting of a limestone mine in their hollow, and Friends of the Cheat was asked to take stands on various environmental issues not only within the watershed but also throughout the state. As Bassage remembered, "Our early successes were intoxicating. The feeling of really making a difference, of getting regular recognition for our efforts, and new opportunities to grow our organization at frequent intervals was incredibly fulfilling."[26]

Friends of the Cheat was involved in numerous activities throughout the watershed, including building interpretive trails and an interpretive center on the Cheat, conducting stream inventories, helping other local watershed organizations, holding workshops and meetings, establishing a VISTA/AmeriCorps program, producing a documentary on issues about the watershed, and working with the EPA to develop TMDL determinants, developing rails-trails recreational access, conserving habitat, and maintaining river access for boaters, among other things.[27] To keep its members apprised of these activities, Friends of the Cheat published a newsletter twice yearly. The Friends of the Cheat also started an annual Cheat River Festival in 1995. Aware of the need to raise the profile of the efforts under way to restore, protect, and promote the Cheat watershed, the members of Friends of the Cheat wanted to reach out to the community to celebrate and share its victories and defeats on a yearly basis. The Cheat River Festival is a popular spring event and also serves as a major fund raiser for Friends of the Cheat. Local music and food were highlighted. A silent auction or raffle featured local goods and crafts. Different agencies, organizations, and retailers set up information booths to highlight their accomplishments. Puppet shows provided education to children about the surrounding ecosystem, the impacts of AMD, and cleanup efforts.

The difference between Friends of the Cheat and the River of Promise is subtle but important. According to Bassage, "If Friends of the Cheat is made up of the people who care about the watershed, then River of Promise is made up of people who care and can do something about it." River of Promise is the written agreement. Friends of the Cheat is the leader of and a participant in the River of Promise, but several members of the River of Promise are not members of Friends of the Cheat. Bassage chaired the River of Promise partnership and compared his role to that of a coach of an athletic team: "The athletes went out and did all the work. I tried to keep them on task and direct them to the right objectives."[28] Keith Pitzer, executive director of Friends of the Cheat, saw himself in a similar role in 2008: "Officially, I chair meetings. In reality, I try to steer involvement and commitment of various agencies for projects along the way."[29]

The River of Promise agreement integrates participants among the many levels of governance throughout the watershed into the effort to restore the Cheat. Signing the River of Promise pledge—a document that articulates a shared commitment to clean up the Cheat watershed—was the centerpiece of the first Cheat River Festival held in 1995. At the festival a ceremony was held where the original six signatories—the Friends of the Cheat, Anker Energy Corporation, USOSM, West Virginia Rivers Coalition, the West Virginia Division of Environmental Protection (WVDEP), and the West Virginia Division of Natural Resources (WVDNR)—publicly declared their collective support for addressing AMD in the basin. The participants in the River of Promise understood the importance of the different actors within the hierarchy that make up the Cheat River watershed governance system and created a structure that allowed all of these actors to come together.

The costs for cleaning up an abandoned mine site ranged from thousands to tens of millions of dollars on an annual basis, depending on the size of operation and the sustained output of acidity from the site. Estimates for cleaning up the entire Cheat watershed, the most adversely affected in West Virginia, were placed in the hundreds of millions of dollars.[30] One of the complications in treating AMD is that once a site begins producing acidic water, it can continue for an indeterminate time and require treatment for decades, if not centuries. The financial pressure on state agencies to clean up abandoned sites is great, and the Cheat River watershed was but one of many severely affected watersheds in the state. At the time, the WVAML program received approximately $24 million per year, and only $2.4 million of that was set aside per year to address AMD abatement.[31] Scarce financial resources, multiple abandoned mines, limited technologies, and liability issues all affected the ability of state agencies to take a comprehensive approach to the problem of AMD in the Cheat River watershed. While state and federal agencies undertook piecemeal efforts at remediation, wholesale cleanup was an impossibility given the numerous sources of pollution, property rights issues involving landholders of the various mining claims, and the numerous parties who either caused or were affected by the AMD in the watershed. River of Promise was the catalyst for the various agencies that had responsibility for AMD to focus their mission and concentrate in a specific watershed. Under the status quo, no one was particularly happy with water quality in the Cheat River. Existing trends suggested that water quality was not improving and might very well continue to degrade under existing conditions. River of Promise quite simply offered an alternative to those who wanted to effect positive change. As Greg Adolfson, an environmental resources specialist with the WVDMR, recalled, "What we realized was that if we could all do what our respective programs were meant to do, we could really all pull together and make a bigger difference."[32]

Adolfson came up with the idea for the *River of Promise* in 1994 after the T&T blowout.[33] Rejecting the idea, Adolfson's division head at the time felt that any effort to address AMD issues on the Cheat would be a waste of time and money due to the immense scope of the problem and the enormous costs affiliated with a cleanup effort. A change in political leadership several months later led Adolfson to try again. In 1995 he made his pitch to a new division head soon after the Cheat had been named to American Rivers list of the country's top-ten most endangered rivers. Adolfson approached his boss to see if there was value in bringing together various public, private, nonprofit, research, and community people who had a vested interest in working to mitigate the AMD damage on the Cheat. The vision was one of a "shared commitment and cooperative effort of necessary participants to gather the right data to enable us to begin to make good decisions about where we invest our resources in areas impacted by AMD," recalled Adolfson. He approached Steve Brown, a wildlife planner in the WVDNR, who immediately saw the potential for reestablishing fisheries and expanding recreational opportunities on the Cheat, if it could be restored. Both men realized it was imperative to work with community members if such an effort was to have a chance of success.[34]

Friends of the Cheat was in its formative stages, and Bassage saw the appeal of pulling together the various participants who possessed the resources and will to change the future of the Cheat. The timing was fortuitous and other entities throughout the watershed also were predisposed to participate in the River of Promise effort. West Virginia Rivers Coalition, a statewide nonprofit river advocacy organization, was supportive. West Virginia Rivers Coalition had been established in 1991 and provided financial and technical support to Friends of the Cheat in its early years.

On the federal level other initiatives were under way. The USOSM established the Appalachian Clean Streams Initiative in 1994, which funds cooperative agreements between the USOSM and nonprofit groups for local AMD programs. Prior to 1994 USOSM had not prioritized AMD. Bob Uram, appointed director of the agency that year, wanted to spend more money to clean up streams polluted with acid mine drainage. Under previous USOSM policies, acid mine drainage was considered a lower priority project, unless the polluted stream was directly used for drinking water. Uram said that under his new policy, mine cleanups could be considered high-priority projects if "the problem to be reclaimed affects the protection of general welfare, i.e., the problem area is located in the immediate vicinity of a residential area or has an adverse economic impact upon a local community."[35] With this in mind, Uram created the Appalachian Clean Streams Initiative and was personally vested in not only Appalachian Clean Streams Initiative's success but also the success of the River of Promise and Friends of the Cheat. As Uram proclaimed, "Friends of the Cheat and Appalachian Clean Streams Initiative grew up together. This was one project we supported most. Of all projects this one was most strongly based around community redevelopment. This was a place where people saw it as not just cleaning up streams, but having an impact on the whole watershed."[36] Funding for such efforts was imperative, and Uram devoted much time to lobbying Congress and industry to get them to see it was in their interest to fund such a program. Since it started, the Appalachian Clean Streams Initiative has participated in 161 cooperative agreements in eleven states contributing more than $14 million to various initiatives. As of 2006, 92 projects had been completed. An additional 20 new watershed cooperative agreements were planned for 2007 for a total of $1.5 million.[37] Rick Buckley, USOSM program specialist and coordinator of the West Virginia Appalachian Clean Streams Initiative program, understood that River of Promise could provide a means to integrate the various efforts that were under way throughout the watershed. "Office of Surface Mining recognized early on that there was a lot of activity in the Cheat but no opportunity to share information. Cleaning up AMD is an expensive process, and River of Promise would allow us to share resources and spread our money farther," Buckley observed.[38]

In addition to the interest from state and federal agencies, industry also was intrigued by the idea. John Faltis, the owner and operator of a local coal company, Anker Energy Corporation, saw the appeal of River of Promise. Faltis was "pretty visionary" according to Bassage, and Faltis's wife had been involved in a commercial whitewater operation prior to their marriage. Faltis was predisposed to new ways of looking at the problem of AMD, and River of Promise presented him with a vision that resonated with Faltis's own desires: "John told us that he had been looking for an opportunity for his company to do something to help address the sins of the coal industry's past. John believed that as long as streams were still running orange, it was effectively a black eye for the coal industry. And he wanted to do what he could to get rid of that black eye."[39] Faltis decided to put his energies into the nascent River of Promise to see where it would lead. The appeal of River of Promise was that it presented an alternative that worked better than any of the status quo options at the time. The status quo policy meant continued degradation of the Cheat, no emphasis on new technologies to try to remedy AMD, and ad hoc efforts to remediate the watershed.

In early 1995 the initial interested participants—Adolfson from West Virginia Department of Environmental Protection (WVDEP), Buckley from USOSM, Faltis from Anker Energy, Roger Harrison from West Virginia Rivers Coalition, Bassage from Friends of the Cheat, and Steve Brown from the WVDNR—gathered at the Anker Energy offices in Morgantown. Together they drafted the River of Promise document that articulated the shared commitment to the watershed. Participants then had to take the document back to their home agency, organization, or company to gain approval for it. In May 1995, during the first Cheat River Festival, John Faltis, president of Anker Energy Corporation; Robert Uram, head of the USOSM; Eli McCoy, deputy director of the West Virginia Division of Environmental Protection; Charles Felton Jr., director of the West Virginia Division of Natural Resources; Dave Bassage, executive director of Friends of the Cheat; and Roger Harrison, executive director of the West Virginia River's Coalition, all gathered on the center stage to publicly sign the River of Promise agreement.[40] Since then, more than twenty groups have signed on to the agreement, including more state and federal agencies, academics, conservation groups, and local government. Meeting quarterly and chaired by Friends of the Cheat, the River of Promise task force coordinates and initiates AMD remediation projects throughout the watershed. The National Mine Land Reclamation Center, a research unit located at a nearby West Virginia University, is an integral River of Promise partner, gathering water quality data, developing conceptual designs for projects, and conducting postconstruction monitoring and evaluation.

In addition to having personal commitment from a variety of participants throughout the nested structure of the governance system, River of Promise was designed to be comprehensive of interests related to water quality concerns in the watershed, including community members and nonprofit organizations not usually considered in such an effort. River of Promise worked, Adolfson said, "because is was inclusive, people were eager and willing to work on it, and there was a great desire to work together. We shared a similar vision and the same goals. We wanted to make progress and maintain those results."[41]

The only interests that appeared to oppose the River of Promise effort were some environmental groups who saw efforts of Friends of the Cheat in working with the coal industry as collaboration with the enemy. One Friends of the Cheat board member, who represented environmental interests, ended up resigning his seat over the issue. Given the relationship he was building with Faltis and others, Bassage and the rest of the board were willing to accept the resignation and take their chances by embarking on this new way of doing things.

The River of Promise is a short, two-page document that details the problem of AMD in the Cheat watershed and the responsibilities of the signatories. To achieve the shared vision for the restoration of the Cheat River, the partners identified and jointly committed to several action items. These included expanded efforts to identify significant sources of acid pollution in the watershed, increased public awareness of the extent and impacts of acid pollution in the watershed, working together to target streams that contribute significant acid pollution, selecting or developing effective technologies to mitigate that pollution, working in concert to secure funding for acid pollution mitigation projects, implementing financially and technically effective acid pollution mitigation projects, monitoring the status of water quality and fisheries in the watershed and sharing data, and promoting the recreational use of the river and the contribution of that use to the local economy. The River of Promise allowed the various entities to leverage resources more effectively and avoid duplication in effort. Restoring the Cheat was an expensive proposition, and River of Promise would allow the participants involved to share resources and spread money further.[42]

River of Promise was effective because of the contributions of people and interests involved. Citizen support was also important and was evident in the establishment of Friends of the Cheat—a community-based group. "There is often resistance when government comes in," says Bassage. "We invited them in and gave them guidance."[43] Agency involvement at both the state and federal levels allowed resources to be managed and pooled for effective cost savings. Industry participation was an additional asset. Involving industry meant that people did not have to choose sides in the environment versus jobs debate that often framed these issues. University researchers infused efforts with the latest technologies and understanding of AMD mitigation and reclamation techniques. West Virginia Rivers Coalition gave River of Promise a higher profile with environmental groups throughout the state. The West Virginia Division of Natural Resources was interested in the recreational, and especially fishing, benefits that would come with improved water quality on the Cheat and its tributaries. The WVDNR's participation was important from the standpoint of recreation and wildlife interests throughout the state.

According to several participants in the River of Promise, the agreement works on account of several factors. These include personal commitment, diverse representation, local engagement, and having a tangible agreement. Rick Buckley, West Virginia coordinator for USOSM's Appalachian Clean Streams Initiative, states that it takes "extraordinary personal commitments" by everyone involved to make these relationships work:[44] "The people that participate in River of Promise want to see it succeed, and that is what makes a difference."[45]

In analyzing this case, it is clear that while the personal commitment to participate has been important, so too was the agency structure and support that buttressed that individual commitment. The structure of the USOSM and its mandate were crucial to the way its personnel could interact with local watershed efforts. The agency as a whole had to support the move in the direction toward local watershed initiatives. According to Buckley, the local watershed approach was easier for an agency like Office of Surface Mining because the agency as a whole is small.[46] It was easy for Buckley to call up the director of USOSM or to have direct communication with individuals higher in his agency. The commitment of Uram, coupled with the size of the agency, gave the program legitimacy not only with other employees within USOSM but also within West Virginia as well. In turn, Buckley could make a personal commitment to River of Promise and be supported by the hierarchy of his own agency.

Having a tangible agreement also was constructive given the voluntary nature of the work. Signing the agreement, especially in a public venue in front of the media, meant the agency or organization was under greater pressure to honor it. While agreeing to work together was acceptable, the signed agreement "is the government equivalent of a handshake."[47] For instance, the River of Promise statement was a useful instrument for Buckley to take back to his higher-ups in the agency and leverage additional resources. "It is helpful for me with my superiors to say, 'We signed this document and made a commitment,'" And he adds that signing the commitment "has given us a sense of ownership in the process."[48]

The Friends of the Cheat has been engaged in numerous projects since its inception. Through its partnerships with many state, federal, and other nonprofit groups, as embodied in the River of Promise, Friends of the Cheat has been able to leverage an estimated $6 million to $12 million in studies and reclamation projects to the watershed. The tangible products from the River of Promise agreement are varied. These include improved water quality in the main stem of the Cheat and its tributaries, new social infrastructure in terms of the River of Promise partnership, improved recreation in the watershed, greater involvement of the coal industry in wanting to remediate AMD problems, greater knowledge about the conditions under which AMD mitigation technologies work, and a national focus on the Cheat watershed.[49] Many of the reclamation projects undertaken in the watershed have experienced varying degrees of success. Several of the technologies employed to treat the AMD are experimental passive systems of treatment. In some instances, the projects have been very successful at first and then, for any number of reasons, have become less effective in their treatment of AMD. In other cases, projects meet or exceed design expectations. Trial and error have been essential in working through the complexities associate with treating AMD. Recalled Adolfson, "It was an experiential learning process. We got out on the ground and learned what worked by being on the ground."[50] River of Promise focuses on pooling information among the many participants and evaluating their endeavors. Consequently, all participants learned more quickly about what worked under certain conditions and what did not.

As a voluntary agreement River of Promise was quite successful in channeling resources to the Cheat that otherwise would not have been available or would not have been used as efficiently. Among other accomplishments, the River of Promise has resulted in projects totaling $250,000 from Anker Energy, $1.4 million from the USOSM, $500,000 from the EPA, $140,000 from WVDEP, and $600,000 from the USACOE.[51] WVAML dedicated $5.4 million to new projects in the Cheat watershed in 2002. WVAML has been a reluctant partner in River of Promise, unwilling to sign the formal agreement but participating with funding and projects nonetheless. The general effectiveness of River of Promise has varied over the years, and much of this has hinged on the ability to keep the varied participants involved. Initiating the innovation involved in the River of Promise agreement has proven easier than sustaining it. Changes in political and administrative leadership within and among the various organizations and agencies have posed the greatest challenges.

Most significantly, changes in political leadership affected the involvement of state agency participants. New gubernatorial leadership under Republican Cecil Underwood in 1997 combined with changes in administrative heads created a situation that prohibited Adolfson from being involved in River of Promise. Other agency officials were prevented from spending time or money on travel to community meetings, thereby effectively starving River of Promise from state involvement. Changes in the leadership in the WVAML resulted in less participation from this agency and cultivated an agency culture of community avoidance. In 1997 John Faltis, owner of Anker Energy, was killed tragically in a helicopter crash. In 2000 Dave Bassage left Friends of the Cheat to work for state government as a small business ombudsman on the issue of environmental innovation. Bassage was suffering from burnout from working primarily in a volunteer capacity for eighty to one hundred hours a week: "I had started out as a dedicated, perhaps fanatical, volunteer, then transitioned into a paid executive director making very low pay but still committed to working eighty- to one hundred–hour weeks trying to do most of the work myself. When I attempted to scale back my hours to something more reasonable, it was not received well by the board, nor could they see the need to offer a salary of $20,000 or more."[52] Friends of the Cheat took nearly two years to fill his position.

During 2000–2001, Friends of the Cheat (FOC) limped along. Bassage remembers that the group was really struggling at that time: "FOC really could have gone the other way during that time after I left. We had a crisis period, and I really could have been the bad guy that doomed the group when I chose to leave." As Bassage recalled, it took the board a long time to come to terms with the fact that to find a competent, well-qualified executive director, it would have to pay a competitive salary. In the meantime, without coaching from Friends of the Cheat, River of Promise was not as active or as directed. The board of directors kept some projects hobbling along but not at the same pace as when Bassage had been fully engaged. "Morale was low. . . . No one was providing strong leadership."[53]

In late 2001 the board came to terms with the need to find a competitive salary for an executive director. Keith Pitzer, a watershed resident and Friends of the Cheat board member, accepted the Friends of the Cheat executive director position. Pitzer recalled that what motivated him then "was the need of the organization." He had been on the Friends of the Cheat board and served as the chair from 1998 to 2000. He was aware that Friends of the Cheat was struggling and with some encouragement from other board members began to see a role for himself. Under Pitzer's leadership, Friends of the Cheat and River of Promise regained momentum. Pitzer recalled that the budget had suffered greatly over the previous year and half and so that became an instant priority for him. His other priority was "driving ROP [River of Promise], keeping or regaining confidence in our partners there and getting projects planned that would bring a cash flow to the organization."[54] Pitzer revitalized Friends of the Cheat after nearly two years of foundering. "Keith stepped in, and he has been great. He has paced himself well and not burned himself out. He really gives you the sense of a steady hand at the helm. Keith is fairly unflappable," observes Bassage.[55]

While maintaining focus on AMD remediation work in the watershed, Pitzer expanded the mission of the organization to include work on a recreation-based economy. This vision includes a thriving trout fishery in the restored streams, reliable river access for the boating community, and a network of trails that can support biking, hiking, and camping: "FOC has broadened its activities to include projects that ensure public access on and off the Cheat River and Big Sandy. This resonates with the boating community. FOC also took the lead in advocating and fund raising for development of Rails to Trails on abandoned railroad corridors in the watershed. This again broadened awareness of and support for FOC."[56]

Under Pitzer's leadership the group has undertaken an extensive watershed water quality mapping project: "Our water quality monitoring and mapping project is second to none in West Virginia and has been presented at several trainings and conferences."[57] Using a Geographic Information System (GIS), the group collected water quality information from more than one hundred AMD drainage sites throughout the watershed and plotted them on a map of the watershed. As of 2007 they had collected 560 specific sample points of which 375 were AMD sources.[58] With multiple sampling dates for many sites, the database provided information needed to prioritize sites for treatment. This helped the group identify where AMD problems are concentrated and which sites are responsible for the worst impairment in the tributaries. The mapping and monitoring project guides strategic planning for all current and future River of Promise projects.

Outreach and watershed education also have been a big priority under Pitzer. Starting in 2001, Friends of the Cheat began leveraging interns from the year-round, full-time USOSM/VISTA/AmeriCorps program and the USOSM summer interns program to take summer educational programs to 4-H and scouting camps in the watershed. Programming concentrates on stream quality, macro-invertebrates, and the causes of stream degradation. Since 2002 FOC has held an annual water festival for elementary schools that promotes water quality awareness and education.[59] At the high school level, Friends of the Cheat has done modules on stream monitoring and AMD treatment. In 2005 Friends of the Cheat began offering an annual AMD tour, which takes people to different treatment sites all over the watershed. In 2008 one of the USOSM/VISTA interns presented to the American Society of Mining Reclamation National Conference on the accomplishments of Friends of the Cheat.[60]

Under Pitzer, "a lot more ground work is being done," observed Bassage, who in 2009 was vice president of the board: "When I was there we had one or two projects at any given time. Now there are five or six in progress. There is more money being put into projects. Expanding into rails to trails and land management has also been an emphasis of Keith's. He is a good grant writer and a good project manager."[61] Financial records support Bassage's observation. For the period of 1995–2000, when Bassage was executive director, Friends of the Cheat had a total income of nearly $500,000. From the period of 2002–2008, when Pitzer was executive director, Friends of the Cheat had a total income of nearly $1.9 million. Achieving financial stability was a top priority for Pitzer, who saw it as essential before diversifying Friends of the Cheat's mission to rails to trails, education, and river access projects.

Pitzer, like Bassage, is quite proud of what Friends of the Cheat and River of Promise have accomplished: "FOC had a good reputation and prominent position among watershed groups thanks to the leadership of original director, Dave Bassage. I think we have continued that and built upon it. We've won numerous state awards, including Watershed of the Year and WVDEP's Environmental Excellence Award."[62]

In 2007 Friends of the Cheat completed its tenth AMD treatment project. These ten projects targeted four tributaries of the Cheat. Pitzer estimates that Friends of the Cheat is directly responsible for a total investment of nearly $2 million into reclamation projects since 1995. In addition to cleaning up the watershed, these projects funnel money into the local economy, as most of the design, engineering, and construction work is done by local businesses. He estimates that millions more have been directed to the watershed based on the work done by Friends of the Cheat.[63] Projects in progress in 2008 include an EPA Targeted Watershed Initiative grant for $835,000 that will focus on the Muddy Creek Drainage upstream of the T&T site. In 2002 President Bush asked the nation's governors and tribal leaders to nominate proposals to support community-based approaches to clean up the nation's watersheds. In 2005 Congress appropriated $9 million for the Targeted Watershed Grant Program, which was conceived to encourage community-based approaches to restore, preserve, and protect the nation's watersheds and to promote strong public and private partnerships that lead to measurable environmental results. Friends of the Cheat was one of twelve grant recipients chosen from a list of 100 nominations nationwide. Muddy Creek is the largest contributor of AMD to the Cheat main stem. This project will remove twenty-seven stream miles from the impaired list of streams and could result in a smallmouth bass fishery from Muddy Creek downstream.[64]

Under Pitzer's leadership, the relationship with WVAML continued to be difficult. In 2007 the federal Abandoned Mine Land Program was reauthorized by Congress. The federal AML program collects a tax on each ton of coal produced to pay for reclamation of sites abandoned before the passage of the SMCRA of 1977. Beginning in 2008, the reauthorized program doubles the amount of funding to the states. States are allowed, but not required, to set aside up to 30 percent of each year's payout for water quality treatment. Previously they had been allowed to set aside only 10 percent. Political pressures within each state determine how much is actually set aside for water quality. The program will sunset in 2022 with no mechanism for continuing it. Friends of the Cheat has been particularly keen to figure out what this means for stream restoration and watershed funding in West Virginia. Pitzer met with WVAML's director Charles Miller, WVDEP's secretary Stephanie Timmermeyer, and WVDEP's director of land reclamation Ken Ellison to clarify how water quality would be affected. Pitzer stated that what he heard was "in general positive, but noncommittal as to specifics regarding water quality."[65] Friends of the Cheat has advocated strongly for West Virginia to commit the full 30 percent to water quality programs and create an interest-bearing trust fund with a large portion of that funding. Once the federal AML fund is terminated in 2022, Friends of the Cheat wants to be able to fund operation and maintenance of active and passive treatment systems into perpetuity. Additionally, it would like to see a portion of the funding go to a watershed grant program for watershed organizations to fund water treatment projects and monitoring at a local watershed level.[66]

The WVAML has moved forward to deal with some aspects of water quality treatment. Three projects are planned for the watershed, but the agency has not involved Friends of the Cheat in its planning. The approach chosen by WVAML is in-stream lime dosers. Pitzer objects to this approach because "in-stream dosing is not restoration in any true sense of the word. It can improve water quality at some point downstream to the degree that fish could be stocked there. In-stream dosing also requires continued operation/maintenance costs and relies on a mechanical device that could fail. This is not the sort of restoration the watershed community envisions for our streams and rivers." A statewide AMD advisory committee was formed by WVDEP to advise where and how the projects could take place. Pitzer sits on the committee and noted that "planning on three small watershed dosing approaches has moved forward without committee involvement."[67]

Pitzer has been frustrated in trying to get an AMD project implemented on Lick Run, a tributary of the Cheat. Initially working with Friends of the Cheat as their local watershed partner, the USACOE obtained a $500,000 appropriation courtesy of U.S. Rep. Allan Mollohan in 2002. After four years of performing ground survey work and meeting with Friends of the Cheat a few times, the USACOE failed to design a blueprint for the project. Pitzer, clearly frustrated with the relationship and outcome, said, "There is a saying about the Corps: 'They're slow, but they're expensive.'" The $500,000 appropriation is a lot of money for a small group like Friends of the Cheat, which has a demonstrated record of performing on the ground. "This is an example of an agency with no sense of or means to take local input," Pitzer said.[68] "I don't know how many meetings [with Corps officials] have been canceled."[69] USACOE has stood in the way of progress and is "a huge, unworkable bureaucracy that doesn't know a thing about acid mine drainage." Without USACOE approval and sign-off, the project cannot move forward. "The Lick Run project is dead in the water."[70]

Since 1999 Frank Jernejcic, West Virginia Division of Natural Resources fisheries biologist, has conducted fish surveys and water quality testing throughout the Cheat main stem to Cheat Lake. Cheat Lake now has a thriving bass fishery and hosts a bass fishing tournament. The upper part of the Cheat has documented good fisheries, but as AMD entered downstream the fisheries were degraded. Over time the Cheat Lake fishery has improved and now ranks as one of the top five waters for bass fishing in West Virginia. Testing for pH values from 2004 to 2006 revealed levels that should have tolerated fish throughout the Cheat canyon. In 2005 fish catches by the WVDNR confirmed the presence of seven species. Jernejcic sees the River of Promise as having a profound impact throughout the watershed: "The major payoff is the restoration of a sport fishery that my generation had forgotten."[71] In 2007 paddlers found river otters for the first time. Fish-eating bird species such as the great blue heron and osprey are now seen throughout the Cheat Canyon.[72]

The innovations that began in 1995 persisted into 2009 and adapted to new circumstances along the way. River of Promise experienced times of greater and lesser effectiveness, and this posed implementation challenges. Weathering the change in the executive director position within Friends of the Cheat, as well as changes in political leadership, River of Promise maintained enough continuity to resurge in 2002. Having key people in place, notably the executive director of Friends of the Cheat, was crucial to keeping the team of participants focused on their goals. Reflecting on the fifteen years that Friends of the Cheat has been in operation, Bassage felt that "the philosophy we chose to adopt from the outset 'seek partnership not conflict' has worked well. We separated ourselves from other environmental groups. We didn't want to divvy up the world into good guys and bad guys. We also had a long-range vision. This allowed us to focus on the marathon, not the sprint. Those two philosophies—seeking partnership and having a long-range vision—have served FOC well."[73]

Pitzer sees it a bit differently. He feels that the original mission of the organization was key to Friends of the Cheat's success, but strategically diversifying the activities taken on by the group also has been essential to broadening awareness of Friends of the Cheat and expanding its base of support. "The defined mission of the organization was focused enough, yet broad enough to guide the organization over a period of years," he reflected. "Taking the lead in AMD construction management was crucial because it brought administration funds to the organization." As the executive director, Pitzer was worried that an organization with one narrow focus would run out of steam: "Support grows weary of the same issues, especially if [it needs to be sustained] against considerable odds."[74] To deal with this, Pitzer broadened Friends of the Cheat activities to take on public river access to connect better with the boating community, fisheries restoration to connect with the fishing community, and rails-to-trails development to connect with the biking, hiking, and recreation crowd.

APPLYING THE ANALYTIC FRAMEWORK

The analytical framework laid out in chapter 1 is applied here to the Friends of the Cheat case study. The three macro categories of individuals (motivation, norms and harmony, and congruence), structure (rules and communication, incentives, opening, and resistance), and culture (shocks, framing, and legitimacy) are laid over the details of the case to illustrate how these factors were or were not accounted for in the implementation of this innovation.

Individuals

Motivation The impetus for pursuing an innovative approach often rests on discontented individuals who are capable of devising an alternative to the existing status quo.

The status quo situation in this case was a state regulatory agency that was reluctant to tackle water quality problems associated with AMD and a prevailing belief that many of the tributaries to the Cheat, as well as the main stem, would continue to run orange and remain devoid of life. The WVAML program did not prioritize water quality issues. Moreover, the problem was fragmented throughout the state with no real catalyst to focus action. Many potential participants could play a role in addressing AMD water quality problems, but there was no easy solution for integrating the many players. Altogether the lack of action on behalf of the WVAML program and the lack of a mechanism to integrate potential stakeholders created a vacuum in which others could take and sustain action.

Capable leadership existed at many different levels in several organizations, and these leaders were highly motivated to change the status quo. Dave Bassage with Friends of the Cheat, Greg Adolfson with WVDEP, Steve Brown with the WVDNR, Bob Uram and Rick Buckley with USOSM, and John Faltis with Anker Energy all were critical to the success of the initial effort. The executive directors, Bassage and Pitzer, and the board of directors were essential to the continued implementation of the effort.

Bassage was inspired by his love of the outdoors and the lure of making a living that would combine his river experience with advocacy work. Adolfson was motivated by the ability to achieve something on the ground and make a difference. Brown was encouraged by the promise of a restored fishery and recreation-based economic opportunities in the region. Uram was personally vested in the USOSM Appalachian Clean Streams Initiative and the promise of restoring the Cheat watershed, as evidenced by his attendance at the original signing of the River of Promise document and continued support for lobbying Congress for the money to support the Appalachian Clean Streams Initiative. Buckley saw potential in how Friends of the Cheat and River of Promise could facilitate federal work at the watershed level. He was motivated by the promise that his agency and others could use their collective resources more efficiently to accomplish remediation work. Faltis wanted to give back to the community and be seen as a progressive coal owner and operator. River of Promise also afforded the opportunity to experiment with new AMD remediation technologies. An Anker Energy employee and local landowner in the Cheat watershed, Troy Tichnell, explained that "the appeal for Anker was a way to give back, to do something. [Anker] always gave money and time, but reclamation allowed them to put their skills to better use."[75]

It is clear from the outset that motivation among the group was self-reinforcing to some degree. "I really felt like all of us were doing something incredibly important—something that would last," recalled Bassage.[76] Bassage made clear that efforts by the community needed to be complemented by equal efforts on the agency side, "What's needed from the community organization's side is a perceived need for change and a strong sense that their participation in any process will be more than just token . . . employees of the agency must have a sense of personal buy-in to the change process. Many of them are hardened by experiences with agency and/or poorly informed citizenry."[77] It was clear from others that this commitment existed at both the state and federal levels. As recalled by Rick Buckley, there were "extraordinary personal commitments by everyone."

However, motivation to participate in Friends of the Cheat and River of Promise has not been consistent over time. The Friends of the Cheat and the River of Promise faced numerous challenges to maintain its focus and overcome challenges. Following Faltis's death in 1997, River of Promise members were concerned about Anker Energy's continued participation. Tichnell stepped in to oversee the company's role and ensure that Anker Energy's perspective was represented. He now sits on the Friends of the Cheat board. Tichnell commented that the continuing motivation to be involved in the River of Promise was to carry out Faltis's vision after his death. Over time, some board members have stepped down, and new ones have taken their place. The group has benefited from new members who were motivated to take on new or sustain existing projects. Charlie Walbridge, board president in 2009, has been a key fund raiser and primary advocate for keeping salary rates competitive. Other members have been consistently involved and provide a degree of institutional memory about projects and relationships.

When Bassage stepped down from the executive director position in early 2000, the group lost its principal leader and an important participant in the mutually reinforcing motivation that prevailed. Without clear leadership to catalyze action, most participants were less motivated to work.

In late 2001 Pitzer, a board member, took over as executive director. Under his capable leadership, many within the group were once again motivated to work. Reflecting on when he came on board, Pitzer recalls, "I think people were ready to have someone in charge . . . to make decisions, to commit to projects and make things happen on the ground." Pitzer was motivated to take the position originally because the organization was in dire need and he was looking for a position closer to home that would avoid his current daily commute to the Shenandoah Valley in Virginia. As of 2009 his motivation is "driven by the shared commitment of those stalwart partners that are there through success and failure and by the sense of place and identification that comes with living in this area."[78]

Motivation to participate was affected by political leadership within agencies. For instance, leadership change in the WVDEP altered the ability of Adolfson to participate in River Promise. Adolfson had trained people below him who were capable of filling his shoes upon his departure, including Jennifer Pauer in the governor's Stream Partners Program. Others within the WVDEP Non-Point Source Program were highly motivated to continue to work with Friends of the Cheat and have provided consistent support. Pitzer emphasizes, "Program policies and mandates certainly exist, but the attitude that one works with has at least as much to do with using those policies and the language they contain. In West Virginia, [US]OSM's Clean Streams Initiative has involved many watershed groups in activities, trainings, etc. . . . In other states, it's a silent program. It's still people that make a difference."[79]

Norms and Harmony The underlying social norms that drive River of Promise are the shared commitment to improve the watershed. These norms are held mutually among the principal players and reinforced at quarterly meetings, with the Cheat River Festival, and in the projects undertaken by the group. Predisposition toward change can be influenced by the desire to minimize conflict in the workplace. If change is perceived to cause disagreements, then there is a tendency to avoid change. River of Promise was a patchwork of many different organizations and agencies. Some of those agencies and participants were threatened by the community-oriented focus in the watershed effort and emphasis on improving water quality. For instance, the prevailing culture with the WVAML program was top-down decision making that did not focus on water quality. WVAML did not want to alter its decision-making style or schedule of projects to accommodate a community-based, stakeholder approach embodied by Friends of the Cheat or River of Promise. At times some participants had to back off of their roles within River of Promise when a change in political leadership or agency mission was less conducive to community-oriented work. At those times agency norms clashed with the norms of the River of Promise, and those participants needed to break from River of Promise. Disharmony prevented more active participation. Because of these clashes, it became important for like-minded people to find each other and work together. As observed by Pauer, "People are afraid of change, that their workload will change and that they will have to do something different. People who think alike in the agency need to band together—create our own culture of doability."[80] Buckley found that his organization wholly supported his participation, as did others like Anker Energy and the WVDNR. In spite of this disharmony, the River of Promise has carried on with those who continued to share the vision and collaborative ideals embodied in the agreement.

Congruence When the dominant values in an agency clash with the values of individuals who are expected to carry out a mission, then implementation of a mission is less likely. In the case of River of Promise, there was not one prevailing agency through which implementation took place. Government agencies were not in charge but part of a larger stakeholder effort that was "coached" by a local nonprofit group. Federal, state, and local public, private, nonprofit, and research-oriented participants interacted with each other in multilateral and bilateral settings. Multiple agencies and organizations coordinated to undertake remediation projects. Consequently, congruence is not a very powerful explanatory factor in this case.

Structure

Rules and Communication Compliance with an innovation can be increased if there are effective administrative rules and clear communication and information exchange. The mission statement for Friends of the Cheat is clear and concise: "The mission is as relevant today as it was when we came up with it. It is one sentence. It is easy to commit to memory."[81] The primary set of administrative rules for River of Promise is a two-page, voluntary agreement that spells out the responsibilities of the twenty signatories and the joint commitment to several action items: "River of Promise was focused on establishing priorities and divvying up responsibilities. To be a participant you were expected to identify your niche and step up to the plate and fill it."[82] In the earlier years, a strategic plan prioritized tasks in the watershed and was revisited based on resource availability, funding opportunities, and political change. According to Pitzer, "ROP still meets quarterly. We are less vital in terms of generating ideas, new policy, new takes on treatment. If we had greater participation from WVU [West Virginia University] so as to generate ideas in a true think tank model, I think it would serve us better. ROP is still very functional. We have a clearinghouse four times a year to discuss and commit to new projects."[83] Between quarterly meetings, minutes from the meetings are still circulated, as are agendas for upcoming meetings. Specific tasks are reviewed during quarterly meetings that allow the participants to coordinate and talk about what has or has not been accomplished in the interim and to plan for the upcoming months.

Friends of the Cheat has an organizational structure that consists of an executive director, two additional full-time staff, and a USOSM/VISTA employee. In the summer they have additional interns.[84] Staff work in the same office and the small group size facilitate easy communication. The Friends of the Cheat board is the main governing body for the group and consists of seven members. The board meets every six weeks. Membership meetings are not held, but the group communicates with the membership through its website, biannual newsletter, and the annual Cheat Festival. Bassage says, "Keith is very good at communicating key issues. Board meetings are pretty informal. Most work is done through consensus. We don't get bogged down in process. We stay focused on the mission and let that be the guiding force."[85]

Incentives Resources can be used to induce behavioral change in the direction consistent with innovation. Three types of incentives seem relevant in encouraging innovation in the watershed—money, technical skill, and mutual support and friendship. It is not clear that these incentives were used in a deliberate manner to effect change in a given direction by one specific actor with a clear vision, per the rational choice model. Rather, various incentives created a critical mass to forge a partnership that would allow resources to be used most efficiently throughout the watershed. The coincidental confluence of participants with incentives appears opportunistic rather than deliberate.

In terms of funding and technical support, several organizations were willing to pitch in to assist in the Friends of the Cheat and River of Promise effort. Friends of the Cheat was the beneficiary of good timing in this regard. Several programs to assist watershed groups were coming into effect just as the group was getting off the ground. West Virginia Rivers Coalition, a statewide nonprofit river advocacy organization, had been established in 1991 and provided financial and technical support to Friends of the Cheat in its early years. The WVDEP established a watershed grant program in 1995 to encourage groups to form and support its work. On the federal level, the USOSM established the Appalachian Clean Streams Initiative in 1994, which funded cooperative agreements between the USOSM and nonprofit groups for local AMD programs. Since its inception Friends of the Cheat has obtained funding from the EPA through 319 funds and its Targeted Watershed Grant Program, as well as a variety of grants from local, state, and national nonprofit organizations that support river, recreation, and water advocacy work. Funding has been an especially key component in continuing to motivate work. The same is true for River of Promise. According to Pitzer, "ROP all depends on the participation of its partners and especially the partners that can bring money to the table. If we don't have the money to make the matches to do the project, ROP ceases to be effective. We have other important partners like WVDNR, who participate actively and help us with all the fisheries work, but they don't have money to bring to the table. Without the money we can't do work on the ground."[86]

While funding served primarily to provide an incentive for Friends of the Cheat to keep moving forward with projects, sharing technical skills and knowledge has served several members of the group well. Friends of the Cheat and the River of Promise have become pioneers in applying passive and active AMD remediation systems in a variety of contexts. Each system must be appropriate for the problem posed at the site. Sometimes this means a closed, anoxic system; other times it means an open limestone pit. Anker Energy donated its machines and knowledge to learn about new AMD remediation technologies. The National Mine Lands Reclamation Center has been a key participant in using experimental designs at AMD sites, refining them and improving them over time. All of the participants with River of Promise are beneficiaries from this learn by doing approach.

Lastly, collaboration, friendship, and a shared sense of commitment and responsibility serve as the final incentives that facilitate the implementation of River of Promise. Friends of the Cheat and its River of Promise partners are clearly collegial. They enjoy each other's company and the sense of accomplishment they have achieved together. The opportunity to leverage resources collectively and more efficiently appealed to many participants from public agencies where resources are hard to come by and the scope of the problems is enormous. These people want to invest their time and money in something that will produce results, and the collaborative potential with River of Promise held out that likelihood. The yearly celebration at the Cheat River Festival allows everyone to relax and publicly celebrate the previous year's accomplishments.

Opening When the political structure is open, there is greater opportunity to foster change. When the political structure is closed, opportunities for change are constrained. Friends of the Cheat worked through local, state, and federal political structures to effect change. The group faced situations over time where some political structures closed, thereby sealing off those opportunities, while other structures opened up. Friends of the Cheat and River of Promise needed to operate strategically under these circumstances. They would concentrate their efforts where they would bear the greatest fruit while acknowledging that some avenues would be closed to them. For instance, Greg Adolfson came up with the idea for the River of Promise in 1994, but the WVDEP division head at the time felt that any effort to address AMD issues on the Cheat would be a waste of time and money. Adolfson waited for a change in political leadership to try again. This time Adolfson made his pitch right after the Cheat had been named to American Rivers list of the country's top-ten most endangered rivers in 1995 and the new division head was more amenable to participating in the River of Promise.

In 1996 a new governor took office and appointed new heads to state agencies. At that time, Adolfson was prohibited from participating in River of Promise, and some state agencies became less amenable to community-based approaches to watershed remediation. Consequently, state involvement and opportunities to seek funding or technical assistance from the state were hindered. This caused Friends of the Cheat and River of Promise to focus more on federal resources from the USOSM and EPA. In 2001 a new gubernatorial administration under Democrat Bob Wise took office and signaled a more receptive approach to community-based environmental management. Consequently, opportunities at the state level opened again. In 2008 Pitzer commented that since his tenure with the group began, the administrative leadership within the WVDEP has been supportive indirectly if not directly of the type of approach embodied by Friends of the Cheat and the River of Promise. Jennifer Pauer has been in place for the entire life of the West Virginia Stream Partners Program and successive secretaries of the WVDEP have been supportive. Pitzer also has found the WVDEP Non-Point Source Pollution program to be a staunch supporter since he assumed leadership of the group.[87]

The WVAML Program represented the dominant state-level political structure most relevant to the Friends of Cheat and River of Promise mission. However, this structure was closed to the group from the outset and continues to remain so. WVAML controls the lion's share of state resources that can be directed at abandoned mines and AMD. However, the agency has been reluctant to partner with Friends of the Cheat, even though the agency sporadically attends River of Promise meetings. "[WV]AML is not good about communicating where they are working in our watershed, so that limits the opportunities to do this sort of value added onto their work," observes Pitzer. If they could better coordinate with where WVAML is working in the watershed, there would be greater efficiencies to the money spent on remediation: "We could do the water quality work and they could do the reclamation." Without WVAML's cooperation, Friends of the Cheat has chosen to work with partners where the political structure is open: "We have much more collaborative relationships and true partnerships with [US]OSM and WVDEP/Non-Point Source Program. They are always there to provide the matching funds we need to get the project moving."[88]

While some state agencies have been intermittently open, most federal agencies have been consistently open and supportive of change. Friends of the Cheat and River of Promise have worked constructively with the USOSM reliably for many years: "The [US]OSM has always been a true partner, not only in funding through the Watershed Cooperative Agreement Program, but in information, encouragement and expertise."[89] The EPA became more supportive in the early 2000s and has remained a staunch supporter. Friends of the Cheat has had a more difficult relationship with the USACOE. Political structure has effectively closed off the opportunity to make progress on the Lick Run project. The key to Friends of the Cheat and River of Promise implementation over the years has been having a diverse group of stakeholders at the local, state, and federal levels. Multiple partners has meant that when one partner no longer wishes to participate and that structure closes, Friends of the Cheat has been able to switch its focus to another partner where the political opportunity was more open and welcoming. Diversification is key. By seeking openings with other agencies at the state or federal level, Friends of the Cheat and River of Promise have maintained implementation over time.

Resistance   Existing institutions can be opposed to new practices. For Pitzer the greatest challenge with Friends of the Cheat and River of Promise is "getting buy-in and participation by all agencies involved in mine-related reclamation in the watershed." Two agencies in particular have been resistant to Friends of the Cheat's community-based, collaborative model: "Progress hasn't always been maintained [with] WVDEP, [WV]AML and the [US]ACOE."[90]

At the state level, the WVAML was resistant to Friends of the Cheat and the River of Promise. This resistance was the function of three processes. First, WVAML saw Friends of the Cheat and River of Promise as infringing on WVAML's authority. The agency is very hierarchical with a top-down decision-making structure and does not have a good history of public involvement or community outreach. Second, WVAML's historical mission had not focused on AMD and never gave priority to the treatment of water or addressed water quality issues associated with AMD. WVAML officials state that water quality is not the main focus of the law, and so legally they need to concentrate on the highwalls, open portals, and vegetative reclamation processes. Third, the treatment methods and outcomes from AMD work are uncertain and potentially expensive. The criteria for judging success are more ambiguous for working with AMD in contrast to closing a mine portal or revegetating a strip mine site. Consequently, WVAML has been reluctant to take on these politically risky projects.

Resistance by the WVAML was limited to its reluctance to participate. It did not seek to actively obstruct efforts by Friends of the Cheat and River of Promise. Observes Bassage, "They have made things more difficult than they could have been. AML wasn't well suited for what FOC was trying to do. We were a nuisance to them."[91] Pitzer's experience concurs with Bassage's: "There have been three directors of the AML program since 2001. All have paid lip service to FOC, and all have failed to share the commitment represented by ROP."[92] Friends of the Cheat continues to seek a more collaborative working relationship with WVAML but has not succeeded.

An opportunity to change the relationship between WVAML and Friends of the Cheat may arise out of the recent reauthorization of the federal Abandoned Mine Lands program, the projected increase to states AML coffers, and the potential to direct 30 percent of those funds to water quality work. The reauthorization provides an opportunity for WVAML to rethink its objectives, but it is unclear whether it will alter their current practices. History is not encouraging.

Those within Friends of the Cheat are optimistic that the time might be right for their relationship with AML to change: "The people who have been most resistant to AML taking on water quality projects are on the verge of retirement." With the right leadership and staff AML could play a more active and supportive role in cleaning up AMD and maximizing the funding legally available to do AMD work: "There is certainly opportunity for them to take a leadership role in this area if they decided to."[93] However, Pitzer emphasizes that in 2008 "frustration continues."[94]

Friends of the Cheat has also experienced resistance from the USACOE. Pitzer feels that both WVAML and USACOE look at the problems in the watershed from a very narrow perspective that only fits within their bureaucratic framework. "They fail to see the picture more holistically or understand or want to understand what it means to work with a community group that has limited resources," he says. "If something doesn't meet their specific criteria, then they can't proceed. They don't think about fisheries, economic potential, restoration, or the impact on the community." Having received a $500,000 earmark from West Virginia's Democrat congressman Mollohan, the USACOE conducted studies for a remediation project but never completed blueprints or any work on the ground. During the four years of trying to work with USACOE, Friends of the Cheat claimed to have met all of its demands, including signing on as the local sponsor, which meant assuming long-term responsibility and liability for operation and maintenance of the site, purchasing the site, and securing the match prior to the implementation of the project—all expenses that were incurred without the payoff of a project. In the meantime, the USACOE employee who was the project manager retired and has not been replaced.

Culture

Shocks A dramatic event can provide an opportunity for learning and new action. The T&T mine blowout witnessed and videotaped by Randy Robinson in 1994 was the primary impetus for the formation of the Friends of the Cheat and the River of Promise. The blowout served as a focusing event that allowed those with a predisposition to change the situation to meet and organize. The second blowout in 1995 continued to focus attention on Muddy Creek and the degradation in the Cheat. When American Rivers Inc., a national river conservation organization, named the Cheat to its top-ten list of the nation's most endangered rivers in 1995 after the second blowout, state officials were persuaded to take action.

Framing Framing processes can define problems such that they stimulate action. Often, if people feel aggrieved they can be stimulated to change the status quo. Friends of the Cheat framed the challenge as one that would focus on the problems in the watershed and provide workable alternatives for dealing with those problems. The organization intentionally did not want to demonize T&T Coal and the coal industry. Rather, it wanted to create a sense of potential in the watershed. As summarized by Bassage, "A clean, healthy environment is easy to agree upon, and having an open-armed philosophy really helped."[95] Framing the problem broadly to restore, protect, and promote the outstanding qualities of the Cheat allowed the group to tap into and harness the predisposition to effect change in the watershed, as evidenced by the continuing commitment and participation of the coal companies, whitewater boaters, local landowners, residents, and researchers. The mission was framed to focus on the end state of a cleaner, functional watershed that a diverse group of stakeholders could agree upon, not on the process of laying blame. For this reason, Friends of the Cheat works not only on AMD remediation issues but also on providing watershed education, creating a recreation-based economy, and restoring fisheries, among other issues. The group also made an effort to keep its collaborative, community-based approach in the public eye: "Periodic, high-profile events like the Cheat Fest also really helped keep us in the media and in front of the community periodically."[96]

Because Friends of the Cheat was broadly collaborative in its foundation and mission, this created a nonthreatening environment for most regulatory agencies, the coal industry, researchers, and other nonprofit organizations to organize under the River of Promise agreement. Previous environmental groups had been polarizing, making collaboration difficult. Framing River of Promise as a voluntary, shared commitment was nonthreatening. The problem for addressing the water quality issues in the Cheat watershed prior to the formation of River of Promise had been framed as prohibitively costly and uncertain. River of Promise addressed both the cost and uncertainty issues in novel ways. First, River of Promise leveraged resources among a variety of public, private, research, and nonprofit organizations. In this manner, no single agency was held financially responsible for the entire watershed. Cleanup will still take millions of dollars, but there is greater likelihood of meeting these resource needs through multiple agencies than through only one. The importance of partnership continues to resonate with Pitzer: "This work is far larger than any organization, agency, university institute, or stakeholder group can possibly handle. Only by partnering in good faith across these organizational boundaries will we continue to make progress and enjoy the benefits of an improved environment in the watershed."[97] Likewise, sharing fiscal and technical responsibility for cleaning up the watershed means that no one agency is held singly accountable for the success or failure of this inherently uncertain exercise in remediation.

Legitimacy The social legitimacy of an organization can be enhanced by adopting new practices, thereby encouraging innovation and the perpetuation of new practices.

Friends of the Cheat was a collaborative, community-based watershed group, and River of Promise was a voluntary environmental remediation agreement. These were ideas whose time had come in the mid-1990s. Federal and state agencies, nonprofit groups, private industry, and research organizations saw the value in partnering with a locally based group to enhance their own legitimacy. Pitzer suggested that "neither government agencies nor academia can adequately address local environmental problems without local input. And like politics, all environmental problems are local somewhere." In turn, Friends of the Cheat and River of Promise enhanced their legitimacy by having such a broadly based coalition of stakeholders. In this sense, legitimacy was self-reinforcing for all participants.

The collaborative nature of the group cut both ways. Because Friends of the Cheat decided to collaborate with the coal industry, this gave them legitimacy among some while delegitimizing them among others. Some in the environmental community distanced themselves from Friends of the Cheat, but this in turn legitimized Friends of the Cheat for the state and federal agencies that were interested in a new approach to the problem of persistent AMD. Involving industry also meant that local people did not have to choose sides in the environment versus jobs debate. In this manner Friends of the Cheat was a membership group that did not lead to polarization within the community. Additionally, in the search for innovative techniques for addressing AMD, the group partnered with university researchers. This gave the group technical and scientific legitimacy while also taking advantage of the latest technologies and understanding of AMD mitigation and reclamation techniques.

A balanced and diverse board of directors reinforced the commitment to a truly collaborative and community-based approach. As of 2009 the board continued to have members that represent the coal industry, local landowners, the whitewater industry, environmental activists, teachers, and other local businesses and community interests. This diverse base continues to give the group legitimacy and credibility throughout the county and region. Additionally, the broad membership base gives the group legitimacy as truly locally supported. More than a third of Friends of the Cheat's budget comes from local activities and membership support.

SUMMARY

The summary in table 4.2 categorizes how we can understand why the Friends of the Cheat and River of Promise were successful at times and less successful at other times. The intermittent alignment of individual and structural characteristics is particularly important in providing some explanatory power to the times when Friends of the Cheat and River of Promise were less successful.

Individual characteristics help explain why the innovation was intermittently successful. Individual motivation to participate in the River of Promise waxed and waned over time. Motivation was interdependent among the many participants. Implementation of the River of Promise was contingent upon a strong executive director who

Table 4.2: A Framework for Analyzing Watershed Innovation with Friends of the Cheat and River of Promise

Individuals	Structures	Culture
Motivation: Lack of action by the West Virginia Abandoned Mine Lands Program created a vacuum for action. Numerous individuals at the local, state, and federal levels were motivated to effect changes within the watershed after the T&T blowout. Individuals were less motivated for action during 1999–2001 when Friends of the Cheat lacked an executive director. Motivation resumed with the arrival of a new executive director in 2001.	*Rules and communication:* Rules are simple and straightforward in the two-page River of Promise agreement. FOC is a small agency run by a seven-member board. The small size facilitates easy communication. The clear mission aids continued focus on goal accomplishment.	*Shocks:* The T&T mine blowout provided the impetus for Friends of the Cheat to organize. A second blowout in 1995 put the Cheat on a national list of endangered rivers and brought continued attention to the problems facing the Cheat.
	Incentives: Financial and technical incentives as well as mutual support and friendship stimulated action within Friends of the Cheat and River of Promise.	*Framing:* Friends of the Cheat focused on watershed-wide problems, rather than pillorying the coal industry. River of Promise was framed as voluntary and therefore nonthreatening. River of Promise also helped alleviate concerns about cost and uncertainty associated with remediation work due to its collaborative approach.
Norms and Harmony: There has been some tension in how prevailing norms within agencies or organizations mesh with the prevailing norms of collaboration and community-based remediation in the River of Promise. Some groups have opted not to participate, while others have waited out changes in political administration. Most participants in the River of Promise have been able to harmonize their agency norms with the norms in River of Promise.	*Opening:* Friends of the Cheat and River of Promise have skillfully negotiated political structures to take advantage of openings and avoid closings. Diversified partners at the local, state, and federal levels avoid complete disruption of activities when political change occurs.	*Legitimacy:* Community-based environmental management and a collaborative, voluntary commitment were new approaches that mutually reinforced the legitimacy of all participants, thereby perpetuating the innovative approaches.
Congruence: Not a powerful explanatory factor given the lack of a single-agency and stakeholder-based approach in the River of Promise.	*Resistance:* WVAML program and USACOE have been resistant to Friends of the Cheat and the River of Promise efforts, but they did not actively try to obstruct their efforts.	

was not only motivated himself but harnessed others' motivation. When Bassage left, Friends of the Cheat and River of Promise floundered. Entrepreneurial leaders often are credited with fostering innovation.[98] In this case, Bassage was a driving force. When he left, the weaknesses of that approach became evident. Building an effort on the shoulders of one individual left it vulnerable to that individual's departure. Friends of the Cheat and the River of Promise recovered with the hiring of Pitzer. To some degree the group continues to remain vulnerable to overdependence on one individual. Likewise, norms and harmony influenced individual participation in River of Promise. Change in political leadership at the state level in particular influenced the level of dissonance or harmony individuals experienced participating in a community-based, voluntary remediation agreement. When political or administrative leadership within an agency did not favor involvement, this created tensions for the individuals participating in River of Promise. Periods of withdrawal and engagement by different agency employees affected the work that Friends of the Cheat could carry out. Often, this caused the group to shift its direction or focus toward working more actively with individuals from agencies that had less conflict with the collaborative, community-based norms embodied by the group and in the River of Promise. Congruence as an explanatory factor did not apply to this case study because it was a collaborative effort, and no one agency oversaw implementation.

Structural characteristics also help explain why Friends of the Cheat and River of Promise experienced intermittent success. The categories of openings and resistance provide a better explanation of some of the structural obstacles that have led to intermittent success with Friends of the Cheat and River of Promise, rather than rules and communication and incentives. Rules and communication in the case study are straightforward. Friends of the Cheat is a small organization, and this facilitates easy communication. River of Promise is a two-page agreement with clearly marked responsibilities and signatures. The mission statement is one sentence and understood by the key participants. Incentives do not provide much explanatory value. Incentives do not function here per the vision espoused by rational choice theorists or top-down implementation theorists. There is no central agency conducting or guiding the overall effort. Rather, a variety of participants respond to different types of incentives to remediate the watershed. Financial and technical incentives are key for some, but so are mutual support and friendship. Openings in the political structure, as well as resistance by key agencies, provide some insight into why the group and the agreement have not been continuously implemented over time. As a voluntary group implementing a voluntary agreement, Friends of the Cheat has been dependent on state and federal agencies being open to the River of Promise mission. At times the political structure at the state or federal level has been closed to the innovative opportunity offered by Friends of the Cheat and the River of Promise. Some West Virginia governors have been more amenable to community-based approaches than others. These attitudes were reflected through agency appointments and consequent opportunities, or lack thereof, for promoting community-based watershed management. Friends of the

Cheat has worked with the diverse partners in River of Promise to identify agencies whose political structure was supportive of their mission. By concentrating its efforts with these agencies, Friends of the Cheat has maintained implementation of the River of Promise agreement, although it was not as robust as it could have been had all structures been equally open and supportive of the innovation. Active resistance to the Friends of the Cheat mission and the vision embodied in River of Promise also has created problems in the implementation of the innovation. WVAML is the state agency with the regulatory authority and greatest resources for addressing AMD at the watershed level. With the emergence of Friends of the Cheat and the River of Promise, WVAML has been uncooperative with the group and refused to sign the River of Promise agreement. Preferring to maintain its traditional approach to remediating the non–water-quality aspects associated with abandoned mines, the agency has left Friends of the Cheat and River of Promise without a key partner in the effort to address the persistent challenges of AMD. While WVAML has been resistant to Friends of the Cheat and the River of Promise, the agency has not tried to use its power to actively obstruct or disrupt the efforts of the group. At times, Friends of the Cheat has supplemented the non–water-quality remediation undertaken by WVAML with water quality treatment after WVAML has completed its projects. If WVAML were less resistant to the innovation posed in Friends of the Cheat and River of Promise, the collaboration mostly likely would yield more efficient outcomes and a more fruitful partnership. The USACOE has also been resistant to working more cooperatively with Friends of the Cheat and the River of Promise. Bureaucratic agency structure and a seeming inability to work from a more community-based perspective has led to disengagement from the process. Neither WVAML nor USACOE has actively tried to obstruct Friends of the Cheat or River of Promise efforts in the region.

Cultural characteristics help explain why Friends of the Cheat and the River of Promise have persisted over time, in spite of some of these individual and structural challenges. The initial shock of the T&T blowout focused attention on the problems in the Cheat. A second blowout a year later brought national attention from a river advocacy organization and was sufficient to gain the attention of state leaders. Friends of the Cheat organized after the initial blowout and was able to take advantage of the second focusing event to harness resources and participating agencies and organizations through the River of Promise. Focusing events often can catalyze policy action.[99] In this case, the blowout and subsequent events served this purpose. Friends of the Cheat framed the problem so as not to punish the coal industry but to spotlight an unrealized vision for the watershed. The River of Promise was framed as a voluntary agreement and thus unthreatening in terms of a regulatory solution to the problem of AMD. Additionally, framing the River of Promise as a collaborative endeavor that leveraged resources from numerous agencies helped diversify the risk and uncertainty that would have accompanied only one agency or organization taking on the massive undertaking of remediating the watershed. Finally, Friends of the Cheat emerged at a time when community-based environmental management was very appealing to numerous agencies. The group has derived its legitimacy from its local roots, the collaborative nature of the work, and the voluntary aspect of the agreement. Legitimacy is mutually reinforcing among the many participants. The agencies derive legitimacy from participating with a community-based group. Friends of the Cheat derives legitimacy from the participation of a wide variety of stakeholders.

Friends of the Cheat has experienced intermittent success at different times in the life of its innovation in AMD remediation. Individual and structural characteristics provide a way to understand some of the reasons underlying the hiccups in implementation. At an individual level, motivation was lacking when Friends of the Cheat lost its executive director. Likewise, at an individual level, it was difficult to make progress when individual norms clashed with agency directives and shifts in mission. From a structural perspective, openings and resistance provide a way to understand how implementation was inhibited as some state and federal agencies have been reluctant to participate in the vision embodied by Friends of the Cheat and the River of Promise.

NOTES

1. For instance, iron pyrite (FeS_2), which is common in the overburden in mining, is exposed to air, rain, and snow. This exposure to the elements causes the FeS_2 to break down into its constituent parts of ferrous iron and sulfur. The sulfate ions react with the water to produce sulfuric acid (H_2SO_4).

2. For instance, iron, lead, zinc, copper manganese, aluminum, silver, mercury, nickel, cadmium, and arsenic.

3. Office of Surface Mining Reclamation and Enforcement, "Annual Evaluation Report for the Regulatory and Abandoned Mine Land Reclamation Programs Administered by the State of West Virginia for the Evaluation Year 1995," January 1996; Environmental Protection Agency, "Environmental Protection Agency Region III Coal Mine Drainage Initiative," on file with author, n.d.

4. Sally Wilts, administrative assistant, Friends of the Cheat, e-mail to Toddi Steelman, May 20, 2008.

5. Keith Pitzer, executive director, Friends of the Cheat, telephone interview with Toddi A. Steelman, May 21, 2008.

6. K. Pitzer, "Friends of Cheat," letter, on file with author, n.d.

7. Joseph V. Rees, *Hostages of Each Other: The Transformation of Nuclear Safety since Three Mile Island* (Chicago: University of Chicago Press, 1994).

8. David Bassage, executive director, Friends of the Cheat, in-person interview with Toddi A. Steelman, Bruceton, West Virginia, January 7, 1995.

9. Environmental Protection Agency, "Human Health and Environmental Damages from Mining and Mineral Processing Wastes: Technical Background Document Supporting the Supplemental Proposed Rule Applying Phase IV Land Disposal Restrictions to Newly Identified Mineral Processing Wastes" (1995), www.epa.gov/epaoswer/other/mining/minedoc/damage/metadam.txt (accessed on September 15, 2000).

10. By law, mines abandoned before 1977 do not have to treat the water coming out of their mines and are the responsibility of the state. Mines abandoned after 1977 are legally responsible for the treatment of their water.

11. Brent Wiles, inspector and supervisor, West Virginia Department of Environmental Protection, in-person interview with Toddi A. Steelman, Kingwood, West Virginia, June 25, 1999.

12. Jim Snyder, "The Muddy Creek Story," *Friends of Cheat Newsletter*, May 6, 1995.

13. Lee Chottiner, "Cheat River Endangered: Makes National List, Ranks 8th among Top 10," *Dominion Post*, April 19, 1995. The Cheat River was again named as one of the most endangered rivers in 1996.

14. Bassage, interview (1995); and Snyder, "The Muddy Creek Story."

15. Environmental Protection Agency, "Environmental Protection Agency Region III Coal Mine Drainage Initiative," on file with author, n.d.

16. Jenni Vincent, "Organizations Band Together to Revive Polluted Watershed," *Dominion Post*, November 5, 2000.

17. Gary Bryant (Environmental Protection Agency Region III) letter to Dave Bassage, February 1, 1996.

18. Heather Nann Davis, "Cleanup Money Only Goes So Far," *Dominion Post*, February 26, 1996.

19. Vincent, "Organizations Band Together."

20. David Bassage, telephone interview with Toddi A. Steelman, Raleigh, North Carolina, February 4, 2002.

21. Chottiner, "Cheat River Endangered."

22. Bassage, interview (2002).

23. David Bassage, telephone interview with Toddi A. Steelman, Denver, August 28, 1998.

24. Bassage, interview (1995).

25. David Bassage, "Stream of Consciousness," *Friends of the Cheat Newsletter*, July 1999.

26. David Bassage, telephone interview with Toddi Steelman, April 28, 2008.

27. A total maximum daily load (TMDL) is calculated to determine the maximum amount of a pollutant that a water body can receive and still meet water quality standards. A total maximum daily load for a single pollutant would be the sum of the allowable load of that pollutant from all the point and nonpoint sources.

28. Bassage, interview (2002).

29. Keith Pitzer, telephone interview with Toddi A. Steelman, May 21, 2008.

30. Rick Buckley, telephone interview with Toddi A. Steelman, Raleigh, March 11, 2002.

31. Vincent, "Organizations Band Together."

32. Greg E. Adolfson, telephone interview with Toddi A. Steelman, Raleigh, February 28, 2002.

33. Ibid.

34. Ibid.

35. Ken Ward, "Abandoned Promises: Why America's Coalfields Aren't Cleaned Up. PA Stream Cleanups Overrun AML Budget," *Charleston Gazette*, August 17, 2004.

36. Robert Uram, telephone interview with Toddi A. Steelman, Denver, October 27, 1999.

37. USOSMRE, "Partnerships in Action," annual report, 2006, www.osmre.gov/annualreports/06AR08.pdf (accessed May 19, 2008).

38. Rick Buckley, telephone interview with Toddi A. Steelman, March 11, 2002.

39. Jenni Vincent, "River of Promise Teams with DEP for Cheat Cleanup," *Dominion Post*, November 6, 2000.

40. Heather Nann Davis, "Hundreds Attend Festival," *Preston County Journal*, May 10, 1995, A1.

41. Greg E. Adolfson, telephone interview with Toddi A. Steelman, February 28, 2002.

42. River of Promise, "River of Promise: A Shared Commitment for the Restoration of the Cheat River, West Virginia," draft agreement, on file with author, 1995; and Buckley, interview (2002).

43. Bassage, interview (2002).

44. Rick Buckley, telephone interview with Toddi A. Steelman, Denver, October 5, 1999.

45. Buckley, interview (2002).

46. Buckley, interview (1999).

47. Bassage, interview (2002).

48. Buckley, interview (1999).

49. Bassage, interview (2002); Buckley, interview (2002); and Keith Pitzer, "Working Upstream," *FOC Newsletter*, February 2002, 2–3.

50. Adolfson, interview (2002).

51. Bassage, interview (2002); Buckley, interview (2002); and Pitzer, "Working Upstream," 2–3. FOC Profit/Loss Statements 2002–2007, on file with author.

52. Bassage, interview (2008).

53. Ibid.

54. Pitzer, interview (2008).

55. Bassage, interview (2008).

56. Pitzer, interview (2008).

57. Ibid.

58. K. Pitzer, "Updates on Monitoring, Mapping and All Things AMD," *Into the Canyon*, Summer 2007, 10.

59. Danielle Adams, "The Fourth Year Is the Charm," *Into the Canyon*, Fall 2005, 9.

60. Pitzer, interview (2008).

61. Bassage, interview (2008).

62. Pitzer, interview (2008).

63. Keith Pitzer, "Friends of the Cheat," letter, on file with author.

64. Keith Pitzer, "FOC Receives Coveted Targeted Watershed Initiative Grant," *Into the Canyon*, Spring 2006, 5.

65. Keith Pitzer, "AML Re-Authorization—Update and Outlook," *Into the Canyon*, Fall 2007, 10.

66. Ibid.

67. Pitzer, interview (2008).

68. Ibid.

69. R. Robbins, "Army Corps' Fees Can Delay, Cancel Projects," *Tribune-Review*, Greensburg, PA, August 19, 2007.

70. Pitzer, interview (2008).

71. Frank Jernejcic, "Validating Cheat River Recovery," *Into the Canyon*, Spring 2006, 11.

72. Pitzer, "Friends of the Cheat."

73. Bassage, interview (2008).

74. Pitzer, interview (2008).

75. Troy Tichnell, telephone interview with Toddi Steelman, April 15, 2002.

76. Bassage, interview (2008).

77. David Bassage, e-mail exchange with Toddi Steelman, September 21, 1999.

78. Pitzer, interview (2008).

79. Ibid.

80. Jennifer Pauer, telephone interview with Toddi Steelman, October 12, 1999.

81. Bassage, interview (2008).

82. Ibid.

83. Pitzer, interview (2008).

84. Ibid.

85. Bassage, interview (2008).

86. Pitzer, interview (2008).

87. Ibid.

88. Ibid.

89. Ibid.

90. Ibid.

91. Bassage, interview (2008).

92. Pitzer, interview (2008).

93. Bassage, interview, (2008).

94. Pitzer, interview (2008).

95. Bassage, interview (2008).

96. Ibid.

97. Pitzer, interview (2008).

98. John W. Kingdon, *Agendas, Alternatives and Public Policies*, 2nd ed. (New York: Longman, 1995); Frank R. Baumgartner and Bryan D. Jones. *Agendas and Instability in American Politics* (Chicago: University of Chicago Press, 1993); Michael Mintrom, "Policy Entrepreneurs and the Diffusion of Innovation," *American Journal of Political Sciences* 41, no. 3 (1997): 738–70; and Tom Birkland, *After Disaster: Agenda Setting, Public Policy and Focusing Events* (Washington, DC: Georgetown University Press, 1997).

99. Marcia L. Godwin and Jean R. Schroedel, "Policy Diffusion and Strategies for Promoting Policy Change: Evidence from California Local Gun Control Ordinances," *Policy Studies Journal* 28 (2000): 760–76; Baumgartner and Jones, *Agendas and Instability in American Politics*; Kingdon, *Agendas, Alternatives and Public Policies*; and Birkland, *After Disaster*.

CHAPTER 5

Misalignment of Institutional Characteristics

Implementing Innovation in Forest Management

THE USFS HAS BEEN THE PRIMARY ACTOR within the forest governance system, as detailed in chapter 2 and depicted in figure 5.1. Even though the agency was decentralized, it consolidated decision-making authority at the federal level. This centralized base of power was challenged in the 1960s and throughout the 1970s as new constitutive-level laws gave participants outside the agency power to participate in decision making. The rise of environmental groups at the national level was essential to this change. As timber sales slowed at the national level, communities dependent on forest products began searching for alternatives to their social and economic problems. Beginning in the 1980s community-based forestry groups throughout the United States saw the need to organize at the collective level to effect change at the constitutive level. By the mid-2000s the number of community-based forestry groups was estimated at two thousand.[1] Some of these groups and their efforts have been effective in fostering change, while others have not.

It is into this historical mix of actors and influences that the innovations on the Camino Real Ranger District (Camino Real) in New Mexico took place. Placed within the broader context of communal land management in the Southwest (as detailed in chapter 2), this case illustrates the challenges of implementing innovation in a context where institutional characteristics are misaligned. Efforts to manage forests on the Camino Real had been fraught with controversy for decades. The innovations pursued from 1991 to 1998 were in decline by 2009. Community forestry has been characterized as "a process that seeks to reverse historical drawdowns of natural and community capital through reinvestment and redirection of benefit flows toward local groups who have previously not been part of the broader political landscape of

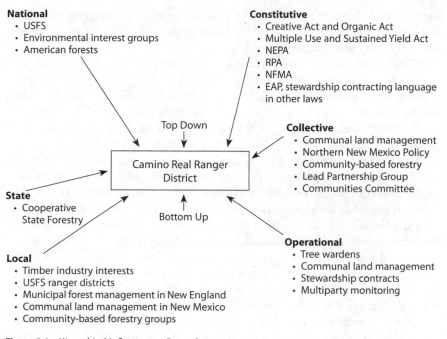

National
- USFS
- Environmental interest groups
- American forests

Constitutive
- Creative Act and Organic Act
- Multiple Use and Sustained Yield Act
- NEPA
- RPA
- NFMA
- EAP, stewardship contracting language in other laws

Top Down

Camino Real Ranger District

Collective
- Communal land management
- Northern New Mexico Policy
- Community-based forestry
- Lead Partnership Group
- Communities Committee

State
- Cooperative State Forestry

Bottom Up

Operational
- Tree wardens
- Communal land management
- Stewardship contracts
- Multiparty monitoring

Local
- Timber industry interests
- USFS ranger districts
- Municipal forest management in New England
- Communal land management in New Mexico
- Community-based forestry groups

Figure 5.1: Hierarchical Influences on Forest Governance

pluralistic political process."[2] The Camino Real case study illustrates the considerable challenges of altering historical structure, culture, and individual incentive structures to create the institutional space for these new practices to thrive. The innovation on the Camino Real was the process of Collaborative Stewardship that resulted in numerous improvements in land management relative to the constituencies serviced by the Camino Real. This process was innovative for both the USFS and the communities that were dependent on the USFS for access to natural resources.

INNOVATIONS IN FOREST MANAGEMENT: VOLUNTARY REGULATION IN THE CAMINO REAL RANGER DISTRICT

The Camino Real is on the Carson National Forest in northern New Mexico. Nestled among the mountains are numerous small, Hispano land grant villages.[3] In addition to the Hispano populations, the Native American Picuris Pueblo is surrounded by the Camino Real on three sides. Conflict, frustration, violent uprisings, and litigation typified the relationships between the USFS and inhabitants of these picturesque mountains and valleys for decades. More than 25 percent of the land in northern New Mexico is under the management of the USFS.[4] Clashes over land and land use were at the heart of most controversies in the region. Consequently, when local communities and the USFS started working together on land use concerns in the early 1990s, it was a noteworthy event.

USFS officials faced decades of challenges from the Hispano landowners and more recently from environmentalists over management practices on public lands. Hispano residents and environmentalists used civil disobedience, violence, the legal system, and general protests to affect the way forests were managed in northern New Mexico. At various times since the 1940s, the USFS responded to these demands with innovative policies to better serve local populations. However, each time, the innovations faded under the internal pressures of the agency to serve larger industrial forest interests or the interests of its own bureaucracy. The most recent attempt to respond to local populations emerged out of the work of a new district ranger, Crockett Dumas. Environmentalists had been challenging timber sales on the Camino Real when Dumas arrived as the ranger in 1990. Hispano residents confronted employees for neglecting the public they were allegedly supposed to serve. Dumas realized he needed the help of the local people if he was going to be an effective land manager. Working with these groups, Dumas crafted a series of voluntary policy innovations that allowed both the USFS and residents to achieve their desired goals. After receiving high-profile, national attention in the form of recognition and awards from Vice President Al Gore's Reinventing Government Team in 1997, and the Harvard University/Ford Foundation Innovations in American Government in 1998, these innovations unraveled and by 2009 existed only in weakened forms within the Camino Real.

This case study documents a form of voluntary regulation on the Camino Real. Government participants worked with community residents to forge new policies that better served local needs. The policies were new codes of practice without any legal formality. Peer pressure among agency officials and community members alike worked to uphold standards of behavior once the new policies were established. The innovative practices on the Camino Real became known as Collaborative Stewardship and embodied a variety of voluntary public land management activities. Unlike the other case studies in chapters 3 and 4, the Camino Real involves an innovation that slowly withered. Individual, structural, and cultural characteristics help explain why Collaborative Stewardship was unable to sustain implementation over time.

A NARRATIVE ACCOUNT OF THE CAMINO REAL RANGER DISTRICT AND COLLABORATIVE STEWARDSHIP

Activist Hispano community members and environmentalists gained power in the 1960s to 1980s to call attention to the failure of the USFS to serve local publics in their national forests (see table 5.1 for chronological history of significant events). Hispano residents invigorated by the Chicano movement in the 1960s, and joined by environmentalists in the 1980s, became formidable adversaries for the USFS.

Table 5.1: Chronological Developments in Collaborative Stewardship on the Camino Real Ranger District

Date	Significant Chronological Events
1948	Congress establishes Vallecitos Sustained Yield Unit to create local jobs from local resources on local national forests.
1960s and 1970s	Civil disobedience and uprisings in the region.
1972	Northern New Mexico Policy places an emphasis on local communities. National Forests asked to recognize the unique cultural connection of the Hispano descendants to the land.
1970s	Back to the land movement; hippies begin to settle in the region.
1980s	Growing network of environmentalists in the region.
1987	Max Córdova becomes head of Truchas Land Grant.
1987	Alamo-Dinner sale begins.
1990	Crockett Dumas arrives as new district ranger of Camino Real. John Bedell is forest supervisor.
1991	Controversy over Alamo-Dinner sale causes Dumas to question how vegetation is being managed.
1991	Horseback diplomacy begins; changes to small timber use permits quickly follow.
1991	Andy Lindquist takes over as new forest supervisor.
1993	Regular meetings with USFS and community residents take place at Los Siete, Córdova's weaving cooperative.
1994	Leonard Lucero takes over as forest supervisor.
1995	Collaborative Stewardship fully formed—easier permitting for firewood, forest restoration, and reorientation of timber sales to local communities with fewer ecological impacts.
1995	Judge Carl Muecke orders halt to all timber harvesting in Region 3 in response to suit brought by local environmentalists concerned for Mexican spotted owl.
1996	Dumas violates injunction to mark trees for local communities so they can gather firewood.
1996	Judge Roger Strand lifts ban on logging.
1996	Dumas and Carveth Kramer create East Entrañas Ecosystem Management Plan.
1997	Stewardship plots started.
1997	Collaborative Stewardship wins Vice President Al Gore's Hammer Award for Re-inventing Government.
1998	Grass banks started.
1998	Collaborative Stewardship is a finalist for the Harvard/Ford Foundation Innovations in American Government Award.
1998	Jealousies begin to undermine relationships.
1998	Dumas transfers to a ranger district in Utah—where he wanted to retire.
2001	Community holds conference to fulfill obligation to the Harvard/Ford Foundation Innovations award.
2009	Not much remains of the original innovations that were part of Collaborative Stewardship.

Protests and litigation drew attention to their plight and prevented the USFS from managing vegetation on national forests. Recognizing the sorry state of affairs between the community and the USFS, Crockett Dumas and his employees engaged in a process called horseback diplomacy. Getting on their horses, or in their trucks, USFS employees went out into the community. By listening to people, agency employees devised responses to address the multiple concerns that were important to the community. These policy innovations became known as Collaborative Stewardship, which emerged gradually and was not expressed as a concrete policy until the mid-1990s. Collaborative Stewardship initially was typified by changes in permitting policies for personal timber use by the communities, avoiding appeals and litigation, reducing the size of timber sales, and creating additional local employment opportunities through smaller nature of the timber sales. Later, grazing reforms and forest restoration were added to the changes.[5]

Landownership issues have fueled much of the conflict in northern New Mexico. It is important to understand the rich history that undergirds present-day relationships to the land. As discussed at length in chapter 2, this history is infused with a tradition of communal landownership and subsistence-level use that largely has been ignored by the USFS. Resentment from the loss of these communal lands and infringement on subsistence traditions permeates relationships with the agency, especially in the Santa Fe and Carson national forests in New Mexico. In the 1940s Congress recognized the unique dependence of local peoples in these regions on the land by creating the Vallecitos Federal Sustained Yield Unit. The intention was to produce local jobs from local resources. When multinational corporations were favored for timber contracts over local, small timber operations, the seeds were sown for discontent. Civil disobedience and uprising during the 1960s led to national attention for the region and the creation of the Northern New Mexico Policy, which once again called for the national forests to work with local communities and recognize their unique dependence on the resources in the region.

During this same general time frame, a new group of inhabitants began to migrate to northern New Mexico. Hippies and members of the "back-to-the-land" movement found the villages in the area embodied their idealistic notion of a more simple life. Often embracing environmental values, these new residents were interested in maintaining a quality of life that was compatible with their lifestyle choices and began to draw greater attention to the environmental impacts that logging had on the natural resources in the region. By the 1980s and early 1990s a network of local, regional, and even national environmental groups were present in the region. Working through legal processes and appealing or opposing proposed timber sales, local and regional environmental groups began to affect the way the USFS conducted its business.

Over time the Northern New Mexico Policy lost its momentum. Higher-level reviews within the agency determined that implementation of a policy that provided special treatment for one area and group of people was illegal. As recalled by Pat Jackson, a USFS lawyer, "The report came up with things we could not do under the law. So we didn't do them. They were things that we wanted to try and do and get special dispensation from Congress or the administration to do, but under the statutory requirements of the day we couldn't do some of the stuff."[6] With the demise of the Northern New Mexico Policy and the rise of the environmentalists, the Hispano communities gained an ally in the fight against industrial timber operations on the forest.

The Truchas Land Grant is one of the recognized communal properties that remains close to the Carson National Forest. About 319 families, or 1,200 people, live on the Truchas Land Grant. The land totals about fourteen thousand acres and adjoins the Camino Real.[7] Max Córdova became president of the Truchas Land Grant in 1987 and hails from one of the original 14 families that settled the region some 250 years ago. The people in Truchas, much like many residents in other land grant communities, subsist on what they can get from the land. Many people earn between $7,000 and $12,000 per year. They use wood from the forest for heating and cooking. They use wild herbs and piñon nuts as part of their diets. They use rocks, logs, and gravel for building their homes. They hunt for deer, rabbit, grouse, turkey, and fish to put food on their tables. Córdova's recollections of the USFS as he grew up are of a strong-armed agency eager to demonstrate its power over locals. Antagonism typified contact between the communities and the agency, and the arrival of a new district ranger in 1988 was regarded with a little apprehension.

Dumas arrived on the Camino Real in 1990 to find controversy in several places. Morale among USFS employees was low, employees were unproductive, forest health was declining, and the policy in the Camino Real was to cater to industrial forest operations with high-volume timber sales.[8] These large timber sales and the paperwork to support them were taking years to complete. The sales did not serve the local Hispano communities because they were too large for the scale of the communities' smaller timber operations. Environmentalists concerned about declining biological diversity and forest health appealed and then sometimes litigated the proposed sales.

Many agree that it was the Alamo-Dinner timber sale that was a catalyst for change. The sale was started in 1987 before Dumas's arrival. As recalled by a USFS public affairs officer at the time, a public meeting had been scheduled. "The ranger [prior to Dumas] asked me to come over and facilitate a meeting," recalled Carveth Kramer. "He said it was going to be around eight to ten people." The ranger had sorely underestimated controversy over the sale, because a few hundred people showed up—"You couldn't have planned it worse from my perspective. . . . I was really afraid of physical harm." The loggers verbally abused the community. The community retaliated in kind against the loggers. The environmentalists attacked the USFS: "I knew I was dead when I looked at the ranger, and he wouldn't come up [and help me]."[9] Not long after this disastrous public meeting, the old ranger left under duress due to threats to his personal safety. It was into this contentious environment that Dumas arrived.[10]

Córdova and other people from the land grant went to see Dumas early after his arrival to share with him concerns about access to fuel woods and road closures. Truchas is situated at approximately eight thousand feet, and the winters are hard.

People use wood to heat their houses and cook their food, as they have for centuries. Each family burns an average of nine cords of wood to stay warm through the long, cold months. Access to the wood is important not just for convenience but for survival. Córdova, in his role as president of the land grant, "decided to try something new. A new ranger was in, and we went to see him. We had problems with the one before. The one before came out to see me and said, 'Max, I don't want any problems.' When the new ranger came in, we went to see him. He sat there and didn't say twenty words."[11] Thus, the relationship between Córdova and Dumas did not bear much fruit until two years later. As in the relationship with the Hispano population, Dumas also faced antagonism from the environmental community.

In the late 1980s and early 1990s local environmentalists such as La Comunidad and Carson Forest Watch were becoming increasingly vocal in their opposition to timber sales on the forest. The Alamo-Dinner sale in particular had catalyzed great opposition, and when Dumas stepped into his new district ranger role on the Camino Real, he realized that the agency "had lost trust with the people it was supposed to serve."[12]

The opposition to the timber sales provided the incentive for Dumas and the USFS employees on the Camino Real, namely Wilbert Rodriguez and Henry Lopez, to rethink their entire approach to forest management in the district. Dumas enlisted help from the USFS regional office to put together a comprehensive survey. He needed to be sure he reached everyone possible, according to USFS regulations. Working with his staff, Dumas engaged thirty-eight of his forty-two employees to go to every household in the district. He called this "horseback diplomacy." The forest supervisor at the time, John Bedell, was supportive of Dumas's efforts.[13]

In March 1991 the Camino Real employees set out on foot and on horseback to talk to representatives of the twenty thousand residents of thirty-two rural northern New Mexico communities who lived on or adjacent to the Carson National Forest. In this manner the USFS employees began to understand the concerns of their publics better and integrate their interests in a policy to better serve them. They arrived at the homes of residents in pairs—one Spanish and one English speaker. They held cards that reminded them, "I am going to people's homes to listen," to keep them focused on their mission. As Dumas recollected, "The employees participated with different degrees of intensity. . . . The ones that were intense about it seemed to get the most satisfaction out of it." At this time the relationships between the Hispano community and the district began to change. Dumas recalled USFS employee Wilbert Rodriguez saying that for a change, "We're wearing the white hats!"[14] Córdova confirmed the positive effect it had within the communities, "I thought it was good community relations. . . . [Dumas] has this mentality that the mountain doesn't come to Muhammad, Muhammad goes to the mountain. He told staff to get out of their trucks and see what people want."[15]

The door-to-door visits lasted two months, but horseback diplomacy continued in a more informal form for much longer. The home visits led to regular meetings between community members and the USFS in 1993. In addition to working as president of the land grant, Córdova ran an artist's cooperative, called Los Siete, devoted to traditional weaving. Córdova organized fourteen meetings at Los Siete, which were attended by a core group of about twenty people, including USFS representatives.[16] At these meetings, Córdova says they made great progress on the permitting problems and other issues, including timber sales. In the meeting Dumas continued his informal "horseback diplomacy" to the villages, and Córdova often accompanied him.

Dumas worked closely with Córdova, who also must be credited with assisting in the success of the outreach effort. Córdova was open to being approached by the USFS in a new way, as indicated by his initial visit to Dumas in 1990. Córdova represented a new generation of leadership on the land grants, and given how terrible the relationships had been with the USFS in previous years, he felt it could not get any worse, so why not try something new? Carvath Kramer observed, "Max was not enamored with the USFS at all at that time and didn't think very highly of us. . . . Crockett had started these discussions and developed a relationship where they both changed. . . . This occurred over a period of time, and Crockett decided to get out of commodity production and saw timber and oriented to providing wood to small communities."[17] As the channels of communication opened between Córdova and Dumas, each began to see the other's viewpoint. Greater understanding about the need for small projects and the impacts that a few small changes in firewood permitting could have on the lives of the community members helped smooth relationships.

While engaged in their community outreach campaign, the employees on the Camino Real learned of various problems facing the community. For instance, one set of problems related to the cutting of firewood, *vigas* (cross beams in home building), and *latillas* (posts for roof supports and fences).[18] People from the villages use the forests to provide building materials for houses and need permits to get wood from the forest. For years, residents had been experiencing problems with the location, timing, and number of permits issued by the USFS.[19] Permits were issued too late in the year for residents to cut firewood and have it seasoned in time for the winter. Likewise, permits were offered for sale at the Carson National Forest headquarters in Taos, which meant that locals had to drive long distances from their villages to obtain the permits. Too few permits were issued to meet the needs of the community members. Consequently, residents would drive long distances to Taos to line up at two or three o'clock in the morning to secure a permit to cut wood.[20] Thus, Collaborative Stewardship began with the USFS listening to people's concerns about firewood, vigas, and latillas, and devising responses to them.

After progress had been made on the personal firewood issue, Córdova and Dumas began working on forest restoration efforts—another constituent part of Collaborative Stewardship. From Dumas's perspective they were thinning the forest and making the forest healthier—doing ecosystem management. This point of view differed from the communities in substance, but not in practice: "We were managing the forest—the by-product for the communities was that they got all the things they wanted."[21]

Dumas and his employees were meeting with the community on a regular basis. Through the meetings, Córdova and Dumas realized that the places where the fuelwood cutting was taking place could be undertaken to better benefit the environment. Córdova remembered, "Forest restoration work started in 1993, and it started looking at areas and cutting firewood. The second year it turned to more . . . cutting the right trees, measuring, monitoring." Córdova clarified that "forest restoration and logging are two different things. In forest restoration you leave the best, while in logging you take the best." The goal was to cut down the density of trees, clear out the slash, and open the canopy. The cut trees that were cleared could be used for vigas, latillas, firewood, or other wood products. The initial results from the forest restoration efforts surprised Córdova. "We started out cutting wood, and the rewards were enormous. Habitat came back, endangered species came back, trout, elk, . . . piñon nuts, turkey. . . . More snow falls on the ground and stays; we have streams that are running that didn't run before." Córdova added that traditional medicinal herbs were found in the region again. What was most important to Córdova was that capacity building and education accompany the opportunity to work at an appropriate scale in the forest.[22] For Córdova community health was inextricably tied to forest health. He wanted his people to understand why restoration was important and to develop competency in the skills to carry out restoration efforts. Kramer felt Dumas connected with this larger vision of community development: "He had small greenwood fuel areas that were right by the communities and then educated the people in the communities as to why they [were] doing this."[23]

The Alamo-Dinner sale that had ignited the ire of locals and environmentalists was retailored to meet the needs of smaller timber companies in the area. In October 1991 the sale, no longer facing opposition from locals, was authorized to proceed. Kramer recalled, "Crockett came in and redid that sale so it would be redesigned to get products to the locals and not the mill in Espanola."[24] However, in June 1992 a notice about the La Cueva Timber sale of 9,500 acres was sent out. The Cueva, Ojos-Ryan, and Angostura were large sales designed for a few big operators, rather than smaller community operators, as the Alamo-Dinner sale had been.[25] Not surprisingly, these timber sales were appealed and litigated by locals. At this point the USFS employees on the Camino Real began to realize that *all* timber sales would have to be approached differently. For the most part, this meant reorienting large projects with products going outside the community to small projects with products used in the small local communities.[26] From Crockett's perspective, he was engaging in "inappropriate spending of taxpayers' dollars and the use of employees because we weren't producing anything." He concluded, "Let's not spend our money on attorneys and planning, and spend our money more wisely."[27] At about this time a local journalist and community activist, Mark Schiller, went to interview Dumas: "Crockett said he was sick and tired of every project that the USFS was promoting was appealed and litigated and that obviously the era of big timber was over."[28] This frustration led to and sustained a change in approach to timber sales—another component of Collaborative Stewardship.

During these early years Collaborative Stewardship had support from Dumas's superiors. A new forest supervisor, Andy Lindquist, took over the Carson from 1991 to 1994. Lindquist was supportive of Dumas's efforts and gave him a promotion in place—a highly unusual accomplishment since the USFS typically does not promote without a transfer to a new locale. In 1994 a new forest supervisor took over—Leonard Lucero. Dumas's relationship with the new Lucero was much more contentious.[29]

In 1994 Dumas had been working with Carveth Kramer, the forest planner, on some new ways of planning with communities. Dumas and Kramer were looking for a way to make plans that were smaller and more dynamic. Kramer was trying to move this idea forward at the forest level, and Dumas wanted to move the idea forward on his district. Their pilot effort became the East Entrañas Ecosystem Management Plan. In the fall of 1994 Dumas met with Lucero to present the idea, and Lucero rejected it without explanation. This nonsupportive attitude extended over time to other activities that Dumas was experimenting with. Gradually Lucero reduced the budget for the program on the Camino Real. He opposed the way Dumas was working with the local communities. Cutting resources for outreach activities (horseback diplomacy and meetings) began to strain some of the relationships Dumas was trying to build. During Lucero's tenure the total number of employees on the Camino Real was slashed from forty-two to seventeen. Lucero's and Dumas's priorities differed, and so did the budget allocations. As Dumas recalled, "Leonard didn't have any ownership in innovations and was subversive." Dumas had a "good relationship, trust, and respect from Andy [Lundquist], but not from Leonard."[30]

In 1995 Collaborative Stewardship was composed of policies that focused on easier permitting for firewood, forest restoration, and a reorientation of timber sales to local communities with fewer ecological impacts. At this time Collaborative Stewardship faced a major challenge. The U.S. Fish and Wildlife Service designated the Mexican spotted owl as a threatened species in 1993, and in 1994 the agency released a plan that proposed to designate 4.8 million acres in the New Mexico and Arizona regions as critical habitat.[31] Approximately 2,700 owls are located throughout the Southwest, and 1,000 were believed to live in New Mexico or Arizona.[32] The designation of the Mexican spotted owl and the identification of its habitat gave environmentalists the ammunition they needed to restrict logging in old-growth forests in the Southwest. A suit brought by the Forest Conservation Council, Forest Guardians, Southwest Center for Biological Diversity, Greater Gila Biodiversity Project, Biodiversity Legal Foundation, Carson Forest Watch, Maricopa Audubon Society, Robin Silver, and Diné Citizens against Ruining Our Environment was intended to force a reevaluation of the standards and guidelines for timber, grazing, recreation, and wildlife programs in the region. In response to this suit, U.S. District Judge Carl Muecke, on August 24, 1995, ordered a halt to all timber harvesting in Forest Service Region 3. The injunction was issued to allow the USFS, in conjunction with the USFWS, to assess the cumulative biological impacts on the spotted owl from the many timber sales in the region. The sweeping injunction affected any tree-felling project on the eleven national forests in the region, including the Carson and Santa Fe.[33] The order effectively put twenty-six timber sales and eighty-five million board feet of timber off limits from the Southwest timber industry and represented 80 percent of the volume under contract at that time. The injunction also had the effect of constraining the collection of personal-use timber—including firewood.

Nearly one hundred families in the mountain villages did not have adequate firewood for the upcoming winter months, and twenty-two of them were in immediate need of wood because of low or nonexistent fuel supplies.[34] A survey of homes revealed that the families were short 1,800 cords of wood to get them through the harsh winter. Córdova expressed his aggravation: "People don't understand that we have a real crisis up here. That is what's so frustrating. We can't seem to get through to them."[35] In response to the restrictions, a group called Herencia de Norteños Unidos organized to protest the callousness of the environmentalists toward Hispano communities.

In October 1996 federal judge Carl Muecke ordered the USFS and environmentalists to meet until they reached an agreement on the Mexican spotted owl. Facing continued restriction on firewood gathering and entering the second winter facing an unpredictable supply of firewood, residents needed to collect wood. Córdova needed to know whether Dumas was going to support the policies under Collaborative Stewardship, namely, the ones that facilitated cutting personal-use timber. Córdova placed a call to Dumas: "I am going to send my people to cut wood. You can either send people to mark trees, or we are just going to cut the trees." Dumas replied, as remembered by Córdova, "Max, you don't understand. A federal judge has handed down an injunction that we cannot violate." To which Córdova replied, "Hey, the federal judge doesn't live here. We need help."[36] Dumas agreed to send his people to mark the trees and told Córdova that he would probably lose his job in the process. The next day Córdova and his people cut and hauled wood to meet their needs. By supporting Córdova and his people's needs for fuelwood, Dumas supported Collaborative Stewardship. On Wednesday, December 4, 1996, federal judge Roger Strand lifted the controversial ban on logging from the eleven national forests.[37]

Dumas's decision to violate the injunction by marking the trees for cutting was controversial. Dumas was highly praised in the surrounding communities for supporting the policy and understanding their plight: "Crockett made a lot of courageous decisions . . . he stood up to the forest supervisor."[38] Those within the USFS were less enthusiastic. Kramer articulated this perspective: "There is a feeling by many in the organization that no matter how bad things are you can't violate a law. . . . You draw the line right there. You don't violate the law. I think if you talked to most other Forest Service employees, they would tell you the same thing."[39] But Dumas was not afraid to take appropriate risks: "If you want to lead, at some point you need to take appropriate risks."[40] He did what he thought needed to be done. The decision felt right to him.[41] He recalled that he had the support of Michael Dombeck, USFS chief at the time, and Phil Janeck, who was associate chief at the time. He also remembered that Lucero made it clear he did not support Dumas.[42] Dumas was warned by the USFS regional office that he was on his own after violating the injunction. They would not protect him if someone did take legal action against him.[43] The decision created tension between those on the Camino Real Unit and other units on the Carson National Forest: "It created a lot of animosity between that unit and the rest of the forest that still exists."[44]

Even though Dumas violated the injunction by marking the trees for Córdova and his people to cut, he was not prosecuted and did not lose his job. Dumas's extensive and loyal support in the community insulated him from any action taken against him. As recalled by local community activist Luis Torres-Horton, "Without the community, Crockett would have gone to jail. The [forest supervisor] wasn't about to touch Crockett."[45] Henry Lopez, one of Dumas's employees, concurred, "If they put him in jail, they would have had to put me in jail and the community in jail."[46]

When the injunction halted all timber cutting on the Carson National Forest, the employees on the Camino Real realized once again the need for a different approach to timber management in area. Not only did they need to pay heed to the local community, but they also needed to provide greater attention to ecosystem dynamics, and especially the habitat for the Mexican spotted owl. The goal was to devise a "customer-driven and -supported program that meets the customer's needs, while improving forest conditions without expensive and lengthy litigation."[47] Working with Kramer, who had become the Carson National Forest planner, Dumas and many community members came up with what they characterized as an "informal amendment" to the existing forest management plan.[48] The district was divided into nine ecological and social management areas and analyzed from the perspective of what practices would achieve conditions desired by the community. What resulted was the East Entrañas Ecosystem Management Plan, which formalized some of the outcomes from the innovative practices embodied in Collaborative Stewardship. These practices included working with local people to provide easier access to firewood, emphasis on forest restoration, and reorientation of timber sales to local communities. The vision was partnerships with local community members in various projects. Cooperative agreements with the Forest Trust (an environmental and community development nonprofit), La Montaña de Truchas Woodlot (a Hispano-owned timber company), Picuris Pueblo (a Native American community), the Santa Barbara Grazing Association (a local trade group), and the Valle Grande Grass Bank (a conservation nonprofit) resulted in successful thinning and restoration projects, which benefited local ranchers and the villagers who relied on fuelwood and other forest resources.[49]

The East Entrañas Ecosystem Management Plan was the closest Collaborative Stewardship came to codification. Since 1991 Collaborative Stewardship evolved piecemeal from redesigned timber sales to more user-friendly firewood permitting to forest restoration practices to grazing improvements. Until then, Collaborative Stewardship had been an unnamed mix of practices. The East Entrañas plan was twelve pages long with a twenty-three-page addendum that detailed social conditions and maps. Articulated on the second page were the goals, including a desire to manage with "an emphasis on local wood products (latillas, vigas, firewood, small-saw timber sales)." Also expressed was a desire to focus on smaller projects oriented toward local use rather than large saw timber sales into the future.[50]

Small projects and good communication were the key to keeping timber moving, improving forest health, and serving local populations on the Camino Real. All of these efforts were inordinately dependent on Dumas to keep the channels of communication open and provide the authority for continued implementation.

After the East Entrañas plan was written, Collaborative Stewardship continued to evolve. In 1997 the USFS began to issue stewardship plots to interested parties. These were one- to four-acre allotments that people cut timber from to get the firewood and then piled the slash. The best trees were left to grow after the plot had been cleared. The area was then set for prescribed burning in the winter. Henry Lopez, forest technician on the Camino Real and lifelong local resident, was in charge of the project and came up with the idea. Lopez commented that many people from the community use the stewardship blocks—Anglos, land grant peoples, other community members, men, women, young, and old.[51]

In 1997 the innovations on the Camino Real began to attract attention from outside the district and forest. The district and the community received then Vice President Gore's Hammer Award for Reinventing Government for their ability to cut red tape and make government work more efficiently. The innovative policies were found meritorious on the grounds that they overcame the litigious nature of timber sales and worked with the local community. Since 1993 not one timber sale or project had been appealed or litigated.[52] When they won the award, Córdova remembered, "We had a big party with 500 people [at Los Siete]. That motivated us to do more work and get things done."[53]

A grass bank initiative in the Penasco area around the Camino Real emerged in 1998 when the Quiveras Coalition, a regional environmental organization, was invited by the local Rio Pueblo/Rio Embudo Watershed Protection Coalition to give a workshop in the area. One hundred people attended to learn about how economically viable ranching and an ecologically healthy range land could coexist.[54] Grazing groups noticed that forage was decreasing, the weight of their cattle was declining, and the density of trees was increasing, thereby posing a wildfire threat.[55] Environmentalists were concerned about declining water quality in the streams when the cattle got in them and the degraded land from overgrazing. Bill DeBuys was featured as one of the speakers and invited local ranchers to move their cattle to the Valle Grande grass bank to allow restoration work on their lots within the national forest. The local Santa Barbara Grazing Association then held a meeting with the permittees and petitioned for 203 cows to be moved to the grass bank. Restoration activities on the Santa Barbara Allotment within the Camino Real then were planned, such as thinning and prescribed burns with the USFS. Restoration work would take two to three years and entail three thousand treatment acres.[56] The project would provide local jobs, and permits would be sold to reduce fuels in the area. The effort was funded through the USFS, the EPA, and the New Mexico Environmental Program, mostly through EPA 319 funds of the Clean Water Act that can be used to address non–point-source pollution.

In 1998 Harvard's Innovations in American Government Award, done in partnership with the Ford Foundation and the Council for Excellence in Government, honored Collaborative Stewardship when it made the final cut of ten among 1,400 award applications nationwide.[57] The award recognized that Collaborative Stewardship provided a creative solution to a pressing social and economic problem, while also being novel, effective, and transferable to other places. The award came with $100,000 to promote the innovative practices to others. "Having [our program] become an Innovations in American Government winner [was] the highlight of my thirty-year career as a federal employee," Dumas said.[58]

Max Córdova identified the award and the subsequent plan to disseminate the innovation as the beginning of the end of Collaborative Stewardship: "Everything was moving along really well, and then they entered our project in the Kennedy School of Government [contest]."[59] Within the Camino Real and on the Carson National Forest, jealousy undermined relationships following the national awards honoring Collaborative Stewardship. Friction between Dumas and the forest supervisor, as well as his own employees, led to hard feelings and resentment. Recalled Córdova, "About three months after we got the [Harvard] award, I got a call from [someone] on the Camino Real staff and [that person said the staff] felt Dumas was ramming the [dissemination] proposal down [their] throats and this was not what [they] wanted to do. . . . Then I realized we were in trouble."[60] Others concur that Dumas was a bit autocratic in his ways, including Dumas himself. "Crockett pretty much wrote the whole scenario out. He was going to bring in experts on Collaborative Stewardship. We fought him on that," remembered Kay Mathews, a local journalist and community activist.[61] At this stage a wave of jealousy and infighting was released that signaled Dumas's departure and the demise of Collaborative Stewardship.

Córdova attributed some of the dissention to *la envidia*, envy, or in his words, "some people cannot appreciate their own blessings for worrying about the blessings of others." Córdova felt that "The [forest] supervisor had wanted more ownership and recognition. . . . Everyone wanted a feather in their cap."[62] *La envidia* is a widespread and vicious sentiment in northern New Mexico. Jealousies insinuated their way into many relationships, not just those associated with Collaborative Stewardship. Recalled Dumas, "Professional motivation and job satisfaction were overridden by *la envidia*, and that is what happened with Leonard and many of the other rangers. I was the odd person out, and they didn't want to rock the cradle."[63]

Dumas did try to promote his people, but he was constrained by his forest supervisor, Leonard Lucero. Promotion in place is hard to do within the USFS. And Lucero would not let Dumas promote Henry Lopez because of Lopez's close ties to the community. Since the forest supervisor had to sign the promotions, he controlled the decisions. "Henry was a great employee—I wish I could have done more for him," lamented Dumas. "The more you brag about your employees, the more Leonard hates them." Dumas advocated for the others who were willing to be transferred to be promoted: "The ones that were more mobile went on to bigger and better things."[64] By 1998 most of the original employees who had been involved in Collaborative Stewardship had left except for Henry Lopez.

Dumas had strong feelings that his employees needed to be part of the program, and this also may have given rise to hidden resentments. As district ranger, he felt he needed to be realistic: "You are never going to have 100 percent support . . . but if people weren't on board with the train, they were run over by it." In short, Dumas was the conductor, and the employees needed to get on board with his vision. Dumas acknowledged that "this probably caused some hard feelings." Dumas could have done a better job of sharing the glory. A neighboring district ranger observed, "A lot of people are necessary to make [the innovation] go. . . . A lot of what Crockett likes to lay claim to is not what Crockett has done but what people working for Crockett have done."[65] That said, in hindsight, it is clear that Dumas was essential to the innovations that happened on the Camino Real.

In 1998 Dumas transferred himself from the Camino Real to another ranger district in Utah. His wife had been unhappy in northern New Mexico, and the Dumases had a horse farm in Utah to which they wanted to return. Dumas had chosen to live in the community and had been the only district ranger who had chosen to live among the community. Building those relationships was good for Collaborative Stewardship, but it was hard on his wife.[66] Dumas felt that he no longer had the support of his superiors for his policies. Dumas was quite adamant that he was not forced out. According to Henry Lopez, regarded by some as Dumas's right-hand man, Dumas left because he had some problems with people on his own staff. He did not focus on promoting his own people from within his district, and this created some resentment.[67] Córdova was mostly mystified as to what happened and how quickly everything went wrong: "Dumas was a unique fellow. The innovations [awards] gave him credit for what he had done. The biggest surprise to me was that people didn't like to give credit."[68]

In reflecting on his own experience, Dumas commented that he had been "on the Camino Real nine and a half years. And if you wanted to move up in the organization then you have to move on every two and a half years." If you do that "then you never have to live with your mistakes." Dumas had to live with his mistakes, but he also got to live with his accomplishments. Explaining his decision to stay put for such a long period of time in spite of the professional drawbacks, he said, "You want to go to bed feeling good at night. I had an intense land management ethic—keeping the soil in place and managing the watershed, but you have to involve the public in that. Once I got up to the level where I could make those decisions, I wanted to make good decisions and effect things on the ground."[69]

Under Collaborative Stewardship the share of timber sales going to large businesses decreased, while the percentage of timber going to personal use increased. Between 1992 and 1994 large businesses received the largest share of distribution on the

Carson, with 36 percent of the total volume. Between 1997 and 1999 personal use permits received the largest share, claiming 78 percent of the total volume, and large businesses received only 3 percent of the distribution. In 1994, 600 personal-use firewood permits were sold, as were 1,216 cords of firewood. In 1996, 739 permits were sold, and 1,478 cords of firewood were collected. Small and medium-sized businesses received the largest portion of contract timber sales on the Carson National Forest with a 16 percent share of the distribution.[70] The same could not be said for the neighboring Santa Fe National Forest. Every year since 1993, large businesses on the Santa Fe received at least 80 percent of the contract volume. During the period 1992–1994, large businesses received 19 percent of the total volume, and in the period 1997–1999 this portion grew to 29 percent.[71] The volume going to small and medium businesses during the same time frame also grew from 3 percent to 5 percent. In addition to the changes in timber sales, personal-use firewood problems also were addressed. Forest health projects were created and implemented. After the court injunction was lifted at the end of 1996, six separate forest health projects on approximately 1,500 acres of land supplied over 3,000 cords of woods to local communities. Nine wildlife and fisheries projects were completed without appeal or litigation.[72]

After Dumas's departure some elements of Collaborative Stewardship continued. The stewardship plots program was expanded. On the Carson National Forest, because saw-timber production had been replaced by ecosystem management that produced small-diameter wood products, the overall budget was reduced from about $16 million to $6.5 million for fiscal year 1999. This meant that the Camino Real did not have the funding to conduct the archaeological and wildlife surveys for ecosystem management areas that provided fuelwood and wood products to communities and local contractors.[73] In 2001 two hundred acres had been treated in the stewardship plots, and Lopez was seeking approval for two more areas of five hundred acres each. At that time, Lopez was having trouble getting the new district ranger to get the environmental assessment completed so the areas could be rolled out to the community.[74] "Demand on the district for stewardship blocks far exceeds our ability to prepare them," Lopez said. He expressed additional frustration with the staff reorganization throughout the Carson National Forest that designated the timber staff as a forestwide team, which Lopez felt inadequately addressed Camino Real timber needs, such as the stewardship program and small thinning contracts.[75] The consequences for Collaborative Stewardship were real. Córdova's La Montaña de Truchas was hamstrung on several of its projects because the district was unable to complete necessary paper work. From Córdova's perspective, "The stewardship plots started out really well and then fizzled out."[76]

In April 2001 the community held a conference to fulfill its obligation to diffuse the innovation as part of its obligation as a recipient of the Harvard/Ford Foundation Innovations award. Córdova summarized, "In October 2000 we were supposed to lose the money. . . . We asked for an extension to March 2001."[77] A group of community organizers and USFS employees rallied to put on a workshop. The controversy over

Dumas remained alive: "When we were planning the innovations program, the employees came here and said if Dumas is coming then we don't want to have any part. So then I said if Dumas doesn't come, then I won't come either. So finally a compromise was reached that he would be invited, but not allowed to speak."[78] The experts who did speak were the residents themselves—local farmers, ranchers, woodlot operators, and USFS personnel who had been involved directly in Collaborative Stewardship. In many ways, this was a victory in itself—the community spoke in its own words about what it accomplished. The goal was to share successes and failures. During the two-day "unconference," as they called it, concerns were raised about the future of the stewardship plot program and the Santa Barbara Grazing Allotment Rehabilitation Project. All the USFS professional staff who had been present when the innovations were initiated had left, contributing to delays and misunderstandings that threatened the projects. Local residents who worked as technicians and office staff provided some level of continuity, but they could not drive the work.[79] Another problem addressed was how communities could maintain a meaningful voice in the collaborative process, which many felt had not been sustained with the new district ranger.

While personal-use timber access was much better for the land grant peoples, Córdova felt that forest restoration and stewardship plots slipped after Dumas left: "We were better off a year ago than now. I think there has been a decline." When Dumas left, "all of the people here have an idea that [forest restoration] is something else." For instance, some USFS employees think forest restoration is embodied only in the stewardship blocks, but according to Córdova, "that doesn't allow the community to build its own capacity, and there is no training going on to enhance people's skills or help them understand the ecological importance of what they need to do and why." The linkages between the community health and forest health were lost: "My feeling was that the USFS never really understood the true nature of what we were trying to do [after Dumas left], how we were trying to connect community health to forest health."[80]

Community outreach and horseback diplomacy were the two strategies that facilitated understanding of community needs that then could be targeted through actions that constituted Collaborative Stewardship. Upon Dumas's departure these strategies broke down. Since Dumas left, "we haven't had a single meeting. . . . It's hard to get anyone from the administration to come." The departure of administrative personnel on the Camino Real underscores a persistent problem within the USFS related to community relationships—turnover in agency personnel. Community outreach strategies are built on trust that is gained through contact with locals. Countless hours of understanding, education, patience, and trust are vested in these relationships and are irreplaceable once one of the parties is transferred elsewhere. The frustration is evident: "We built all that base and then lost it. Setback after setback after setback." The one employee who has maintained some consistency is Henry Lopez. "If Henry left it would be bad," proclaimed Córdova.[81] "Henry deserves a lot of credit—he's very sincere. . . . He tried to get work done on the ground," remarked Mark Schiller. He was less complimentary of the district ranger who followed Dumas: "[She] gives lip service to [Collaborative Stewardship], but she hasn't been very supportive."[82]

In the years since, continued budget cuts to the USFS meant fewer staff and more contracting out to accomplish work previously conducted by staff. The upshot, according to Kay Mathews, writing in 2005, was a continued loss of local input in the Camino Real, which once again resulted in mistrust and alienation between the agency and local community members. Remaining staff had less time to get out into the community because of demands in the office and increased paperwork.[83] In 2006 the Camino Real got another new district ranger. Max Córdova and Mark Schiller went to visit the new ranger and asked if he would consider reviving the practice of working more actively with the community. The response they received was noncommittal.[84]

After he left the Camino Real, Dumas continued to advocate for the USFS to move from the "autocratic/authoritarian to the convening/facilitating modus operandi for the most successful way of doing natural resources business on the ground and for the taxpayer without appeals and litigation." In 2002 he commented, "We have been unable to gain very much ground as far as [USFS] cultural change over the dozen or so years we have been working on it."[85]

The unraveling of Collaborative Stewardship cannot be attributed to any one factor. Dissension among employees on the Camino Real, tensions within the Hispano community, lack of support from USFS administrators, and changing budget situations all contributed to the decline: "While many of us gave Collaborative Stewardship our best shot, it's hard to know how long the program could have been sustained, with or without Dumas, given the complex relationship between the USFS and the communities."[86] Skepticism, cynicism, and doubt typify sentiment about the potential for future collaborative efforts. Mark Schiller went so far as to say that Collaborative Stewardship was "deliberately dismantled" because the USFS transferred all the personnel who had been involved in it. Henry Lopez was the only person left in 2008 who had been part of the initial effort. Schiller communicated that the USFS was now transferring Lopez, too. "Henry is the last resource on the Camino Real who was sensitive to community concerns," Schiller lamented.[87] The community circulated a petition to keep Lopez on the district. The leaders within the Hispano community were exhausted, too. Ike DeVargas, a local Hispano activist, reflected that "you're also not going to see any kind of change in USFS policy to benefit the communities without some kind of community-based leadership, and there isn't any now. . . . All of the former community leaders have been beaten down and dispirited. . . . We're old and tired. It's a sad commentary."[88]

APPLYING THE ANALYTICAL FRAMEWORK

The analytical framework laid out in chapter 1 is applied here to the Collaborative Stewardship case study. The three macro categories of individuals (motivation, norms and harmony, and congruence), structure (rules and communication, incentives, opening, and resistance), and culture (shocks, framing, and legitimacy) are laid over the details of the case to illustrate how these factors were or were not accounted for in the implementation of this innovation.

Individuals

Motivation If the impetus for innovation rests on discontented individuals, then Max Córdova and Crockett Dumas were primed to act. To innovate, individuals should be free to devise alternative solutions, and Dumas was in a stronger position to take action than Córdova, who ultimately was dependent on the USFS. The status quo in this case was gridlock on the Camino Real. USFS employees could not do their jobs, environmentalists were blocking timber sales because they were unhappy with the ecological consequences of forest management, and Hispano communities were not able to get the timber products they needed.

Córdova and others within the Hispano communities were motivated to change because Collaborative Stewardship was better than the status quo. The land was essential to the well-being of these communities. For Córdova, it was worth a trip to the new district ranger's office to see if progress could be made on the issues faced by his community. He had nothing to lose. The relationship with the USFS could only get better between the agency and the Hispano communities. Once Collaborative Stewardship was under way, satisfaction in working together and effecting change carried its own momentum. Progress on the permitting issue for firewood, vigas, and latillas gave way to progress on forest restoration, stewardship plots, and grazing improvements. The group celebrated after the Gore Award, and this created additional drive to persevere.

Frustration with the inability to get work done within the Camino Real resulted in a predisposition for change among Dumas and his staff. Dumas wanted to be free of the constraints in order to carry out his mission, which he saw as managing vegetation on the land.[89] Dumas's motivation was job satisfaction. Until he was able to do his job, he would not be satisfied. He realized that as long at the environmentalists appealed and litigated timber sales he would be unable to manage the land with which he was charged in his district. Dumas realized that if he had the support of local communities, then he would be able to accomplish his goals on the Camino Real. Dumas and other USFS staff were motivated because Collaborative Stewardship allowed them to get timber sales moving on the district and gave them a sense of personal satisfaction. Collaborative Stewardship was a means to accomplish work on the district. Lucero's cuts to the Camino Real and additional downsizing efforts throughout the federal government reduced funding and the number of district employees from forty-two to seventeen.[90] Therefore, the USFS needed to branch out and work with others to accomplish its goals. Henry Lopez and Wilbert Rodriquez, local residents and Camino Real employees, were happy to be wearing the "white hats" for a change. Job satisfaction, camaraderie, and good working relationships with the community provided the stimulus to continue. Others on the forest also were motivated to support Collaborative Stewardship. Carveth Kramer and others in the supervisor's office supported those on the Camino Real with outreach and planning.

The innovation was successful from 1991 to 1999, when Dumas left the district. Without him, many of the practices would not have happened, and in his absence, many of the practices faded. While many were inspired to change, others were not. Notably, the district rangers who followed Dumas were not so nearly motivated to work with local communities. Without the leadership of Dumas, there was not sufficient motivation to continue reaching out to the community or to fight the USFS bureaucracy to accomplish the goals established in Collaborative Stewardship. The innovation was inordinately dependent on Dumas for its success and highlights the vulnerability of an innovation overly dependent on one highly motivated individual. The literature on policy entrepreneurs celebrates the power of the individual to change policy direction.[91] This literature has less to say about how to build a sustainable structure for continued innovative practice in the entrepreneur's absence.

Subsequent district rangers did not participate in community outreach or collaborative efforts. "Everything was in place when the [new district ranger] came, and she could have picked up the ball and run with it," recalled Schiller. But instead, he felt they were given a duplicitous response. After visiting with the new ranger and getting agreement on some local projects, community members later found out that the ranger took the opposite action. As of 2008, the newest district ranger was difficult to find and usually not in the office, making it difficult to make contact. In contrast, Dumas was proactive about reaching out and informed the community about what was going on: "He always kept the lines of communication open, listened, and responded in a reasonably thoughtful way."[92]

Norms and Harmony Individuals' predisposition to support innovation can be affected by a desire to preserve harmony in the workplace. If an innovation causes conflict, then individuals may not be predisposed to support change.

The norms that prevailed historically within the Camino Real were not supportive of collaboration with the local community. Córdova had been frustrated in his relationship, or lack thereof, with the ranger prior to Dumas. The transition to the new norm of collaboration was not discrete but gradual. Employees on the Camino Real had the idea of talking to the community, and when Dumas arrived he carried out that vision, enlisting the help of the public affairs specialists in the USFS regional office. Horseback diplomacy began to open relationships with the community. Employees on the Camino Real began to experience benefits from these relationships. Some employees were more supportive than others. In the early days of Collaborative Stewardship (1991–96), there was support both from the community and within the Camino Real for the innovation.

In 1997 outward signs of dissension began to emerge. The Harvard/Ford Foundation innovation award revealed that not all the employees on the Camino Real or within the community continued to be supportive of the practice or content with

Dumas's leadership. People complained that they were not recognized or were not given enough credit. Jealousy, envy, and distrust infected relationships. Conflict over continued support of the innovation led to acrimony among the many participants.

Congruence The individual level of support for an innovation can be affected by the dominant values in an agency or organizations. If the dominant values conflict with the values promoted at the implementation level, then individuals may find it difficult to support an innovation. For all its rhetoric about working with communities, the broader culture of the USFS is not a hospitable place to engage with outsiders, and the broader USFS culture within which Collaborative Stewardship played out explains partially the failure to sustain the innovation over time.

Dumas relished being different within the agency. He did not wear a USFS uniform or badge. He did not drive a USFS truck. He rejected all the traditional symbols of USFS authority to cultivate relationships in the community. He clearly went against the rules and regulations of the agency during the injunction in 1996. He liked being a bit of a maverick within his own agency. He was willing to defy the more dominant culture because he saw the value in working with the community and continuing to have their support. He was able to enlist the support of groups and individuals outside the agency, whether it was from Vice President Al Gore or the Harvard/Ford innovations people. This external political support provided a buffer for his unconventional practices. His alternative practices did not create tensions for him as an individual until 1997, when he felt he began to lose the support of his superiors and his employees on the district. The district rangers who followed Dumas were not as enthusiastic about working with the community, reaching out, or taking risks.

Dumas was incongruent with the broader agency culture and provided a buffer of support between his employees and the agency that did not value the collaborative, community-based practices. When Dumas left, the broader agency culture once again prevailed, making individual participation difficult.

Structures

Rules and Communication Compliance with an innovative practice can be hindered if administrative rules and communication are not clear and supportive of anticipated actions and expectations. The rules guiding Collaborative Stewardship were never very clear because the approach emerged piecemeal. Opportunities to respond to community concerns arose, and these were addressed in an ad hoc manner. Those engaging in the innovation did not really know they were practicing Collaborative Stewardship per se until they articulated it in the application for the Gore Hammer award in 1996. At that time, the East Entrañas Ecosystem Management Plan was created, which was the primary document that codified the existing and expected actions under Collaborative Stewardship. Dumas left shortly after the policy was documented. The East Entrañas

Ecosystem Management Plan was opposed by the forest supervisor. Consequently, it was up to a new district ranger to pick up where Dumas left off, and antagonism toward Dumas and his efforts under Collaborative Stewardship made this difficult, if not impossible, within the USFS. Since Collaborative Stewardship was not codified or institutionalized in a meaningful way, it was difficult to stabilize expectations and to pass on the practices. Into 2009 there is still a lack of agreement among the many participants about what Collaborative Stewardship actually entailed. Some say it was stewardship plots, some say it was the outreach efforts, others say it was connecting the community to forest restoration, and yet others think it was all of these things.

Communication was dependent on Dumas. He organized his staff to begin outreach efforts typified by horseback diplomacy and meetings at Los Siete. He worked with communities to create responses to their concerns. Others were certainly involved in the process, but everyone took direction from Dumas. This created problems after his departure because no one knew Collaborative Stewardship as well as he did or wanted to practice it from an administrative perspective.

Incentives   Organizations can provide incentives to encourage innovative practices. Dumas promoted Collaborative Stewardship through his position as district ranger. He was limited in the types of incentives he could offer. The primary inducement for USFS workers within the district to support change was an increase in their ability to get work done, which resulted in more genial relationships with the community. These incentives initially made a big difference to those engaging in Collaborative Stewardship. After Collaborative Stewardship started, USFS staff had better morale and productivity, since energy, time, and resources once spent on appeals and litigation were now focused on project design and implementation. People from other communities drove from other ranger districts, sometimes more than one hundred miles, to the Camino Real to do business, which gave staff a sense of personal accomplishment. Absence of complaints from local residents contributed to greater job satisfaction.[93]

Arguably, Dumas could have done a better job using other incentives available to him as district ranger to support the innovation. Some complained that he insufficiently acknowledged their efforts or failed to promote those within the district. Dumas argued that he had limitations on what he could do. Carveth Kramer took three people from the Camino Real to work with him at the forest level. Others were promoted. It was difficult to promote people in place if they wanted to stay where they were. Dumas wanted to promote his people, but he had limited options. Promotions were dependent on Lucero to approve, so Dumas was ultimately constrained by the forest supervisor.

Dumas created an incentive for the Hispano communities to engage in Collaborative Stewardship because he was willing to listen and, perhaps more important, to act on their concerns. Communities knew they were contributing to better forest health in the way they were harvesting products from the forests. More reliable timber was available for communities.[94] Incentives are usually treated as financial inducements. In this case, constrained budgets and the relationship with the forest supervisor limited how Dumas could provide financial incentives. Instead, job satisfaction, friendship, and mutual respect provided incentives for action.

Opening An opening in the political structure can allow marginalized groups an opportunity to foster change. In this case, Dumas opened the political structure on the district to give the Hispano communities a voice in how policy should change. The opening occurred because Dumas had the power as the district ranger to alter the status quo. He opened the political structure to being more amenable to the concerns and ideas that the community had and how the agency and community could work together.

Importantly, the political structure on the Carson National Forest and at the regional level remained closed to the innovations that were taking place. Dumas had no authority beyond his district to alter how decisions were made. As long as Dumas was in place at the district level, he had the force of will to keep access for local communities open. Upon his departure, the political opportunity structure was much less responsive to local concerns once again. Dumas's forest supervisor was unsupportive of Dumas's action. Lucero actively cut Dumas's budget and staff. Dumas was not opposed at the USFS regional level, but he also did not have unqualified support. He was told he was on his own after violating the timber injunction with the spotted owl controversy.

Resistance Existing institutions can be resistant to new practices. Larger power dynamics and vested interests may resist or obstruct change. These dynamics were undeniably at work in the Camino Real case.

The USFS in northern New Mexico did not have an easy history with its local publics. Relationships varied from insurrectionist to merely oppositional (as documented in chapter 2). Creating new patterns in community relationships, as well as serving community needs, was met with skepticism and unease among some within the agency. Two other efforts to serve local communities prior to Collaborative Stewardship failed. The Vallecitos Federal Sustained Yield Unit in 1948, which was intended to provide local jobs and products, failed to hire sufficient labor from the local communities, sat idle, or was contracted to an international multinational corporation. The rebellion in the 1960s caused the USFS to respond with the Northern New Mexico Policy, which detailed ninety-nine policy recommendations for the region. Forest supervisors and district rangers in the Carson, Cibola, and Santa Fe national forests were called upon to recognize the unique cultural connection of the Hispano descendants to the land and support these communities with changes in (a) timber sales to make them more compatible with the needs local communities, (b) grazing policy to accommodate small permit numbers to better fit the needs of the Hispano communities, (c) firewood and building materials policy to provide communities with deadwood and small-diameter trees for poles, posts, and vigas, (d) attention to

Native American ceremonial areas and religious shrines, and (e) attitudes of the USFS employees to acknowledge the uniqueness of northern New Mexico.[95] After financial and political support from the regional and Washington offices declined, and legal challenges made support of the policy untenable, relationships and management practices returned to their previous level of antagonism. In many ways Collaborative Stewardship was an extension, either implicitly or explicitly, of the 1967 Northern New Mexico Policy, since it attempted to serve local populations in many of the same ways and recognized the special cultural connection that Hispano communities had to the land in the Camino Real. And much like the other policies before it, Collaborative Stewardship faded due to the broader resistance within the USFS.

According to Ernie Atencio, a local environmentalist and rancher, Collaborative Stewardship embodied the notion that "rather than the typical top-down imposition of policy, forest management projects are designed to enhance the ecosystem and biodiversity while providing resources and income for community members."[96] To carry out this vision of a more participatory and less autocratic agency, Dumas was willing to risk relationships with other districts, the forest supervisor, and the region.

Dumas had been supported in his early efforts with horseback diplomacy by forest supervisors John Bedell and Andy Linquist. When Leonard Lucero came in as forest supervisor, Dumas had a much more contentious relationship with him. Lucero had opposed the East Entrañas Ecosystem Management Plan and cut the resources going to the Camino Real. Violating the injunction created tensions between the Camino Real and other districts on the Carson National Forest. Some worried that Dumas had gotten too close to the community. Lucero said the regional office told him that Dumas was on his own if someone took him to court for violating the injunction. Shortages in staff and budgets made it increasingly hard to carry out work on Collaborative Stewardship projects after Dumas's departure.

Agency structure provides its own challenges to innovative practices. Many fault the agency rather than Dumas for Collaborative Stewardship's inability to persist. "I think [Dumas] initiated some very innovative stuff," observed DeVargas, a local Hispano activist. "I can really like a person on the ground, but I recognize the agency structure controls things. The agency itself is very, very cumbersome, very out of date."[97] Córdova concurred: "[The USFS] is very bureaucratic. They are so used to doing things in certain ways that they don't want to change. When change does happen, they resist it to the fullest extent."[98]

The Camino Real case illustrates the power of historically vested interests and how they can continue to shape policy, even in light of dynamic, entrepreneurial individuals. Historical institutionalists see a world in which institutions give some interests disproportionate access to the decision-making process, resulting in those groups with access winning out over those without it.[99] While individuals may be discontented with a given situation and seek to innovate, these efforts may be obstructed by larger power dynamics and vested interests. In the Camino Real case, traditional bureaucratic interests overwhelmed the community-based, collaborative efforts instigated by Dumas.

Culture

Shocks Catalytic events or shocks to the system can provide opportunities for alternative courses of action to take form. Shocks do not provide much explanatory power in this case. No single event is responsible for the transition to Collaborative Stewardship. Controversy over the Alamo-Dinner sale began to open Dumas's eyes to the problems in the community. Dumas came to the conclusion that he would be unable to manage vegetation or serve the people in the district if he did not have the support of the local communities, and this provided an incentive for him to change management action. Change was gradual and evolved piecemeal over time.

The controversy over the Mexican spotted owl injunction and Dumas's decision to help the community rather than uphold the injunction may have been a shock to the USFS. For some it clarified how far Dumas was willing to go to the support the community.

Framing Framing processes can affect people's perceptions that there is a problem, thereby instigating action that otherwise might not have taken place. There was no conscious effort early on to frame the initiatives that were taking place on the district. The practices emerged gradually in response to issues raised by the local communities. Later, when efforts were made to summarize all the actions in the awards applications, the innovation was framed as "Collaborative Stewardship." Language was used that catered to the awards criteria—it invoked efficiency gains, litigation avoided, and the meeting of customer needs. When Collaborative Stewardship was recognized with the Gore and Harvard/Ford innovation awards, the innovations were framed as a success, and this helped provide additional motivation for continued implementation on the district, until infighting and jealousy undermined the effort.

Legitimacy New practices can enhance the legitimacy of an organization, thereby leading to the adoption or continued use of that practice. In the case of the Camino Real, legitimacy worked at cross purposes. Collaborating with the community was perceived as legitimate within the Camino Real and by those external to the agency. But getting too close to the community was not considered legitimate by those within the Carson National Forest, especially if it drove an employee to break the law. Dumas saw it as a necessity to build relationships, but others within the agency felt that he was getting too close to the community, and this compromised his professional standing.

Collaborative Stewardship was recognized as legitimate because the approach embodied many of the public management practices that were being touted at the time. The Gore/Hammer Award was presented to teams of federal employees who were thought to have made a significant contribution in support of reinventing government principles. The Harvard/Ford award sought to recognize and promote excellence and creativity in the public sector. Both awards enhanced the legitimacy of what the Camino Real was doing and provided Dumas a measure of political protection from his forest supervisor, who was unsupportive of him and his efforts. The awards also provided legitimacy to those who were engaged in Collaborative Stewardship. Acknowledgment from the outside world of what they were doing made them proud and, for at least a while, provided additional incentive to continue to engage in Collaborative Stewardship practices.

Community outreach was the key to Collaborative Stewardship. The Camino Real could not be responsive to community needs unless the district was engaged in an active dialogue with them. Dumas's close relationship with the community made those in the USFS think of him as a collaborator in the worse sense. In this way Collaborative Stewardship delegitimized the district within the eyes of the broader organization. When Dumas gained a sense that what he was doing was no longer considered legitimate by his superiors and within the district, he put in for a transfer. He was two years away from retirement, and his wife was keen to move.

SUMMARY

The summary from the analytical framework in table 5.2 illustrates the importance of individual, structural, and cultural factors in the emergence and then decline of Collaborative Stewardship on the Camino Real. The misalignment of these characteristics provides some explanatory power for both the early stages when the innovation was successful and the later stages when it unraveled.

Motivation was clearly important, but motivation was disproportionately dependent on Dumas. While Córdova and Dumas were motivated to see change on the ground in the district, only Dumas could carry out the change. Without Dumas to motivate for continued change and fight, navigate, or disarm the bureaucracy, Collaborative Stewardship became susceptible to the inertial forces of the status quo within the USFS. Córdova was clearly motivated to continue advocating for change, but he was not free to carry out reforms or innovative practices on his own. He needed someone with authority within the district to be equally motivated for change.

Individuals were influenced in their support of Collaborative Stewardship by prevailing norms and congruence with the dominant values within the USFS. Collaboration with the community became the norm for about five years, from 1990 through 1996. After this time, jealousy, envy, and distrust weakened relationships on the district and with the community. When accord on the district was undermined, then Collaborative Stewardship was less well supported as an innovated practice. The dominant culture of the USFS was not accommodating to Dumas's collaboration with the community, especially when it led to Dumas siding with the community during the Mexican spotted owl injunction in 1996. When Dumas no longer felt supported by those on his district or by his superiors, his enthusiasm for continuing was dampened, and he put in for a transfer.

Collaborative Stewardship suffered from many structural challenges. It was dependent on Dumas to keep communication flowing. The innovation was not codified until 1996. Even then it lacked support from forest administrators beyond the

Table 5.2: A Framework for Analyzing Forest Management Innovation on the Camino Real Ranger District

Individuals	Structures	Culture
Motivation: Max Córdova and Crockett Dumas were highly motivated to try something new on the Camino Real in response to existing gridlock. Initial success on small projects sustained motivation. Camino Real staff were inclined to continue because of job satisfaction and being liked in the community. Motivation was dependent on Dumas. Subsequent district rangers were not eager to work with the community.	*Rules and communication:* Administrative rules were not clear. The policy was ad hoc in its early years. Collaborative Stewardship was not cataloged until several years into the practice. Communication was clear but dependent upon Dumas, who knew the policy and was motivated to practice it. Without more substantial codification and institutional support at the forest level, Collaborative Stewardship was susceptible to decline upon Dumas's departure.	*Shocks:* There were no shocks in the Camino Real case study. Collaborative Stewardship emerged gradually in reaction to Dumas's realization that he would have to have the support of communities to manage land on the district.
Norms and Harmony: Collaboration was not customary on the district or in the forest. The transition to a more collaborative and community-oriented norm was gradual. These norms were supported until jealousy and envy undermined harmony on the district.	*Incentives:* Friendship, camaraderie, and job satisfaction were the primary incentives used to encourage participation in Collaborative Stewardship. Acknowledgment and greater	*Framing:* Efforts were not made to intentionally frame the innovations that were taking place early on. When the awards applications were written, the effort became known as Collaborative Stewardship and framed to bring attention to the suite of activities that had been taking place. *Legitimacy:* Legitimacy worked both to support and undermine Collaborative Stewardship. The awards enhanced the legitimacy of the

Congruence: USFS culture tends to be insular, not outward oriented. Dumas defied the more dominant culture by going against the injunction and serving the community. Dumas put in for a transfer after he felt he lost the support of the agency. District rangers who followed Dumas have not been risk takers.

recognition of effort by Dumas could have been used more strategically to encourage continued support. Many were promoted but moved out of the area. Financial inducements were hindered by USFS regulations and the forest supervisor.

Opening: Dumas opened the political structure on the Camino Real to participation from the communities. The political structure on the forest and at the regional levels remained closed to more innovative approaches.

Resistance: Historically there had been great tension with the USFS working with local communities. Many within the Carson National Forest were skeptical, uneasy, or unsupportive of Dumas's relationship with the community. Ultimately Dumas had to work within an agency structure that was opposed to his efforts. These forces prevailed after Dumas's departure.

innovations for the district. However, collaborative practices and Dumas's engagement with the community led those within the forest and region to view Collaborative Stewardship as illegitimate.

district. The primary incentives Dumas used to support the policy were satisfaction for a job well done and friendship on the district and with the communities. When district employees felt that they were not appropriately acknowledged or recognized for their efforts, Dumas was left with very few options for inducing continued support for Collaborative Stewardship. Lucero was a real challenge for Dumas. Dumas could have gotten Henry Lopez a promotion if Lucero had supported it, but Lucero felt Lopez, like Dumas, was too close to the community.

Through force of will Dumas opened the political structure on the Camino Real to allow communities to participate in creating alternatives for land management on the district. However, the culture of the USFS was powerful, and the history of enmity with communities on the forest was long. Dumas was unsupported by his forest supervisor for his efforts. Budgets, staff, bureaucracy, and incongruence with the broader USFS culture process all conspired against the continuation of Collaborative Stewardship.

Broader cultural factors do not significantly explain how Collaborative Stewardship faded over time. Their absence may provide some clues about what could have been done differently to provide more enduring change. No shocks were evident to induce change. Rather, change was gradual. Framing was not used to shape action or provide new problem definitions. Legitimacy worked both to support and to undermine the innovation simultaneously. Collaborative Stewardship was legitimized in the world external to the USFS but unsupported inside the forest.

Individual and structural factors appeared to provide a strong explanation as to why Collaborative Stewardship initially rose then fell. The innovation was inordinately dependent on a charismatic manager—Crockett Dumas. Dumas was highly motivated to change the status quo practices on the Camino Real. For a while he successfully harmonized the collaborative norm for his employees. His personal incongruence with the broader agency culture eventually gave way to disharmony for him and his employees. Without Dumas's force of personality to sustain the practices, the innovation withered over time.

From a structural perspective, rules were not codified. Communication was principally oral and was dependent on Dumas. Incentives included satisfaction, respect, and friendship. Financial inducements were difficult to structure due to USFS regulations that tied promotion to transfer and a forest supervisor who was opposed to Dumas's and his protégé's efforts. Dumas pried open the political structure on his district. This structure once again closed upon his departure, in part due to staunch resistance on the forest to collaborative, community-based practices.

Cultural characteristics might have been leveraged more effectively had Dumas been more aware of their significance. Framing could have been used to package and promote more widely what was being done and its significance. The legitimacy of the effort could have been leveraged more effectively outside the Carson National Forest to bring greater recognition to the forest and the region. Shocks do not seem to provide much explanatory power. On the whole, individual, structural, and cultural factors are insufficiently leveraged. This case illustrates how these factors, when misaligned, contribute to the demise of an innovation.

NOTES

1. Trust for Public Land, n.d., www.conservationalmanac.org/forests/map.html (accessed March 2, 2009).

2. Mark Baker and Jonathan Kusel, *Community Forestry in the United States: Learning from the Past, Crafting the Future* (Covelo, CA: Island, 2003), 10.

3. "Hispano" is a colloquial term used by the participants in this research to refer to themselves. The more conventional reference is "Hispanic." I wished to remain true to how the interviewees saw themselves and have thus retained the use of Hispano throughout this chapter.

4. William Hurst, "Evolution of Forest Service Policy for Managing the National Forest Land in Northern New Mexico," paper presented before R-3 Forest Officers at a Northern New Mexico Policy Discussion Forum, March 28, 2001; and William Hurst, "Region 3 Policy on Managing National Forest Land in Northern New Mexico," memo, March 6, 1972.

5. Toddi Steelman and Donna W. Tucker, "The Camino Real: To Care for the Land and Serve the People," in *Adaptive Governance: Integrating Science, Policy and Decision Making*, ed. R. Brunner, T. Steelman, L. Coe-Juell, C. Cromley, C. Edwards, D. Tucker (New York: Columbia University Press, 2005), 91–130.

6. Pat Jackson, in-person interview with Donna Tucker, Albuquerque, NM, October 3, 2001.

7. The original grant of land totaled 314,000 acres of land. The U.S. government recognized 21,000 acres, of which 7,000 were privately owned lands. Consequently, 14,000 acres of land were deeded as the Truchas Land Grant. Max Córdova, in-person interview with Toddi Steelman and Donna Tucker, Truchas, NM, May 21, 2001.

8. Steve Marshall, "Application for Innovations in American Government 1998 Awards Program Semi-Finalist Application/Application #379, Northern New Mexico Collaborative Stewardship Program" (USDA-Forest Service Cooperative Forestry, April 28, 1998).

9. Carveth Kramer, in-person interview with Toddi Steelman and Donna Tucker, Taos, NM, May 26, 2001.

10. Crockett Dumas, telephone interview with Toddi Steelman, October 7, 2008.

11. Córdova, interview.

12. Marshall, "Application for Innovations in American Government 1998."

13. Crockett Dumas, Boulder, CO, December 2–3, 2001.

14. Crockett Dumas, e-mail exchange, November 26, 2001.

15. Córdova, interview.

16. Ibid.

17. Kramer, interview.

18. *Vigas* are cross beams used in the construction of adobe houses, and *latillas* are posts used to support roof structures and in the construction of fences. Vigas and latillas are needed for new homes or to sell to others.

19. Steelman and Tucker, "Camino Real."

20. Córdova, interview.

21. Dumas, interview, 2008.

22. Córdova, interview.

23. Kramer, interview.

24. Ibid.

25. Zoe Miller, "The Northern New Mexico Collaborative Stewardship Program: Fitting an Agency-Led Initiative into the Model of Collaborative Government," term project for Governance and Natural Resources, a seminar at the University of Colorado at Boulder, December 1999.

26. Marshall, "Application for Innovations in American Government 1998."

27. Dumas, interview, October 21, 2008.

28. Mark Schiller, in-person interview with Toddi Steelman and Donna Tucker, Chamisal, NM, May 22, 2001.

29. Crockett Dumas, telephone interview with Toddi Steelman, October 21, 2008.

30. Ibid.

31. Keith Easthouse, "U.S. Agency Wants 4.8 Million Acres for Owl Habitat," *Santa Fe New Mexican*, December 1, 1994, B1.

32. Mike Taugher, "Judge Bars Federal Forest Logging," *Albuquerque Journal*, August 25, 1995, A1.

33. Mike Taugher, "Scientist: Logging Ban Poses Fire Risk," *Albuquerque Journal*, August 30, 1995, A1.

34. Keith Easthouse, "U.S. Agency Wants 4.8 Million Acres."

35. George Johnson, "In New Mexico an Order on Elusive Owl Leaves Residents Angry, Cold," *New York Times*, November 26, 1995, A16.

36. Córdova, interview.

37. Keith Easthouse, "Judge Lifts Ban on Southwest Logging. Loggers Are Relieved, but Environmentalists Vow to Continue Fight against Cutting in Old Growth Forests," *Santa Fe New Mexican*, Dec. 5, 1996, A1.

38. Schiller, interview.

39. Kramer, interview.

40. Dumas, interview, October 21, 2008.

41. Dumas, interview, 2001.

42. Dumas, interview, October 21, 2008.

43. Ibid.

44. Kramer, interview.

45. Luis Torres-Horton, in-person interview with Donna Tucker, Espanola, NM, September 28, 2001.

46. Henry Lopez, in-person interview with Toddi Steelman and Donna Tucker, Penasco, NM, May 21, 2001.

47. Marshall, "Application for Innovations in American Government 1998," 6.

48. Dumas, interview, 2001.

49. Ernest Atencio, *Of Land and Culture: Environmental Justice and Public Lands Ranching in Northern New Mexico*, report by The Quivera Coalition and the Santa Fe Group of the Sierra Club, January 2001.

50. Camino Real Ranger District, "Existing and Desired Conditions and How To Get There—East Entrañas," on file with author, July 13, 1996.

51. Lopez, interview.

52. Marshall, "Application for Innovations in American Government 1998."

53. Córdova, interview.

54. Mark Schiller, "Santa Barbara Rehabilitation Project: Show Us the Work," *La Jicarita News* 7 (March 2002), www.lajicarita.org/02mar.htm#santabarbara (accessed May 4, 2008).

55. Steve Miranda, transcript from "Collaborative Stewardship at Work" conference, Taos, NM, April 27–28, 2001, sponsored by Carson National Forest and Camino Real Ranger District. On file with author.

56. Schiller, "Santa Barbara Rehabilitation Project."

57. Out of the total pool of applicants, one hundred semifinalists are selected in the spring, and twenty-five finalists are announced in the early fall, each of which is eligible for $20,000. The ten winners of the Innovations in American Government Awards are selected by the National Selection Committee, and each receives an additional $80,000.

58. "Northern New Mexico Collaborative Stewardship Wins Innovations in American Government Award," *La Jicarita News* 3, no. 10 (November 1998).

59. Córdova, interview.

60. Ibid.

61. Kay Mathews, in-person interview with Toddi Steelman and Donna Tucker, Chamisal, NM, May 22, 2001.

62. Córdova, interview.

63. Dumas, interview, 2008.

64. Ibid.

65. Kirt Winchester, in-person interview with Donna Tucker, El Rito Ranger District, NM, October 2, 2001.

66. Dumas, interview, 2001.

67. Lopez, interview.

68. Córdova, interview.

69. Dumas, interview, October 21, 2008.

70. Greg Gunderson, "Distribution of Timber Sales on Northern New Mexico National Forests 1992–1999," SCFRC Working Paper 4, Forest Trust, Santa Fe, NM (November 2001).

71. Ibid.

72. Marshall, "Application for Innovations in American Government 1998."

73. Mark Schiller and Kay Mathews, "Collaborative Stewardship on the Carson National Forest: Where We've Been and How Far We Have to Go," *La Jicarita News*, 4, no. 11, December 1999.

74. Lopez, 2001.

75. Mark Schiller and Kay Mathews, "New Southwest Regional Forster Mets with Community People and Local Forest Service Personnel in Truchas," *La Jicarita News* 7 (November 2002), www.lajicarita.org/02nov.htm#regionalforester (accessed May 4, 2008).

76. Córdova, interview.

77. Ibid.

78. Ibid.

79. Kay Matthews, "Editorial: Collaborative Stewardship—Where Do We Go from Here?" *La Jicarita News* 6, no. 5 (May/June 2001); "Collaborative Stewardship At Work: A Two-Day "Unconference," April 27–28, 2001, at the Kachina Inn, Taos, New Mexico, *La Jicarita News* 6, no. 3 (March 2001).

80. Córdova, interview.

81. Ibid.

82. Schiller, interview.

83. Kay Mathew and Mark Schiller, "Local Concerns Slipping through Cracks as Forest Service Becomes More and More Centralized," *La Jicarita News* 10, no. 7 (August 2005).

84. Mark Schiller, "Camino Real Gets New District Ranger," *La Jicarita News* 11, no. 4 (April 2006).

85. Dumas, e-mails, September 3 and November 11, 2002.

86. Kay Mathews, "Book Review: Adaptive Governance: Integrating Science, Policy and Decision Making," *La Jicarita News* 10, no. 9 (October 2005).

87. Mark Schiller, telephone interview, May 14, 2008.

88. "Interview with Antonio 'Ike' DeVargas, Ten Years Later," *La Jicarita News* 10 (December 2005).

89. Dumas, interview, 2001.

90. Marshall, "Application for Innovations in American Government 1998."

91. John W. Kingdon, *Agendas, Alternatives and Public Policies*, 2nd ed. (New York: Longman, 1995); Nancy C. Roberts and Paula J. King, "Policy Entrepreneurs: Their Activity, Structure and Function in the Policy Process," *Journal of Public Administration Research and Theory*, 1, no. 2 (1991): 147–75; Frank R. Baumgartner and Bryan D. Jones, *Agendas and Instability in American Politics* (Chicago: University of Chicago Press, 1993); Michael Mintrom, "Policy Entrepreneurs and the Diffusion of Innovation," *American Journal of Political Sciences*, 41, no. 3 (1997): 738–70; and Michael Mintrom and Sandra Vergari, "Policy Networks and Innovation Diffusion," 1998, 30.

92. Schiller, interview, 2008.

93. Marshall, "Application for Innovations in American Government 1998."

94. Ibid.

95. Hurst, "Evolution of Forest Service Policy"; and Hurst, "Region 3 Policy."

96. Ernest Atencio, *La Vida Floresta: Environmental Justice Meets Traditional Forestry in Northern New Mexico* (Santa Fe Chapter of Sierra Club, 2001), 34.

97. Ike DeVargas, in-person interview with Toddi Steelman and Donna Tucker, Espanola, NM, May 26, 2001.

98. Córdova, interview.

99. Thomas A. Koelble, "The New Institutionalism in Political Science and Sociology," *Comparative Politics* 27 (1995): 231–44.

CHAPTER 6

Fostering Enduring Change

THIS BOOK BEGAN WITH A SIMPLE QUESTION: Why are some innovations implemented, while others are not? The conventional framing of innovation places great weight on the role of the individual. Based on the evidence presented in this book, this emphasis is misplaced. Individuals are clearly important in the innovation process, but there also are limits on what individuals can do within the broader structural and cultural institutional context. Innovative practices are embedded in larger institutional processes that affect effectiveness of innovations, especially during the periods of implementation. Implementing innovation is simply more challenging than conventionally understood. This finding is significant on both theoretical and practical levels. From a theoretical standpoint, innovation often is addressed at the operational level without regard to the broader institutional context in which it is nested. This leads to innovation being treated as a technical phenomenon, abstracted from the conditions that influence implementation. These theoretical assumptions permeate the beliefs of those who practice innovation at the operational level and those who seek to foster innovation at the collective or constitutive level. A more realistic theoretical understanding of the conditions that engender success and failure in the implementation of innovation can contribute to more sound practice.

From a practical perspective, scarce resources are vested in innovative practices. As a society we need to be judicious in how these resources are allocated. Public managers, nonprofit organizations, and foundations invest in new practices. Understanding the conditions that foster a greater chance for implementation success over time is essential for actually improving society at large. Otherwise we are left with a heap of innovative practices that may have showed promise but did not realize their potential. Additionally, when innovation is ineffective, it contributes to innovation fatigue. As innovative practices are devalued through misapplication or misguided use, practitioners and policymakers lose important tools from their already meager policy tool kits. Clearer understanding of the conditions under which innovation stands the best chance of longer-term implementation can help us better prioritize scarce resources and use innovation more wisely.

Many theories suggest how issues come onto the agenda or how policy is changed or how institutions persist over time. Bringing these theories together and leveraging their collective power provides a more comprehensive understanding for how innovation is implemented. No single theory fully captures the dynamics of all three case studies. But collectively the integrated theory provides a more robust framework for understanding the complex dynamics of implementing innovation and how we might better understand these processes to foster more effective social and environmental outcomes in the future.

Chapter 1 laid out factors associated with the implementation of innovation. These conditions are revisited here and presented in table 6.1 to illustrate how each case study met these conditions and what the patterns across the case studies reveal about the potential for facilitating enduring change through innovative practice.

GREAT OUTDOORS COLORADO

Whether consciously or not, GOCO founders and managers dealt positively with many of the implementation factors at the individual, structural, and cultural levels. In this case study, all the factors aligned to mutually support the innovation. The mission of GOCO was to help the people of Colorado "preserve, protect, enhance, appreciate, and enjoy our parks, wildlife, trails, rivers and open space through strategic grants, partnership and leadership."[1] As a quasi-governmental agency formed through the initiative process, GOCO had a dedicated funding source and little oversight from the General Assembly of Colorado. Its mandate was to help cities, towns, counties, nonprofits, special districts, and statewide organizations with land protection. The agency provided direction to local land protection efforts through grant guidelines, but ultimately it was dependent upon local governments and organizations to take action if land protection was to occur. The competitive grants process demonstrated how local, state, and federal agencies and organizations could work together to create a more effective and innovative solution for protecting land.

Culture

From a cultural perspective, individuals are embedded in routines and tend to subscribe to certain frames of meaning that guide their action. To move from an embedded routine, cultural institutionalists see framing events or shocks as op-

Table 6.1: Summary of Individual, Structural, and Cultural Characteristics in Case Studies

Individual	Structure	Culture
Great Outdoors Colorado		
• Highly motivated group • Norms/harmony not an issue because new group • Congruence not an issue because no dominant agency/culture	• Clear rules and communication • Financial incentives support innovative practices • One political structure; political structure opened through initiative process • General Assembly of Colorado, Div. of Parks/Rec, Div. of Wildlife resistant; GOCO tries to mitigate	• Shocks not applicable • Skillful framing motivated voters, elites • Market-based innovation that did not regulate property was legitimate in Colorado's culture
Friends of the Cheat/River of Promise		
• Highly motivated group, driven by the executive director • Norms of collaboration uphold harmony among stakeholders; some individuals defect when norms conflict • Congruence not an issue because no dominant agency/culture	• Rules/communication clear while ex. dir. engaged • Technical, financial incentives supplemented by friendship and project satisfaction to support innovation • Multiple political structures; some open/closed at different times. Strategically work with those most accessible at any given time • Resistance from WVAML and USACOE. Makes remediation more difficult	• Mine disaster provided catalyst for Friends of the Cheat formation; second disaster maintained focus • Mission framed to be inclusive, not demonize mining industry • Collaborative, voluntary approach and participation by coal industry legitimized group
Collaborative Stewardship on the Camino Real		
• Motivated individual. Once Dumas leaves no one has authority to sustain change • Collaborative norms supported within district, not supported by Carson National Forest. Jealousy, envy undermines harmony among individuals on district and in community • District values incongruent with dominant values within the forest. Creates tension for individuals on district to continue innovative practice	• Rules not clear; communication clear but dependent on Dumas • Camaraderie, job satisfaction are primary incentives to support innovation. Acknowledgment, recognition could have been better used. Financial incentives limited • Multiple political structures. Depended on Dumas to open District to innovation. Forest remained closed • Resistance from other districts, forest undermines efforts in the longer term	• Shocks not applicable • Framing not used intentionally. Innovation framed as "Collaborative Stewardship" when applying for awards • Collaboration legitimizes group with external award agencies; collaboration delegitimizes with other districts, forest

portunities for fostering change.[2] New practices can enhance the legitimacy of an organization, thereby providing incentives to undertake innovation.[3] In the GOCO case study, framing and legitimacy were more important than shocks in setting the stage for GOCO to emerge and thrive. There was no clear catalytic event to create a focal opportunity for new action or alternatives. Rather, skillful framing on behalf of the policy entrepreneurs who drove the GOCO initiative process effectively created momentum for collective action. The initiative was framed as an opportunity to rectify the decision by the General Assembly to divert funds away from open space protection. The Citizens for GOCO entrepreneurs allowed the public to believe that change was not only possible but also desirable, through the initiative process. After the formation and implementation of GOCO, framing efforts focused on what the public had gained in the form of open space protection. GOCO was perceived as a legitimate alternative to the land use problem in Colorado because it embraced a market model that fit in well with Republican and Democratic politics alike. The ability to fit within these broader cultural expectations enhanced GOCO's legitimacy as an organization, thereby sustaining it over time.

Structures

Historical institutionalists propose that political structures may not be open to change due to power relationships in existing arenas of action, and active resistance can be expected from those with power. If political structures can be opened and resistance effectively addressed, then innovation may stand a better chance of being implemented.[4] Ensuring clarity in communication and rules, while also providing incentives for desired behavior, is an additional structural factor that facilitates implementation.[5] Citizens for GOCO was constrained by the legislature in terms of open space protection in the state. With this particular political structure closed, Citizens for GOCO sought an opening through another venue—the initiative process. With the passage of the initiative, GOCO was enshrined in Colorado's constitution. Change at the constitutive and collective level is more difficult and less likely to be altered in the future than change at the operational level.[6] This meant that GOCO moved to a higher order of political opening, unlike the other innovations discussed in this book. This more permanent level of political opening protected GOCO from encroachment from other bureaucratic agencies and from being raided by the General Assembly in times of fiscal insecurity. To mitigate resistance from the General Assembly, Citizens for GOCO addressed the legislature's concerns about losing its capital construction moneys. GOCO proposed a phased transition period during the move to the full delegation of funds for open space protection, thus allowing the legislature to pay off existing obligations and providing time to create new alternatives for future capital construction projects. GOCO continued to anticipate resistance from the General Assembly by actively monitoring what happened in the legislature, employing lobbyists, and promoting to legislators what GOCO was doing in their respective counties and districts. Resistance from the Division of Parks and Recreation, as well as the Division of Wildlife, was mitigated initially with the promise of funding for their programs. GOCO experienced continued resistance from the divisions of Wildlife and Parks and Recreation at different times over GOCO's history. The level of resistance to GOCO's mission was contingent on administrative leadership within the respective agencies. As of 2009, the Division of Parks and Recreation was more resistant than the Division of Wildlife. Historically, the reverse was true. GOCO continues to use the incentive of money to encourage cultural change within the Division of Parks and Recreation. The small size of GOCO minimized potential distortion of the rules through layers of bureaucracy. Likewise, day-to-day communication about rules, program, and expectations was straightforward and clear. Incentives were effective in catalyzing behavior at the local level to encourage greater activity for land protection around the state. Incentives continued to be used to overcome resistance and encourage structural changes within the divisions of Parks and Recreation and Wildlife.

Individuals

Individuals are the primary drivers in change processes in rational choice institutionalism. This school of thought suggests that new institutions can be intentionally created by individuals to achieve solutions to collective-action problems.[7] The creation of GOCO fits this theoretical vision well. Highly motivated individuals engineered a new institution that met their needs better than the status quo. GOCO emerged out of discontent with the solution provided by the General Assembly. Key participants in the process, including Citizens for GOCO, the Colorado business community, the divisions of Wildlife and Parks and Recreation, and voters, could see they would be left better off with GOCO than with the continued loss of open space. For the Citizens for GOCO and the current GOCO staff, innovation was and continues to be an option because the benefits of effecting change clearly outweigh the costs of not doing so.

Individuals also are highlighted in public management and policy studies as the primary drivers of innovative efforts.[8] No one individual stands out as the primary policy entrepreneur or manager of the innovation that became GOCO. Different individuals played key roles at different times during the emergence and implementation of the innovation. With a diversified leadership base, multiple people were motivated to keep GOCO moving forward. The redundancy in leadership served GOCO well. GOCO's diversified leadership base meant that individuals could take responsibility for specialized actions to keep the initiative moving forward. Floyd Ciruli was responsible for polling, Ken Salazar consolidated support in the business community, and others worked on media message. These leaders worked in both directive and supportive roles at different times in the life of the innovation. Entrepreneurial leadership was important, but single, individual leaders did not lead the charge at all times. GOCO has had strong, active boards that buttress their executive directors. This finding supports, as well as challenges, some of the literature that focuses on the primacy of the individual. Individuals clearly were important, but GOCO illustrates a group model of entrepreneurism rather than a singular, hero model of entrepreneurism and management.

GOCO was a new program, so it avoided many of the challenges associated with integrating into an existing institutional culture. Congruence in patterns and behaviors and fitting in with existing norms were not problematic because the agency was created anew. As a new agency, GOCO was afforded the opportunity for a de novo approach to establishing norms among individuals working within the agency as well as creating agencywide values.

FRIENDS OF THE CHEAT AND THE RIVER OF PROMISE

Friends of the Cheat and the River of Promise agreement illustrates the intermittent alignment of individual, structural, and cultural factors. This pattern partially clarifies why the group experienced irregular implementation over time. Intermittent alignment of individual and structural factors in particular explains the success the group had at times and the lack of success at other times.

Individual factors affected implementation, notably the lack of an executive director who could motivate action. Likewise, structural factors including political openings and norms and harmony affected the ability to get work done in some places. When all the factors are aligned and mutually supportive, then the prospect of implementing innovation stands the greatest opportunity for success. However, all of these factors and their subcategories are moving targets. When individual, structural, or cultural factors are askew, then the implementation of the innovation faces challenges. Friends of the Cheat demonstrated how these challenges disrupted implementation at times and how the group persisted over time in spite of these challenges.

Individuals

Individuals who are free to devise alternative possible solutions can be motivated to alter the status quo. Friends of the Cheat was started by a group of highly motivated individuals who were committed to "restoring, promoting and protecting the outstanding qualities of the Cheat watershed," as laid out in their mission statement. One person, Dave Bassage, stood out as a charismatic and entrepreneurial leader. River of Promise, the voluntary, written agreement to address the persistent acid mine drainage (AMD) problems in the watershed, was a stakeholder-driven collaborative approach that was dependent upon the actions of numerous entities to function effectively. Rational choice institutionalism suggests that freely contracting individuals can alter the status quo.[9] While the GOCO example fit this model well, Friends of the Cheat/River of Promise does not provide as clean a fit. Individuals created a new group, Friends of the Cheat, and an innovative voluntary agreement, River of Promise, but these innovations had to fit with existing agencies and organizations to make change feasible in the watershed. Friends of the Cheat members were not completely free to change because they had to negotiate the broader federal and state regulatory infrastructure that influenced mining reclamation and water quality. Friends of the Cheat and River of Promise did not control the rules or laws or resources, but they did create norms for their own collaboration in the watershed. GOCO could create its own path because it was a new agency with constitutional authority. Friends of the Cheat did not have this luxury.

The policy entrepreneurship literature often focuses on a single individual who fosters change.[10] The entrepreneurial model of leadership fits the Friends of the Cheat/River of Promise model well, and it also illustrates its flaws. Dave Bassage, as the original executive director, and Keith Pitzer, the second executive director, both provided strong, directive leadership. While the board of directors and other key players provided essential supportive roles, the day-to-day and longer-term effectiveness of the group and the River of Promise agreement rested with the executive director. The vulnerability of this approach was revealed when Friends of the Cheat lost its executive director in 2000 and the group nearly collapsed. The board of directors was able to maintain some degree of continuity until a new executive director was found in late 2001. This model of leadership differs from the GOCO case study. Leadership and motivation for change was sustained by multiple leaders at different points in time in the GOCO case study. This stands in stark contrast to the Friends of the Cheat and Camino Real/Collaborative Stewardship case studies, which were inordinately dependent on single individuals.

In the Friends of the Cheat/River of Promise case study, the individual factors of norms and harmony interacted with openings under the structural factors. Friends of the Cheat/River of Promise had to negotiate the complex web of agencies and organizations that affected the persistent pollution of the watershed. Friends of the Cheat/River of Promise adapted to these situations as appropriate so as to channel their energy and resources at the levels and within the agencies that would be most responsive and productive. In contrast to GOCO, which pried open the political opportunity structure, Friends of the Cheat had to continuously negotiate openings and closings. Historical institutionalism suggests that when the political structure is open, more marginalized groups have an opportunity to foster change.[11] Friends of the Cheat/River of Promise had to work with many different political structures at the local, state, and federal levels. Some of these structures were open and then closed at other times, depending on the administrative or political leadership. When the administrative or political leadership was not conducive to participation in a community-based collaborative restoration initiative, then this created tensions for the individuals who participated in River of Promise. Some individuals defected from participating in River of Promise when it created disharmony for them in their home agencies.

Structure

Top-down implementation theory proposes that rules, communication, and incentives can be used strategically to induce compliance with desired behavior.[12] Rules and communication within Friends of the Cheat/River of Promise were clear and facilitated implementation of innovative practice, as predicted by theory. Incentives were used in the Friends of the Cheat/River of Promise case but not as conventionally understood in the institutional or implementation literature. In contrast, GOCO followed a more deliberate model using financial incentives to achieve an explicit, desired response.

There was no single individual in charge who used incentives deliberately to achieve a specific goal. Rather, a coincidental confluence of incentives was made available by a critical mass of participants and used opportunistically by Friends of the Cheat/River of Promise to achieve their goals. River of Promise is a collaborative effort. The executive director of Friends of the Cheat provided a leadership role that was limited mostly to facilitating action among the rest of River of Promise group. Collective incentives were not directed at individual participants but motivated the group to stay together and involved. In this regard, incentives to participate extended beyond financial and technical resources, which are often considered the most common inducements used to alter a cost-benefit behavioral calculus. Respect, friendship, and a shared sense of accomplishment provided powerful incentives to encourage the group to work together over time.

Historical institutionalism sensitizes us to look for larger power dynamics and vested interests that may resist change.[13] The West Virginia Abandoned Mine Lands Program (WVAML) and the U.S. Army Corps of Engineers (USACOE) provided the best examples of how vested interests and power dynamics can create resistance to new practices. While WVAML and USACOE did not outright oppose Friends of the Cheat/River of Promise efforts, they made Friends of the Cheat/River of Promise work in the watershed much more difficult and less productive than it could have been with their assistance. WVAML was resistant to looking at water quality issues due to its own historical mining reclamation practice or to take input from watershed group. USACOE was resistant to finding ways to engage with a community-based, collaborative effort.

Culture

In terms of cultural factors, Friends of the Cheat provided a textbook example of how a shock or focusing event can provide a catalyst for action.[14] The T&T mine blowout created the impetus for the formation of the Friends of the Cheat. After the blowout, framing was used to consolidate and channel interests constructively. A second blowout helped maintain focus on key issues that had been initiated by the group. Framing an issue appropriately can condition people to take action.[15] Much as with GOCO, framing was used in Friends of the Cheat/River of Promise to motivate and engage participants. Friends of the Cheat framed the problem to focus less on making people feel as if they had lost something and more on how they could gain a clean watershed. Friends of the Cheat/River of Promise built a big tent under which all interests, even the coal industry, could participate. This same framing facilitated legitimacy of the group. Sociological institutionalists propose that organizations will adopt an approach because it enhances the social legitimacy of the organization to outsiders.[16] Restoration of the watershed and a proactive, voluntary collaborative approach were pragmatic responses to a complex problem. They also had the by-product of enhancing the legitimacy of the group. The group was viewed as a legitimate solution both locally and from the perspective of participant agencies and other funding organizations. Importantly, this approach also undermined the group's legitimacy with some of the environmental groups in West Virginia who saw Friends of the Cheat as collaborating with the enemy—the coal industry.

CAMINO REAL RANGER DISTRICT AND COLLABORATIVE STEWARDSHIP

Collaborative Stewardship on the Camino Real Ranger District illustrates the misalignment of individual, structural, and cultural factors. This pattern partially explains the failure of Collaborative Stewardship to thrive over time. Individual and structural factors best explain why the innovation failed over time. The innovation was driven primarily by Crockett Dumas, the district ranger. Once he left, no one was as motivated or had the authority to carry out change. Dumas was able to effect change, but this happened on his district. This left the innovation vulnerable to resistance at the forest level, which eventually created disharmony and incongruence for many of the agency employees engaged in the innovation. Once Dumas left, no one was willing to keep the political structure open to the community, and the innovation slowly fell apart.

Individuals

Rational choice theorists suggest that innovation rests on discontented individuals who are free to devise alternative possible solutions.[17] Dumas was clearly discontented with the status quo situation on the Camino Real. Others were motivated for change, both on the district and within the communities. But Dumas was the only person involved in Collaborative Stewardship with the authority to freely devise an alternative. Since land management fell under the power of the USFS, no one from outside the agency was in a position to foster meaningful change. Innovation would have to be motivated by someone within the agency. As district ranger, Dumas had the authority to devise a new management plan and change policy. Other individuals within the district, notably Max Córdova, had enormous motivation for change. But in this case, motivation needed to be accompanied by the authority to carry out the innovation. This challenges the notion of rational choice institutionalists that anyone can implement change. Without the authoritative support within the broader political structure, grassroots efforts may fail to take root and thrive.

The factors of norms, harmony, and congruence help explain why some individuals were unable to support Collaborative Stewardship over time. A new collaborative norm emerged within the district from 1990 to 1998. Initially, to preserve social harmony on the district, the district employees needed to embrace the collaborative ideal. In Dumas's terms, they needed to get on the bus. However, jealousy, infighting, and envy following the national awards had a corrosive influence within the district and within the community. Once the harmony within the workplace was disrupted, the individuals were less supportive of the innovations. Lack of congruence between the prevailing values with the Carson National Forest and the values that were being pursued on the Camino Real also created difficulties for those who were implementing the innovative policies. Congruence is a more dominant explanatory factor in the Camino Real case study than in GOCO or Friends of the Cheat. A prevailing forestwide culture inhibited innovation at the individual level. A decades-long history of hostility in the region between the USFS and local communities, as well as a Carson National Forest culture that was unsupportive of collaborative norms, led to incongruence for those at the district level who participated in Collaborative Stewardship. These differences were rendered most explicit in 1996 after Dumas violated the timber-cutting injunction. At that time, Dumas served the communities but catalyzed greater opposition to what he was doing within the forest. Some within the agency considered Dumas's actions heresy. These forces eroded the individual motivation for Collaborative Stewardship over time. They also made it difficult for the rangers who followed Dumas to engage in community-based, collaborative activity. Once Dumas felt he had lost the support for his efforts, he left, and the individual motivation for continuing to pursue Collaborative Stewardship declined. Subsequent district rangers did not share Dumas's collaborative ideal or need to reach out to the community.

Structure

Structural factors also provide some explanatory power in clarifying why Collaborative Stewardship did not persist. Top-down implementation theory holds that clear rules and communication will facilitate compliance with innovative practices over time.[18] Collaborative Stewardship was not codified until several years into its practice. Even then, it was written down in the form of an amendment to a plan and award applications. This meant the formal and informal rules were difficult to pass on once Dumas had left. Lack of support for the effort by the forest supervisor left the innovations vulnerable to change or lack of enforcement under a new district ranger. Communication was clear under Dumas, but it was utterly dependent on him. In contrast to GOCO and Friends of the Cheat, Dumas used bilateral communication. Initial communication under horseback diplomacy leveraged many of the employees in the district, but Dumas was the node that connected everyone. The one-on-one outreach helped Dumas understand community concerns. This understanding generated trust among those on the district and community residents, which then facilitated implementation of the innovations in the region. The bilateral communication strategy employed by Dumas and others on the Camino Real was more vulnerable to personnel transfer than a strategy based on multilateral outreach. If the policy had rested on a more diverse set of people from the forest and district, then there might have been a broader collective memory for Collaborative Stewardship. Redundancy could have provided a degree of protection from transfers.

Much as with Friends of the Cheat, incentives were not used intentionally to channel behavior in a given direction. Rational choice institutionalists and top-down implementation theorists suggest that organizations can use incentives or resources to alter individual benefit-cost calculations to encourage innovation.[19] In this case study, incentives to induce compliant behavior did not match up with the vision provided by rational choice institutionalism or top-down implementation theory. Satisfaction from project completion, the ability to do one's job, friendship, respect, and camaraderie all induced compliance with innovative practices on the Camino Real. Financial incentives were not a driver. Some observers have commented that Dumas could have done a better job in acknowledging the work done by others, giving away more of the credit for the innovations, or rewarding those within his own district as additional ways to provide incentives for continuing the innovation. Dumas felt limited in his ability to offer promotions to his staff. USFS practices traditionally did not make promotions without transfer. The forest supervisor was unsupportive of promotions for Dumas's key workers.

Historical institutionalism recognizes that marginalized groups can foster change when the political opportunity structure is open to them. Dumas, through force of his personality and skill, opened the political opportunity structure for the local communities. Without him the communities would not have had access. In this way, motivation for change interacted with the openings for change. However, it was not enough to be motivated—Dumas needed the authority to open the political opportunity structure. Dumas only had the authority to open the political structure at the district level. The political opportunity structure at the forest level remained closed under his forest supervisor, Leonard Lucero. As Goodin theorizes, change is easier at the operational level than at the collective or constitutive level.[20] Dumas was able to effect change at the operational level within the district, but these changes were dependent on his continued presence. He was unable to change policy in a more meaningful way at the collective or the constitutive level within the forest or within the agency. Even though Dumas was able to open the political structure, it was only temporary because there was no mutual support from the forest. As Ostrom suggests, putting operational rules into place without putting into place complementary rules at the other levels results in an in incomplete system of support.[21] Additionally, the Carson National Forest culture was resistant to the notion of community collaboration. The USFS was predicated on a model by which the agency was the ultimate manager of the land. The community contested the claim to the land and asked for a say in how the land was managed. Dumas gave them a voice. In this manner, Dumas defied broader agency values, especially in this region where relationships had been not just hostile but violent. Historical institutionalism maintains that the inertia within existing institutions creates resistance to new practices.[22] While Dumas created some space for innovation to thrive, the force of agency tradition and inertia were too powerful to fight once Dumas was gone. An old Swedish proverb states that "the nail that sticks out gets hammered down." In this case, Collaborative Stewardship was the nail that stuck out within the broader value system of the USFS. It was hammered down after Dumas departed.

Culture

Cultural factors do not offer much explanatory power for the Camino Real case study. Had cultural factors been leveraged more effectively they might have played a role in buttressing the innovations on the district. Shocks were not present. There was no single, focusing event that catalyzed action. Dumas came to a gradual conclusion from the time of his arrival in 1990 to his realization that he would need the support of the community to do work on the district. The timber injunction and Dumas's violation of the injunction could be seen as shocks that catalyzed support within the agency against Dumas. Framing processes were not employed intentionally until the award applications, when the various innovations were grouped under the heading "Collaborative Stewardship." Perhaps framing could have been used more effectively within the agency to promote the innovations in a positive light. Collaborative Stewardship enhanced the legitimacy of the Camino Real with people external to the agency, like those associated with the Gore/Hammer Award and the Harvard/Ford Innovations Award. The USFS Washington office was aware of and supportive of Dumas's efforts, especially after the awards. However, Collaborative Stewardship undermined the legitimacy of the district with those inside the Carson National Forest. After Dumas violated the injunction, many within the agency felt that Dumas had gone too far and had been co-opted by the locals.

THEORETICAL INSIGHTS

When we conceive of innovation as implementation and not just coming up with a good idea, then that leads us to look at what factors might sustain and support innovation. The framework laid out in this book suggests three categories of factors—individual, structural, and cultural—that influence the implementation of innovation. These categories combine scholarship from neo-institutionalism, public management, policy studies, and implementation theory. No one category or school of thought dominates to explain how we might more effectively engage in implementing innovation. Rather, combinations of categories and factors suggest multiple paths for understanding some of the obstacles to and avenues for sounder implementation. Three schools of institutional theory—rational choice, historical, and cultural— propose different mechanisms for change. The case studies covered here indicate that no single theory is adequate.

GOCO adheres to the rational choice institutionalist model better than historical or cultural institutionalist models. It featured freely contracting individuals who changed the status quo, invented new alternatives, and created incentives consistent with change. In contrast, historical institutionalism provided a more complete explanation for the difficulties in the Camino Real case study. Inertia from existing institutions created resistance to new practices. Not all participants had equal access to change through the political opportunity structure. Larger power dynamics and vested interests blocked or obstructed the path of lasting innovation. The path dependence of old practices made innovation more difficult the longer the existing institutions had been in practice. Sociological institutionalism does not provide as full an explanation for one case study as rational choice or historical institutionalism, but it does provide explanatory power for aspects of the case studies. Shocks and frames helped explain how Friends of the Cheat and River of Promise were able to catalyze action for thinking about and devising new alternatives to the problem of AMD. Skillful framing was essential to the passage of the GOCO initiative. Lack of framing may have hurt Collaborative Stewardship. GOCO and Friends of the Cheat/River of Promise were seen as legitimate alternatives and enhanced the validity of the approaches within the broader cultures where they were situated. Collaborative Stewardship enhanced the social legitimacy of the Camino Real with the external world, but delegitimized it in the internal world of the Carson National Forest.

Aspects of public management and policy studies theory are also supported and refuted when applied to these case studies. The literature on policy entrepreneurism and New Public Management puts forth that managers need to actively innovate.[23] The emphasis on the individual manager suggests that these leadership "heroes" can motivate, enable, build capacity, control resources, and scour the environment to facilitate innovation.[24] But this perspective underestimates the influence that structure and culture can have on the potential for longer-term implementation.

Dumas provided the clearest example of the manager ideal envisioned in the public management literature—a strong entrepreneur willing to break rules to make government more efficient and effective.[25] Some have warned that this entrepreneurial ideal can lead to unanticipated outcomes where due process, equal access, and public participation are ignored or marginalized.[26] That was not the case in the Camino Real—the reverse was true. Dumas was a public land manager intent on caring for the land and serving the people. He had to fight his own agency to carry out his stewardship mandate.

Policy entrepreneurs played key roles in all three innovation processes. In contrast to what some in this literature indicate, policy entrepreneurs were diversified across time and tasks leading to more sustained efforts in GOCO. Friends of the Cheat and Collaborative Stewardship adhered to the hero entrepreneur model, but they also revealed the weaknesses of dependency on single leaders. Friends of the Cheat and River of Promise struggled during the times when they lacked an entrepreneur in the executive director position. Dependence on a single policy entrepreneur created vulnerability in the Camino Real case study.

Drawing from top-down implementation theory, clear rules and communication helped explain the success of GOCO and Friends of the Cheat/River of Promise as well as the failure of Camino Real. Likewise, bottom-up implementation theory sensitizes us to the importance of norms, harmony, and congruence in how street-level bureaucrats deal with social pressures and the implementation of innovation. Norms and harmony clearly led to individual defections from the innovation in the Friends of the Cheat/River of Promise and Camino Real case studies. Congruence was not a factor in GOCO or Friends of the Cheat/River of Promise but played a corrosive role in the Camino Real.

Major crises or focusing events often have been identified as providing the catalyst for innovation.[27] In two of the case studies documented here, crises did not play a role in initiating innovation. Blowouts in the Friends of the Cheat/River of Promise clearly provided impetus to change the status quo. No such events were present in the GOCO or Collaborative Stewardship cases. This finding is consistent with findings from a larger study of the Ford Foundation/Kennedy School of Government Innovations in American Government Awards. Sanford Borins found that the most frequent stimulus for innovation were internal problems rather than a crisis. Crisis stimulated innovation in only 25 to 30 percent of the cases he studied, while internal problems accounted for 49 to 64 percent of the innovations.[28]

Framing is a second pathway to instigate change.[29] Framing played an important role in GOCO and Friends of the Cheat/River of Promise to facilitate change. In GOCO, framing helped garner support from key constituencies. In Friends of the Cheat/River of Promise, faming helped build a large umbrella under which many interests could work together. Framing was not leveraged effectively in the Camino Real case study.

Public management literature also has emphasized the importance of collaboration and innovation.[30] One of the most important changes in the past century for many public administrators and managers is the increasing interdependence among agencies and organizations. These themes come through in the case studies documented here. Effectively protecting land, improving water quality, and managing forests requires working across political and ecological jurisdictions. Innovative practices often mean that that people in different organizations and agencies need to work cooperatively. In many of these cases, leadership is as important as followership and collaboration. GOCO could not be effective if its staff did not work cooperatively with local agencies and organizations to protect land. Individual GOCO projects required partnerships. Friends of the Cheat/River of Promise networked and created working relationships for each remediation project to improve water quality. Collaborative Stewardship was not possible without the participation of various community members and agencies to support improved forest and land management. The emphasis on the individual can lead to minimization of the importance of working collaboratively to achieve effective outcomes over time.

The upshot of these theoretical insights is twofold. First, much of the literature has been focused on individuals to the detriment of broader structural and cultural influences. The overemphasis on the individual suggests we need to recalibrate our expectations for what individuals can achieve in terms of lasting innovation. Second, no one theory offers sufficient insight to provide clear action or understanding for how to implement innovation. This is significant because it means there are multiple paths that can potentially obstruct, as well as facilitate, innovation over time. We need to pay attention to the individual, structural, and cultural factors. Together, these theoretical insights mean that we do a disservice to the potential of innovations by placing unrealistic expectations on what individuals can achieve while ignoring the structural and cultural pathways that need to be reinforced to foster implementation over time. The next section details some of the patterns in the case studies so that we draw out the most important lessons for practitioners.

DRIVERS AMONG THE FACTORS AND PATTERNS IN THE CASES

Each case study is driven by different combinations of factors. These combinations of factors result in different patterns. Table 6.2 lays out how the factors align, intermittently align, or misalign within each case study. When the characteristics are consistently aligned—individual, structural, and cultural factors are mutually supportive of the innovation—then the innovation stands the greatest chance of being implemented over time. When the characteristics are intermittently aligned— structural factors do not support individual factors or cultural factors do not support individual or structural factors—then the innovation experiences periodic challenges in its implementation. When the characteristics are misaligned—individual, structural, and cultural factors are out of kilter or work at cross purposes to each other—the innovation stands the least chance of being implemented over time. I explore how different factors drive these patterns and what this may imply for success and failure of innovative practice in different settings.

Great Outdoors Colorado

In GOCO, cultural, structural, and individual factors were mutually supportive and positively reinforcing. Individuals were motivated to undertake change. Cultural legitimacy and framing were used intentionally and skillfully to open the political structure through the initiative process. Individuals anticipated resistance and were

Table 6.2: Consistent Alignment, Intermittent Alignment, and Misalignment of Characteristics in Case Studies

	Consistent Alignment, Great Outdoors Colorado	Intermittent Alignment, Friends of the Cheat/ River of Promise	Misalignment, Camino Real/ Collaborative Stewardship
Individual			
• Motivation	+	+/-	+/-
• Norms/Harmony	NA	+/-	+/-
• Congruence	NA	NA	-
Structures			
• Rules/Communication	+	+	-
• Incentives	+	+/-	+/-
• Opening	+/-	+/-	+/-
• Resistance	+/-	+/-	-
Culture			
• Shocks	NA	+	NA
• Framing	+	+	NA/+
• Legitimacy	+	+	+/-

Motivation → Framing/Legitimacy → Opening →
Rules/Communication → Incentives → Legitimacy → Motivation

Figure 6.1: Consistent Alignment in GOCO Case Study

motivated to counter or neutralize it. A clear set of rules were communicated effectively to grant applicants. Incentives provided motivation for local entities and the agencies to protect land, which provided continued legitimacy for GOCO. Figure 6.1 illustrates this positive feedback cycle.

GOCO encountered resistance with the Division of Wildlife and continued to encounter resistance with the Division of Parks and Recreation. As illustrated in figure 6.2, the GOCO vision of protecting open space was not seen as enhancing the legitimacy of the Division of Wildlife (early on) or the Division of Parks and Recreation (more recently). The incongruence between the divisions' dominant values led to resistance to the GOCO mission and vision. With both the Division of Wildlife and Parks and Recreation the political structures have not been closed, but rather they remained resistant to fully complying with the GOCO mission.

Friends of the Cheat

In Friends of the Cheat/River of Promise the factors align at times but not at others. Figure 6.3 illustrates the pattern that allowed the group to effectively implement the River of Promise in the watershed. In the early years of the organization, shocks motivated individuals to form Friends of the Cheat. The effort to restore the Cheat River was intentionally framed to be inclusive and collaborative. This led to the rules embodied in the River of Promise agreement, which opened access to state and federal political structures. Communication through the stakeholder-based, collaborative approach facilitated compliance with the rules and gave the group and its signatory partners' legitimacy. This legitimacy provided incentives and motivation for everyone to continue to work together through the voluntary agreement.

Misalignment of the factors, as illustrated in figure 6.4, impeded implementation at times. Implementation was consistently stymied by resistance from the WVAML. Engaging in water quality remediation was not seen as socially legitimate by WVAML. This led to incongruence between the dominant values in the WVAML and those

Illegitimacy → Incongruence → Resistance

Figure 6.2: Misalignment in GOCO Case Study

Shocks → Motivation → Framing/Legitimacy → Opening →
Rules/Communication → Legitimacy → Incentives → Motivation

Figure 6.3: Consistent Alignment in Friends of the Cheat/River of Promise Case Study

pursued by Friends of the Cheat through the River of Promise. This incongruence led
to resistance by WVAML and the closure of the political opportunity structure for
the group and their efforts. With no motivation to participate, WVAML consistently
opted out of collaborative or partnership arrangements with Friends of the Cheat and
River of Promise. This same pattern holds true for the USACOE.

Implementation was also obstructed by periodic openings and closings in the political opportunity structure as different individuals opted in and out of participating
in the River of Promise activities, as illustrated in the second pattern in figure 6.4.
As new political or administrative leadership took office, the perceived legitimacy of
the Friends of the Cheat/River of Promise approach would be accepted or rejected.
If perceived as not enhancing the legitimacy of the participating agency, then the
opening would be closed to continued participation by employees in the organization.
The impact on individual workplace harmony would stymie the motivation for the
individual to continue participation in the effort.

Finally, as illustrated in example three in figure 6.4, motivation was lackluster
among other participants after the original executive director left in 2000. Without
a capable executive director to keep open the lines of communication and enforce
the rules in the River of Promise agreement, incentives to participate were negligible.
River of Promise partners were not motivated to continue in the absence of an executive director. This particular negative feedback was rectified once a new executive
director was hired.

In spite of the intermittent alignment of factors as illustrated through the negative
feedbacks in figure 6.4, Friends of the Cheat/River of Promise was able to resuscitate
implementation after even its most pessimistic periods. While implementation was
not as robust at some times as it was at others, it never faced consistent misalignment
and a complete breakdown in implementation.

---

1. Illegitimacy → Incongruence → Resistance → Closed Opening → No Motivation
2. Illegitimacy → Closed Opening → Norms/Disharmony → Stymied Motivation
3. No Motivation → Ineffective Rules/Communication → No Incentives →
   No Motivation

Figure 6.4: Misalignment in Friends of the Cheat/River of Promise Case Study

> Motivation → Opening → Communication → Norms/Harmony →
> Incentives → Legitimacy → Motivation

Figure 6.5: Consistent Alignment in the Camino Real and Collaborative Stewardship

Camino Real

Collaborative Stewardship on the Camino Real was hindered by misalignment of the factors, especially after Dumas's departure in 1999. In the early years of Collaborative Stewardship, however, many of the factors aligned positively, as illustrated in figure 6.5. Individuals, including the district ranger, were highly motivated to change the status quo. The political structure was opened on the district, and the district ranger communicated expectations and kept contact open. This new collaborative norm fostered harmonious working relationships on the district and between the communities, which allowed work to get done and created incentives to continue. The perceived legitimacy of the innovation by groups external to the USFS provided a degree of protection from the broader resistance within the Carson National Forest to collaborative practice. This legitimacy through the award provided additional motivation to continue implementation.

Several patterns contributed to the misalignment of factors in the Camino Real case study as demonstrated in figure 6.6. Pattern one illustrates what happened after the project won the Ford Foundation/Harvard Innovations award in 1998. Jealousy, infighting, and envy led to disharmony on the district and between the district and the communities. Once the harmony was undermined, the incentives for participating in the innovations dissipated, and the motivation for participating in the effort was weakened.

Collaborative Stewardship was not seen as a legitimate practice within the Carson National Forest, as documented in pattern two. This meant the innovation was resisted by the forest within which the Camino Real was situated. This resistance led to incongruence between the larger agency values and the practices on the district. The incongruence created disharmony for the individuals on the district who practiced Collaborative Stewardship. For instance, when Dumas no longer felt he had the

> 1. Disharmony → Lack of Incentive → No Motivation
> 2. Illegitimacy → Resistance → Incongruence → Disharmony →
>   Lack of Incentive → No Motivation
> 3. No Motivation → Lack of Rules/Communication & Closed Opening

Figure 6.6: Misalignment in the Camino Real and Collaborative Stewardship

support of the employees on his district or from his superiors, he left. With disharmony, the incentives of friendship, respect, camaraderie, and job satisfaction faded
away and no longer provided motivation to those who had practiced Collaborative
Stewardship.

Finally, as conveyed in pattern three of figure 6.6, when Dumas left, the motivation
to continue Collaborative Stewardship was greatly diminished. Dumas's departure had
the effect of causing the closure of the political structure because he was no longer
there to keep it open. Likewise, in his absence no one was motivated to clarify and
enforce the rules or keep communication about expectations clear. The district rangers
following Dumas were not motivated to open the political structure.

Comparisons

Similar implementation patterns are present in the GOCO and Friends of the Cheat
cases as demonstrated in the shaded areas of figure 6.7. Implementation is most
effective when individuals are motivated, they use framing processes to convey the
legitimacy of the innovation, and openings are created and codified through rules at
the operational level. For GOCO, rules were additionally codified at the constitutional
level, leading to consistent and reliable rules at the operational level. For Friends of
the Cheat, rules were codified at the operational level in response to opportunistic
openings. In contrast, the pattern in the Camino Real was not mediated by framing
and legitimacy, nor were rules codified.

Without individuals there is no opportunity to initiate or implement the innovations. Many individuals play important roles in the implementation process. Leaders,
like the executive directors with Friends of the Cheat and Great Outdoors Colorado,
Dumas with the Camino Real Ranger District, and Citizens for GOCO all were es-

---

Great Outdoors Colorado
Motivation → Framing/Legitimacy → Opening → Rules/Communication →
Incentives → Legitimacy → Motivation

Friends of the Cheat/River of Promise
Shocks → Motivation → Framing/Legitimacy → Opening → Rules/Communication
→ Legitimacy → Incentives → Motivation

Camino Real/Collaborative Stewardship
Motivation → Opening → Communication → Norms/Harmony → Incentives →
Legitimacy → Motivation

Note: Shaded areas indicate similarities in patterns across case studies.

Figure 6.7: Implementation Patterns That Foster Consistent Alignment in Individual, Structural, and
Cultural Factors

Great Outdoors Colorado
Illegitimacy → Incongruence → Resistance (CO Divisions of Wildlife, Parks & Recreation)

Friends of the Cheat/River of Promise
Illegitimacy → Incongruence → Resistance → Closed Openings → No Motivation (WVAML)

Illegitimacy → Closed Opening → Norms/Disharmony → Stymied Motivation (WVDEP & USACOE)

Camino Real/Collaborative Stewardship
Illegitimacy → Resistance → Incongruence → Disharmony → Lack of Incentive → No Motivation (Carson National Forest)

Note: Shaded areas indicate similarities in patterns across case studies.

Figure 6.8: Implementation Patterns That Contribute to Cultural and Structural Misalignment

sential to their respective innovations. However, these leaders also were dependent on others to facilitate implementation of the innovation over time. Staff, the boards of directors, community members, and participating agencies in each innovative practice played important roles in fostering change. The factors that motivated change for all of these individuals were filtered through a lens of what was or was not perceived as a legitimate cultural solution within the environment in which each person worked.

Specific patterns also appeared to be present where we see misalignment of implementation factors between culture and structures. The perception of illegitimacy is the dominant driver in these processes, as indicated in the shaded areas in figure 6.8. For agencies and organizations the perception of legitimacy drives whether the innovation will be congruent or incongruent with dominant values. If the innovation is incongruent, then the agency may be resistant to the innovative approach. This pattern was evident among the Colorado Division of Wildlife, the Colorado Division of Parks and Recreation, the WVAML program, and the USACOE. If the innovation is perceived as illegitimate, this can lead to the closing of a political structure, which then creates disharmony for those within the agency who wish to participate. These patterns were evident with the WVAML and the USACOE in the Friends of the Cheat case study. Finally, the pattern present in the Carson National Forest indicated that the agency did not see Collaborative Stewardship as legitimate, which led to resistance by the agency and incongruence between the dominant values and individuals wishing to support Collaborative Stewardship at the district level.

A second set of patterns at the individual and structural levels is evident in the shaded areas in figure 6.9. When the Friends of the Cheat executive director left there was no motivation to enforce the River of Promise rules or keep communication

> **Friends of the Cheat/River of Promise**
> No Motivation → Rules/Communication → No Incentives → No Motivation
>   (Bassage leaves)
>
> **Camino Real/Collaborative Stewardship**
> No Motivation → Rules/Communication & Closed Opening (Dumas leaves)
>
> Note: Shaded areas indicate similarities in patterns across case studies.

Figure 6.9: Implementation Patterns That Contribute to Individual and Structural Misalignment

channels open among the stakeholders in the group. Likewise, when Dumas left the Camino Real, there was little motivation to carry on Collaborative Stewardship. The rules were not well codified, and communication about expectations was no longer clear.

It is premature to infer clear, causal explanations based on only three case studies. Nonetheless, these findings point to intriguing relationships among individual, structural, and cultural factors that may provide insight into processes associated with greater and lesser success in the implementation of innovative practices. These findings lay the groundwork for additional research to support, refute, or improve upon the framework established here.

Areas ripe for continued investigation include whether implementing innovation within established bureaucracies follows different patterns than innovations that take place outside of established bureaucracies. Resistance within the Carson National Forest hindered the continued implementation of Collaborative Stewardship. GOCO and Friends of the Cheat did not have to wrestle with being nested completely inside existing bureaucratic structures. GOCO created its own, new structure. Friends of the Cheat had to piece together participants from numerous bureaucracies within its own collaborative framework.

PRACTICAL LESSONS LEARNED

As was stated in chapter 1, this book has clear limitations. The empirical research is derived from three in-depth case studies that were strategically chosen to illustrate the patterns of implementation over time. This means that while these case studies are rich in detail, they are not necessarily generalizable to a broader population. Consequently, the individual, structural, and cultural lessons that follow are qualified as preliminary, not definitive. Nonetheless, this work suggests direction to those investigating how innovation is implemented over time. Future studies might be enhanced by larger sample sizes and the use of regression analysis to identify the significance of individual, structural, and cultural factors. The lessons elaborated on below and listed in table 6.3 suggest some themes that could be built upon or investigated further.

Table 6.3: Practical Implementation Lessons about Individuals, Structures, and Culture

Individuals	Motivation is a necessary, but not sufficient driver of change.
	One person working alone cannot do it.
	Norms/harmony and congruence are more influential on individuals working existing organizations.
	Norms/harmony are affected by agency/organizational leadership.
	Large agencies function by maintaining congruency with their culture.
Structures	More permanent rule structures facilitate continuation of innovative practice.
	Many types of incentives can be used, not just financial and technical, to induce behavior consistent with innovative practice.
	Dealing with multiple structural openings is more difficult than dealing with one opening.
	Multiple openings create multiple opportunities.
	Resistance exists.
Culture	Shocks were not always necessary for innovation to take place.
	Framing processes can condition people to believe they are aggrieved but also that they can take action and be left better off.
	Legitimacy can work to uphold an innovation or undermine it depending on how the innovation is received in that culture.

Individuals

Motivation is a necessary but not sufficient driver of change. In addition to motivation, you need authority and the ability to open the political opportunity structure to foster change. For instance, Camino Real had many motivated individuals, but only Dumas had authority to open the political opportunity structure because the USFS ultimately managed the land. Likewise, Friends of the Cheat had motivated individuals, but they needed to be harnessed by the executive director, who created authority through the collaborative agreement. Finally, GOCO had motivated individuals, but the organization needed authority through initiative process to allow it to open the political process to be effective.

One person working alone cannot do it. The literature on policy entrepreneurship leads us to believe that individuals make a difference, and they can. But force of personality was not enough in the Camino Real/Collaborative Stewardship case study. Dumas was effective for a time, but the structure and culture in which he was working were unsupportive of the efforts. Without him there to keep the political structure open, the innovation collapsed on itself under the pressure of status quo forces within the agency. Likewise, Friends of the Cheat has been inordinately dependent on its executive directors. While they were able to build continuity through a board of directors, this model leaves them vulnerable to the departure of the executive director. GOCO had a broad coalition of individuals working together to create and sustain the innovation over time. GOCO had a multilateral effort to deal with resistance and create incentives that could sustain the agency over time.

Norms/harmony and congruence are more influential on individuals working in existing organizations. Norms/harmony and congruence did not affect GOCO because it was a new organization. Norms/harmony and congruence within the USFS strongly affected Collaborative Stewardship on the Camino Real.

Norms/harmony are affected by agency/organization leadership. Friends of the Cheat/ River of Promise created its own new norm of collaboration. Individuals in agencies where the collaborative norm was unwelcome backed away from River of Promise to keep harmony within their own workplaces. Individuals reengaged when the collaborative norm was more welcome. Dumas created a collaborative and community-oriented norm while he was district ranger. Norms reverted to the status quo after his departure.

Large agencies function by maintaining congruency with their culture. It is difficult to treat one subunit differently than the rest of the units within the agency/organization. Camino Real tried to change persistent practices on the district. Enormous pressures came into play to maintain congruency with the rest of the culture. This was the third time in some sixty years that efforts had been made and had failed to work with local communities in northern New Mexico. The same institutional pressures for conformity destabilized previous attempts to work with local communities with the Vallecitos Sustained Yield Unit and the Northern New Mexico Policy.

Structures

More permanent rule structures facilitate continuation of innovative practice. GOCO was the product of a constitutional amendment. This provided GOCO great protection against change. Friends of the Cheat and River of Promise had a voluntary written agreement with stakeholders. Consequently, they experienced implementation with more active participation by some at times than others. As long as an executive director was able to enforce the voluntary document, it served as an effective tool to facilitate continuation of the innovation. Camino Real/Collaborative Stewardship had no written documentation or codification for many years. The management plan that was formulated only had authority within the district while Dumas was the ranger.

Many types of incentives can be used, not just financial and technical, to induce behavior consistent with innovative practice. Friendship, camaraderie, pride in workmanship, and job satisfaction were important to the innovations featured here. GOCO was the case study that most effectively used financial incentives. Friends of the Cheat/ River of Promise used financial, technical, friendship, and work completion as incentives. Camino Real/Collaborative Stewardship used camaraderie, friendship, and job satisfaction as primary inducements.

Dealing with multiple structural openings is more difficult than dealing with one opening. GOCO had to open the state-level political structure—once the initiative was passed, the structure was open. Friends of the Cheat/River of Promise had to deal with openings at the local, state, and federal levels with multiple agencies. They did not have much power to permanently open structures. The group was always working opportunistically where there was a path of least resistance.

Multiple openings create multiple opportunities. Camino Real/Collaborative Stewardship had to deal with opening the district and forest to create more permanent change. Dumas was successful in opening the district but not the forest. Because there was resistance at the forest level, Dumas had no other avenue to pursue. In contrast, when Friends of the Cheat encountered resistance in one place or agency, the members could shift their efforts to other places where resistance was less likely. While one structure may be easier to negotiate than multiple openings, the multiple openings created the opportunity to work on diversified fronts when resistance was encountered in one place.

Resistance exists. Anticipating resistance and thinking about how it can be mitigated, addressed, neutralized, or by-passed can facilitate continued implementation of innovation. GOCO neutralized the opposition in the General Assembly and continued to keep its finger on the pulse of where things were in the legislature. GOCO continued to work with the Division of Parks and Recreation and the Division of Wildlife to provide continued focus on land protection. Friends of the Cheat/River of Promise tried to work with WVAML for fourteen years. The group continued to keep channels of communication open. Friends of the Cheat/River of Promise continued to work with USACOE to overcome resistance to permitting. Camino Real/Collaborative Stewardship ignored resistance and failed to address it.

Culture

Shocks were not always necessary for innovation to take place. Innovation can take place in the absence of shocks. Friends of the Cheat took advantage of a focusing event to take action and maintain focus on it. GOCO and Camino Real/Collaborative Stewardship did not need focusing events to take action.

Framing processes can condition people to believe they are aggrieved but also that they can take action and be left better off. Citizens for GOCO convinced the public they were aggrieved, and voters took action. Citizens for GOCO also framed GOCO as a positive for business elite and the divisions of Wildlife and Parks and Recreation. Friends of the Cheat/River of Promise framed the remediation of the Cheat Basin as a positive outcome for all stakeholders. Collaborative Stewardship ultimately was framed as a beneficial practice that improved the lives of multiple participants.

Legitimacy can work to uphold an innovation or undermine it depending on how the innovation is received in that culture. The perception of legitimacy upheld GOCO within the broader Colorado culture. The perception of legitimacy upheld Friends of the Cheat/River of Promise outside of the environmental community, which thought Friends of the Cheat was a traitor/collaborator for working with the coal industry. The perception of legitimacy upheld Collaborative Stewardship with groups external to the agency (Gore Award/Harvard Innovations Award), but it undermined legitimacy within the forest, which saw the Camino Real and Dumas as rogue operators.

FOSTERING ENDURING CHANGE

The integrated framework presented here suggests that there are ideal conditions that foster innovation. These include (a) individuals who are motivated and working within workplace social norms and the dominant agency or organizational culture that supports the innovation or the innovative practice; (b) structures that facilitate clear rules and communication, incentives that induce compliance with innovative practice, and political environments that are open to innovation and awareness of resistance and measures to address, mitigate, or otherwise neutralize opposition; and (c) strategies to frame problems to support innovative practice, capitalize on shocks or focusing events if they occur, and use of innovation to enhance legitimacy. These ideal conditions were mostly met in the GOCO case study. They were weakly met in the Camino Real/Collaborative Stewardship case study. They were met more strongly at times than others in the Friends of the Cheat/River of Promise case study.

To the degree that we can extrapolate from three cases, we can infer that it is not often that we face situations where ideal conditions can be met. In those situations, we must learn how to compensate for the weaknesses and build on the inherent strengths of the individual, structural, and cultural factors that are present. We must also recognize that there are situations where innovation might be less likely to take hold. Even the most entrepreneurial of individuals may have difficulty fostering innovation in a hostile culture with closed political and administrative structures. The findings here suggest that the greatest success will come with the potential for building effective structures at the operational and constitutive levels within a culture of legitimacy. Individuals are key to these processes. Individuals working under conditions of weak structures and challenges to legitimacy will face daunting hurdles. Under these conditions, work first needs to take place within the structures and culture before innovation stands a reasonable chance of longer term implementation.

Institutions matter in the implementation of innovation. Structures and culture provide real obstacles for individuals seeking change. The influence of these structures and culture is not readily visible, but they have far reaching consequences. The goal of this book is to create a more comprehensive understanding of the challenges that face the implementation of innovation and the opportunities that lead to its success. Misplaced hope in individuals to the exclusion of the importance of structures and culture will not serve society well. The promise of innovation in the long term can be fulfilled if we have a more realistic understanding of the challenges that face it.

NOTES

1. Great Outdoors Colorado, "Great Outdoors Colorado Strategic Plan," on file with author, April 2002.

2. Irving Goffman, *Frame Analysis: An Essay on the Organization of Experience* (London: Harper and Row, 1974), 21; and Donald A. Schon and Martin. Rein, *Frame Reflection: Toward the Resolution of Intractable Policy Controversies* (New York: Basic, 1994).

3. Thomas A. Koelble, "The New Institutionalism in Political Science and Sociology," *Comparative Politics* 27, no. 1 (1995): 231–43.

4. Peter Hall and Rosemary Taylor, "Political Science and the Three New Institutionalisms," *Political Studies* 44 (1996): 937; and Kathleen Thelen, "Historical Institutionalism in Comparative Politics," *Annual Review in Political Science* 2 (1999): 369–404.

5. Daniel A. Mazmanian and Paul A. Sabatier, *Implementation and Public Policy* (Lanham, MD: University Press of America, 1989); Michael Lipsky, "Standing the Study of Policy Implementation on Its Head," in *American Politics and Public Policy*, ed. Walter Burnham and Sarah Weinberg (Cambridge, MA: MIT Press, 1975); Malcolm L. Goggin, Ann O. Bowman, James P. Lester, and Laurence J. O'Toole Jr., *Implementation Theory and Practice: Toward a Third Generation* (Glenview, IL: Scott, Foresman/Little, Brown, 1990); and Ray J. Burby, Peter J. May, and Robert C. Paterson, "Improving Compliance with Regulations," *Journal of the American Planning Association* 64 (1998): 324–35.

6. Elinor Ostrom, *Governing the Commons* (Cambridge: Cambridge University Press, 1990); and Elinor Ostrom, Roy Gardner, and James Walker, *Rules, Games and Common Pool Resources* (Ann Arbor: University of Michigan Press, 1994).

7. Hall and Taylor, "Political Science and the Three New Institutionalisms"; Thelen, "Historical Institutionalism"; and Douglass C. North, *Institutions, Institutional Change, and Economic Performance* (Cambridge: Cambridge University Press, 1990).

8. John W. Kingdon, *Agendas, Alternatives and Public Policies,* 2nd ed. (New York: Longman), 1995; Nancy C. Roberts and Paula J. King, "Policy Entrepreneurs: Their Activity, Structure and Function in the Policy Process," *Journal of Public Administration Research and Theory*, 1, no. 2 (1991): 147–75; Gerald T. Gabris, Robert T. Golembiewski, and Douglas M. Ihrke, "Leadership Credibility, Board Relations, and Administrative Innovation at the Local Government Level," *Journal of Public Administration Research and Theory* 11 (2000); and Fariborz Damanpour and Marguerite Schneider, "Phases of the Adoption of Innovation in Organizations: Effects of Environment, Organization and Top Managers," *British Journal of Management* 17 (2006).

9. Hall and Taylor, "Political Science and the Three New Institutionalisms"; Thelen, "Historical Institutionalism"; and North, *Institutions, Institutional Change, and Economic Performance*.

10. Kingdon, *Agendas, Alternatives and Public Policies*; Baumgartner and Jones, *Agendas and Instability in American Politics*; Mintrom, "Policy Entrepreneurs"; and Michael Mintrom and Sandra Vergari, "Policy Networks and Innovation Diffusion: The Case of the State Education Reforms," *Journal of Politics* 60, no. 1 (1998): 126–88.

11. Hall and Taylor, "Political Science and the Three New Institutionalisms," 937; and Thelen, "Historical Institutionalism in Comparative Politics."

12. Robert T. Nakamura and Frank Smallwood, *The Politics of Policy Implementation* (New York: St. Martin's, 1980); Paul Berman, "Thinking about Programmed and Adaptive Implementation: Matching Strategies to Situations," in *Why Policies Succeed or Fail*, ed. Helen M. Ingram and Dean E. Mann (Beverly Hills, CA: Sage, 1980); Daniel A. Mazmanian and Paul A. Sabatier, *Implementation and Public Policy* (Lanham, MD: University Press of America, 1989).

13. Hall and Taylor, "Political Science and the Three New Institutionalisms"; Thelen, "Historical Institutionalism in Comparative Politics"; and Thomas A. Koelble, "The New Institutionalism in Political Science and Sociology," *Comparative Politics* 27 (1995): 231–44.

14. Baumgartner and Jones, *Agendas and Instability in American Politics*; Kingdon, *Agendas, Alternatives and Public Policies*; and Tom Birkland, *After Disaster: Agenda Setting, Public Policy and Focusing Events* (Washington, DC: Georgetown University Press, 1997).

15. Goffman, *Frame Analysis*, 21; Donald A. Schon, and Martin Rein, *Frame Reflection: Toward the Resolution of Intractable Policy Controversies* (New York: Basic, 1994).

16. Thomas A. Koelble, "The New Institutionalism in Political Science and Sociology," *Comparative Politics* 27, no. 1 (1995): 231–43.

17. Hall and Taylor, "Political Science and the Three New Institutionalisms"; Thelen, "Historical Institutionalism in Comparative Politics"; Douglass C. North, *Institutions, Institutional Change, and Economic Performance* (Cambridge: Cambridge University Press, 1990).

18. Nakamura and Smallwood, *The Politics of Policy Implementation*; and Mazmanian and Sabatier, *Implementation and Public Policy*.

19. North, *Institutions, Institutional Change*; Margaret Levi, "A Logic of Institutional Change," in *The Limits of Rationality*, ed. K. S. Cook and Margaret Levi (Chicago: University of Chicago Press, 1990), 402–18; Thomas A. Koelble, "The New Institutionalism in Political Science and Sociology," *Comparative Politics* 27, no. 1 (1995): 231–43; Goggin et al., *Implementation Theory and Practice*; and Burby et al., "Improving Compliance with Regulations."

20. Robert Goodin, *Institutions and Their Design* (Cambridge: Cambridge University Press, 1996).

21. Ostrom, *Governing the Commons*.

22. Hall and Taylor, "Political Science and the Three New Institutionalisms"; Thelen, "Historical Institutionalism in Comparative Politics"; and North, *Institutions, Institutional Change*.

23. Osborne and Gaebler, *Reinventing Government*; F. Berry, "Innovation in Public Management: The Adoption of Strategic Planning," *Public Administration Review* 67, no. 3 (1994): 322–30.

24. G. T. Gabris, R. T. Golembiewski, and D. M. Ihrke, "Leadership Credibility, Board Relations, and Administrative Innovation at the Local Government Level," *Journal of Public Administration Research and Theory* 11 (2000); Fariborz Damanpour and Marguerite Schneider, "Characteristics of Innovation and Innovation Adoption in Public Organizations: Assessing

the Role of Managers," *Journal of Public Administration Research and Theory* (2008) (advance access); and Damanpour and Schneider, "Phases of the Adoption of Innovation in Organizations," *British Journal of Management* 17 (2006).

25. Linda R. deLeon and Robert Denhart, "The Political Theory of Reinvention," *Public Administration Review* 60, no. 2 (2000): 89–97.

26. Larry Terry, *Leadership of Public Bureaucracies: The Administrator as Conservator* (Thousand Oaks, CA: Sage, 1995); and H. G. Frederickson, *The Spirit of Public Administration* (San Francisco: Jossey-Bass, 1997).

27. James Q. Wilson, "Innovation in Organization: Notes Toward a Theory," in *Approaches to Organization Design*, ed. James D. Thompson (Pittsburgh, PA: University of Pittsburgh Press, 1966); and Martin A. Levin and M. Bryna Sanger, *Making Government Work: How Entrepreneurial Executives Turn Bright Ideas into Real Results* (San Francisco: Jossey-Bass, 1994).

28. Sanford Borins, "Loose Cannons and Rule Breakers, or Enterprising Leaders? Some Evidence about Innovative Public Managers," *Public Administration Review* 60 (2000): 6.

29. Irving Goffman, *Frame Analysis*, 21; and D. A. Schon and M. Rein, *Frame Reflection: Toward the Resolution of Intractable Policy Controversies* (Basic Books, New York, 1994).

30. Eugene Bardach, *Getting Agencies to Work Together: The Practice and Theory of Managerial Craftsmanship* (Washington, DC: Brookings, 1998); Robert Agranoff and Michael McGuire, *Collaborative Public Management: New Strategies for Local Governments* (Washington, DC: Georgetown University Press, 2003); Eugene Bardach, "Developmental Processes: A Conceptual Exploration," in *Innovation in Government: Research, Recognition, and Replication*, ed. Sanford Borins (Cambridge, MA: MIT Press, 2008), 113–37; and Rosemary O'Leary and Lisa B. Bingham, *The Collaborative Public Manager: New Ideas for the Twenty-first Century* (Washington, DC: Georgetown University Press, 2009).

Index

Note: Page numbers in italics represent tables and figures.

acid mine drainage (AMD), 102–12, 121, 125, 134n1; and Cheat River Watershed, 106–7; Friends of the Cheat treatment projects, 22, 103–4, 115, 117, 118–20, 130; oversight of, 102–3, 106–7, 111–12; treatment methods, 107, 119, 133; and WVAML, 106–7, 119, 121, 126, 127–28, 133. *See also* Friends of the Cheat/River of Promise case study

Adolfson, Greg, 111, 112–13, 115, 116, 121, 122, 126

Alamo-Dinner timber sale (Camino Real Ranger District), 143, 144, 146, 162

alignment of factors in case studies: Camino Real and Collaborative Stewardship, 179, *186, 189*, 189–90; consistent, 185–92, *186–92*; Friends of the Cheat/River of Promise, 176, *186*, 187–88, *188*; Great Outdoors Colorado, 172, 185–87, *186–87*; implementation patterns that foster alignment, *190–92*; intermittent, 185–92, *186–92*; misalignment, 185–92, *186–92*

Allard, Wayne, 81

Alliance for America, 42

American Farm and Ranch Protection Act, 44

American Farmland Trust, 43, 78

American Forest & Paper Association, Sustainable Forestry Initiative program, 5

American Forests, 59, 60

American Rivers Inc., 106, 111, 126, 128

American Society of Mining Reclamation National Conference, 117

Anderson, Norma, 82

Anker Energy Corporation, 112–13, 115, 121, 122, 125

Appalachian Clean Streams Initiative, 111–12, 114, 121, 125

Atencio, Ernie, 161

Baker, Mark, 52

Bardach, Eugene, 12

Bassage, Dave, 107–9; and Friends of the Cheat, 107–9, 116, 117–18, 120, 121–22, 124, 127, 129, 132, 176–77; and River of Promise agreement, 110, 112–13, 114, 116, 120

Bedell, John, 144, 161

Biodiversity Legal Foundation, 147
Blue Ribbon Coalition, 42
Bonneville Power Administration, 49
Borins, Sanford, 184
bottom-up implementation theory, 9,
    11–13, 16, 184; and belief systems,
    12; and forest governance, *139*;
    and individual motivational factors,
    12–13; and land use governance, *71*;
    and policy entrepreneurs, 12; and
    watershed governance, *102*
Braithwaite, John, 6
Brown, Steve, 111, 112, 121
Buckley, Rick, 112, 114–15, 121–22,
    123
Bureau of Land Management (BLM),
    3, 31–32, 36, 61–62n2
Bureau of Reclamation, 46, 47, 49
Bush, George H. W., 36
Bush, George W., 118

CALFED program, 50
California Coastal Commission, 78
California Department of Natural
    Resources, 78
Camino Real Ranger District and
    Collaborative Stewardship case
    study, 23, 138–70, 179–82, 189–90;
    April 2001 community conference,
    153–54; and broader culture of the
    USFS, 158, 160, 161, 163, 166,
    181–82; chronological developments,
    141; community health and develop-
    ment goals, 146, 154; and Córdova,
    143–46, 148–55, 156, 161, 163,
    179; and Dumas, 140, 142, 143–55,
    156–67, 179–83; Dumas's decision
    to violate injunction, 148–49, 160,
    161, 162, 180, 182; Dumas's promo-
    tion in place, 147, 151–52, 159; and
    East Entrañas Plan, 147, 149–50,
    158–59, 161; forest restoration

efforts, 145–46, 150–51, 154; grass
    bank initiative, 150–51; and hier-
    archical influences on forest gover-
    nance, *139*; history of landownership
    issues, 57–59, 139–44, 160–61;
    horseback diplomacy and community
    outreach strategies, 142, 144–45,
    154, 157, 161, 163, 180–81; infight-
    ing and jealousy *(la envidia)*, 151,
    157–58, 180; the Los Sietes meet-
    ings, 145; Mexican spotted owl issue
    and timber injunction, 147–49, 160,
    161, 162, 182; narrative account,
    140–55; national awards and rec-
    ognition, 140, 150–51, 153, 156,
    157–58, 162–63, 182; personal-use
    firewood permits, 143–44, 145, 148,
    153; post-Dumas, 153–55, 157,
    158–59, 160, 180; stewardship plots
    program, 150, 153, 154; and timber
    sales/timber management, 143, 144,
    146–47, 149–50, 152–53, 162; and
    Truchas Land Grant, 143–44, 167n7;
    and voluntary regulation, 139–40
Camino Real Ranger District and
    Collaborative Stewardship case study
    (applying the analytical framework),
    155–67, *164–65*, *173*, 179–82;
    alignment of factors in case study,
    179, *186*, *189*, 189–90; congruence,
    158, 163, *164–65*, 166, 180, 184;
    cultural factors, 162–63, *164–65*,
    166, *173*, 182, 183, 184; framing,
    162, *164–65*, 166, 182, 183, 184;
    incentives, 159–60, *164–65*, 166,
    181; individual factors, 156–58,
    163, *164–65*, 166, *173*, 179–80;
    legitimacy, 162–63, *164–65*, 166,
    182, 183; motivation, 156–57, 163,
    164–65, 166, 179–80; norms and
    harmony, 157–58, 163, *164–65*,
    166, 180, 184; opening in the

political structure, 160, *164–65*, 166, 181; resistance, 160–61, *164–65*, 166; rules and communication, 158–59, 163–66, *164–65*, 180–81, 184; shocks, 162, *164–65*, 166, 182, 184; structural factors, 158–61, 163–66, *164–65*, *173*, 180–82

Carson, Rachel, 33

Carson Forest Watch, 144, 147

Carson National Forest (northern New Mexico): injunction halting timber cutting, 147–49, 160, 161, 162, 180; personal-use firewood permits, 143–44, 145, 148, 153; stewardship plots, 153; and Truchas Land Grant, 143–44; and Vallecitos Federal Sustained Yield Unit, 58, 142. *See also* Camino Real Ranger District and Collaborative Stewardship case study

Carter, Jimmy, 42, 106

case studies, 19–24; and alignment of factors, 172, 176, 179, 185–92, *186–92*; application of framework to, 19–20; combinations of factors and patterns in, 185–92, *186–92*; "innovative practice" as unit of analysis, 20; limitations of the research, 24; methods of data collection, 21, 22, 23; selection, 19–20, 24; three patterns of implementation response, 19–20. *See also* Camino Real Ranger District and Collaborative Stewardship case study; Friends of the Cheat/River of Promise case study; Great Outdoors Colorado (GOCO) case study

Cheat River Festival, 104, 109–10, 113, 123, 125

Chemical Manufacturers Association, Responsible Care program, 5

Chesapeake Bay Foundation, 43

Ciruli, Floyd, 75, 86, 87, 90, 92–93, 175

Citizen's Clearinghouse for Toxic Waste, 37

Citizens for GOCO, 20–21, 74–77, 86, 87–88, 93, 174

Civilian Conservation Corps, 47

Clark, Brad, 50–51

Clary, David, 55

Clean Water Act and amendments, 48, 49, 50, 51, 151

Clean Water Action Plan, 50

Cleveland, Grover, 53

Clinton, Bill, 38, 69n138

Club 20, 81

coal mining: and acid mine drainage (AMD), 102–12, 134n1; oversight, 102–3, 106–7, 111–12, 118, 133; the SMCRA, 106–7, 118; and the USOSM, 102–3, 111–12; and West Virginia's history, 101–2; and the WVAML, 106–7, 119, 121, 126, 127–28, 133, 178. *See also* Friends of the Cheat/River of Promise case study

Coastal Zone Management Act (1972), 35

Collaborative Stewardship. *See* Camino Real Ranger District and Collaborative Stewardship case study

collective level innovation, 15, 29n74, 30–31, *31*, *38*, 38–39; and forest governance, *139*; and land use governance, *71*; and watershed governance, *102*

Colorado Cattlemen's Agricultural Land Trust, 43, 80

Colorado Department of Natural Resources, 92–93

Colorado Division of Parks and Outdoor Recreation, 75, 77, 86, 87–88, 90, 91, 96, 175

Colorado Division of Wildlife, 75, 77, 78, 80–81, 83, 86, 87–91, 92, 96, 175

Colorado Divisions of Parks and Outdoor Recreation, 78, 88–89
Colorado's Front Range and land protection challenges, 20–21, 70–71, 72–74, 84–85, 88–89, 97n3
Colorado State Parks, 81
Colorado Youth Corps Association, 80
commodity management, 31–32, 34, 35, 55, 56
Communities Committee, 59
Community-Based Environmental Protection, 2–3
community-based forestry movement, 59–61; appropriations and funding, 60–61; collaborative processes, 61; contracting and procurement, 61; defining, 138–39; foundational goals, 60; four priority action items, 60–61; historical precedents in New England, 57; historical precedents in the Southwest, 57–59; legislation incorporating movement goals, 61; NEPA and ESA implementation, 61; organizational meetings (1995-2001), 59–61; and Progressive Era forest management, 54; and stewardship contracting, 61, 150, 153, 154; and the USFS, 54, 59, 61, 138. See also Camino Real Ranger District and Collaborative Stewardship case study; forest governance system (evolution of)
La Comunidad, 144
congruence, 17–18, 18; Camino Real and Collaborative Stewardship case study, 158, 163, 164–65, 166, 180, 184; Friends of the Cheat/River of Promise case study, 123, 131, 132, 184; GOCO case study, 94, 95, 95, 176, 184; practical implementation lessons, 194
conservation easements, 44, 78
Conservation Fund, 43

Conservation Trust for North Carolina, 43
Conservation Trust Fund (Colorado), 72, 74, 77
constitutional-level innovation, 15, 29n74, 30–31, 31, 38, 38–39; and forest governance, 139; and land use governance, 71, 76; and watershed governance, 102
Córdova, Max, 143–46, 148–55, 156, 161, 163, 179. See also Camino Real Ranger District and Collaborative Stewardship case study
coregulation, 6, 6–7
Corps of Engineers. See U.S. Army Corps of Engineers (USACOE)
Council on Environmental Equality, 35
Creative Act (General Revision Act) (1891), 53
cultural factors in innovation, 17–18, 19, 182–83; alignment of factors in case studies, 172, 176, 179, 185–92, 186–92; Camino Real and Collaborative Stewardship case study, 162–63, 164–65, 166, 173, 182, 183, 184; framing, 17–18, 19, 85–86, 94, 95, 129, 131, 133, 162, 164–65, 166, 172–74, 178–79, 182, 183, 184, 195–96; Friends of the Cheat/River of Promise case study, 128–30, 131, 133–34, 173, 178–79, 183, 184; GOCO case study, 84–86, 94, 95, 172–74, 173, 183, 184; legitimacy, 17–18, 19, 85, 94, 95, 114, 129–30, 131, 134, 162–63, 164–65, 166, 174, 179, 182, 183, 196; practical implementation lessons, 193, 195–96; shocks, 17–18, 19, 84–85, 94, 95, 128, 131, 133, 162, 164–65, 166, 172–74, 178–79, 182, 184, 195; and sociological institutionalism, 14, 16, 19

cultural institutionalism. *See* sociological institutionalism

Daily, Richard W., 75, 78, 93
Dana, Samuel T., 54
DeBuys, Bill, 150
DeVargas, Ike, 155, 161
Diné Citizens against Ruining Our
Environment, 147
Dombeck, Michael, 148
Downstream Alliance, 107
Dumas, Crockett, 140, 142, 143–55,
156–67, 179–83; decision to violate
timber injunction, 148–49, 160,
161, 162, 180, 182; departure
from Camino Real Ranger District,
152, 163; promotion in place, 147,
151–52, 159. *See also* Camino Real
Ranger District and Collaborative
Stewardship case study
DuPont, 44

easements, conservation, 44, 78
East Entrañas Ecosystem Management
Plan, 147, 149–50, 158–59, 161
Ellison, Ken, 118
"embeddedness," 14
"eminent domain," 40
Endangered Species Act (ESA), 50, 61
Environmental Action, 33
environmental and natural resource
governance system (historical evolution of), 30–69; broad overview,
31–39; pre-1960s, 31–32; the 1960s
and 1970s, 33–35, 138; the 1980s
and 1990s, 35–39; case law and
new legislation, 34–35, 37; changing public mood, 33–34; Clinton's
"reinventing government" agenda, 38;
commodity management approach,
31–32, 34, 35, 55, 56; decentralization and shift in regulatory approach,
35–36, 63n20; early conservationist
and preservationist groups, 32; early
regulatory efforts and standards, 34;
forest governance, 52–61; grassroots
groups, 36, 37; hierarchical pressures
and innovation, 30–31, *31*; innovations at constitutive, collective, and
operational rule levels, 30–31, *31*, *38*,
38–39; land protection governance,
39–45; new nontraditional actors and
strategies, 33–35; pollution concerns
and creation of EPA, 33–34; public
participation in decision-making
processes, 37–38; and scientific management, 32, 34–35, 54; watershed
governance, 45–52
Environmental Defense Fund, 33
environmental movement and interest
groups: and forest management,
55–57, 138, 140–43, 144; and
Friends of the Cheat, 108–9, 113
Environmental Policy Institute, 33
Environmental Protection Agency
(EPA): and Clean Water Act, 48, 49;
and Clinton's "reinventing government" agenda, 38; and Community-
Based Environmental Protection,
2–3; early regulatory efforts and
standards, 34; establishment of,
33–34; and forest restoration work in
Camino Real, 150–51; and Friends
of the Cheat/River of Promise, 115,
118, 125, 127; regulatory approach
and movement toward decentralization, 36; Targeted Watershed
Grant Program, 118, 125; TMDL
procedures, 49; voluntary regulation
programs, 7; and watershed management, 50, 51
"Euclidean zoning," 40

Faltis, John, 112–13, 116, 121, 122

Federal Energy Regulatory Commission, 49

Federal Land Policy and Management Act (1976), 35

Federal Sustained Yield Unit Act (1944), 58

Federal Water Pollution Control Act (1948), 47–48

Felton, Charles, Jr., 113

Fernow, Bernard, 54

Fish and Wildlife Service. *See* U.S. Fish and Wildlife Service (USFWS)

Ford, Gerald, 42

Forest Conservation Council, 147

forest governance system (evolution of), 52–61; community forestry, 57–61; creation of the USFS, 53–55; custodial management, 53–54; early conservation movement, 53–54; environmental era, 55–57; "forest reserves," 53; grassroots groups, 37; historical precedents, 57–59; new tools and innovations, 52; Progressive Era, 53–55; scientific forest management, 54; timber production/commodity management, 31–32, 55, 56. *See also* Camino Real Ranger District and Collaborative Stewardship case study; community-based forestry movement; U.S. Forest Service (USFS)

Forest Guardians, 147

Forest Management Act (Organic Act) (1897), 53

Forest Service. *See* U.S. Forest Service (USFS)

Forest Trust, 149

framing, *17–18*, 19; Camino Real and Collaborative Stewardship case study, 162, *164–65*, 166, 182, 183, 184; Friends of the Cheat/River of Promise case study, 129, *131*, 133,

178–79, 184; GOCO case study, 85–86, 94, *95*, 172–74, 183, 184; practical implementation lessons, 195–96; and sociological institutionalism, 14, 16, 19

Friends of the Cheat/River of Promise case study, 22, 101–37, 176–79, 187–88; AMD treatment projects, 22, 103–4, 115, 117, 118–20, 130; and American Rivers list, 106, 111, 126, 128; and Bassage, 107–10, 112–14, 116, 117–18, 120, 121–22, 124, 127–29, 132, 176–77; Cheat River Festival, 104, 109–10, 113, 123, 125; chronological developments, *105*; coal mining and West Virginia's history, 101–2; core principles, 103; diverse and balanced board of directors, 109, 121–22, 130; education and outreach, 117; and fishing/whitewater recreation, 108; and hierarchical influences on watershed governance, *102*; industry participation and collaboration, 108–9, 112, 113, 114, 121, 122, 130, 179; mission, 108–9, 116–17, 120, 123–24, 129; narrative account, 104–20; and Pitzer's leadership, 116–20, 121, 122, 124, 125, 126, 127–28, 129, 130, 177; and political leadership changes, 115–16, 126, 132, 177; the River of Promise agreement, 103, 104, 110–20, 121–34, 176–77; the SMCRA and Abandoned Mine Land Program, 106–7, 118; the T&T mine blowout (1994), 104–6, 111, 128, 133, 178; and the USACOE, 115, 119, 127, 128, 133, 178; and the USOSM, 102–3, 111–13, 114, 127; and voluntary regulation, 101–4; water quality mapping and GIS monitoring, 117;

water quality testing and fish surveys, 119–20; and WVAML, 106–7, 115, 116, 118–19, 121, 123, 126, 127–28, 133, 178

Friends of the Cheat/River of Promise case study (applying the analytic framework), 120–34, *131*, *173*, 176–79; alignment of factors in case study, 176, *186*, 187–88, *188*; congruence, 123, *131*, 132, 184; cultural characteristics, 128–30, *131*, 133–34, *173*, 178–79, 183, 184; framing, 129, *131*, 133, 178–79, 184; incentives, 124–25, *131*, 132, 178; individual characteristics, 120–23, 130–32, *131*, 134, *173*, 176–77; legitimacy, 114, 129–30, *131*, 134, 179, 183; motivation, 120–22, 130–32, *131*, 134, 176; norms and harmony, 123, *131*, 132, 134, 177, 184; opening political structures, 125–27, *131*, 132, 134, 177; resistance, 113, 127–28, 130, *131*, 132, 133, 134, 178; rules and communication, 123–24, *131*, 132, 178, 184; shocks, 128, *131*, 133, 178–79, 184; structural characteristics, 123–28, *131*, 132–33, 134, *173*, 178

Friends of the Earth, 33

Gaebler, Ted, 12
General Land Office, 61–62n2
Geographic Information System (GIS), 117
Gibbs, Lois, 33
Goffman, Erving, 14
Goodin, Robert, 15, 181
Gore/Hammer Award for Reinventing Government (1997), 140, 150, 156, 158, 162, 182
Grabosky, Peter, 6
Greater Gila Biodiversity Project, 147

Greater Yellowstone Coalition, 43
Great Outdoors Colorado (GOCO) case study, 20–21, 70–100, 172–76, 185–87; agency size and mission, 91; and bonding authority, 83, 84; business community supporters, 76, 86; and capital construction fund, 76, 77, 89; chronological developments, *73*; Citizens for GOCO, 20–21, 74–77, 86, 87–88, 93, 174; and Colorado's land protection challenges, 20–21, 70–71, 72–74, 84–85, 88–89, 97n3; and Conservation Trust Fund, 72, 74, 77, 78; critics, 82–83; and Division of Parks and Outdoor Recreation, 75, 77, 86, 87–88, 90, 91, 96, 175; and Division of Wildlife, 75, 77, 78, 80–81, 83, 86, 87–91, 92, 96, 175; forming the agency, 78; funding GOCO, 77–78, 89; and the General Assembly, 72–74, 81–82, 87, 89, 92–93, 174–75; and GOCO Citizens' Committee, 74, 93; and GOCO Trust Fund, 74, 77, 87; grant programs and funding criteria, 78–81, 82, 88–89, 91, 98nn36,37; and influences on land use governance, *71*; and initiative process, 21, 74–77, 84, 86, 93, 174; and leadership turnovers, 81; and Legacy grants, 79, 80, 81; and lottery proceeds, 72–74, 75, 76, 77–78, 82, 83, 84, 85–86, 89; narrative account, 72–84; and policy entrepreneurs, 96, 175–76, 184; and private property rights, 85; projects funded, 80–81; public planning meetings and revised strategic plan (2002), 91–92; and resistance, 76–77, 81–82, 87, 89–91, 92–93, *95*, 96, 174–75; and state bureaucratic agencies, 80, 87–88; successes and support, 83–84, 85, 89, 94

Great Outdoors Colorado (GOCO) case study (applying the analytical framework), 84–96, *95*, 172–76, *173*, *186–87*; alignment of factors, 172, 185–87, *186–87*; congruence, 94, 95, *95*, 176, 184; cultural characteristics, 84–86, 94, *95*, 172–74, *173*, 183, 184; framing, 85–86, 94, *95*, 172–74, 183, 184; incentives, 87–89, *95*, 175; individual characteristics, 92–94, *95*, 96, *173*, 175–76; legitimacy, 85, 94, *95*, 174, 183; motivation, 92–93, 95, *95*, 175; norms and harmony, 93–94, 95, *95*; opening the political structure, 87, *95*, 174; resistance, 76–77, 81–82, 87, 89–91, 92–93, *95*, 96, 174–75; rules and communication, 91–92, *95*, 174, 184; shocks, 84–85, 94, *95*, 172–74, 184; structural characteristics, 87–92, 94–96, *95*, *173*, 174–75

Green Lights/Energy Star programs (EPA), 7

Greenpeace, 33

Gunnison Ranchland Conservation Legacy Project, 80

habitat protection programs, 44

Harrison, Benjamin, 53

Harrison, David, 75, 80, 86, 87–88, 92–93, 94

Harrison, Roger, 112–13

Harvard University/Ford Foundation Innovations in American Government Award (1998), 140, 151, 153, 157–58, 162, 169n57, 182

Hassell, Milo Jean, 58

Hays, Samuel P., 54

Healthy Forests Restoration Act, 61

Hereford, John, 81, 83

Herencia de Noreños Unidos, 148

Hetch-Hetchy Dam controversy (1955), 32

historical institutionalism, 13–14, 15–16, 18–19, 161, 183; and Camino Real case study, 181–82, 183; and structural factors, 18–19, 174, 177, 178, 181–82

Historic Structures Tax Act (1976), 44

history of environmental and natural resource governance system. *See* environmental and natural resource governance system (historical evolution of)

"horseback diplomacy," 142, 144–45, 154, 157, 161, 163, 180–81

Hurst, William, 58

I-25 Conservation Corridor Project, 80

incentives, *17–18*, 18; Camino Real and Collaborative Stewardship case study, 159–60, *164–65*, 166, 181; collaboration and friendship, 125, 178; financial support, 124–25, 132, 178; Friends of the Cheat/River of Promise case study, 124–25, *131*, 132, 178; GOCO case study, 87–89, *95*, 175; practical implementation lessons, 194–95; and rational choice institutionalism, 18, 181; technical support, 124–25, 132, 178

individual factors in innovation, 16–18, *17–18*, 182–83; alignment of factors in case studies, 172, 176, 179, 185–92, *186–92*; Camino Real and Collaborative Stewardship case study, 156–58, 163, *164–65*, 166, *173*, 179–80, 180, 184; congruence, *17–18*, 18, 94, 95, *95*, 123, *131*, 132, 158, 163, *164–65*, 166, 176, 180, 184, 194; Friends of the Cheat/River of Promise case study, 120–23, 130–32, *131*, 134, *173*, 176–77, 184; GOCO case study, 92–94, *95*, 96, *173*, 175–76, 184; motivation, 16, *17–18*, 92–93, 95, *95*, 120–22,

130–32, *131*, 134, 156–57, 163, *164–65*, 166, 175, 176, 179–80, 193–94; norms and harmony, 16–18, *17–18*, 93–94, 95, *95*, 123, *131*, 132, 134, 157–58, 163, *164–65*, 166, 177, 180, 184, 194; practical implementation lessons, *193*, 193–94; and rational choice institutionalism, 16, 175, 176, 179–80
initiated regulation, *6*, 7; and GOCO, 21, 74–77, 84, 86, 93; and land protection governance system, 44; and state watershed management, 50–51
innovation: and collaboration, 184–85; defining, 4–8; four categories of innovative arrangements, 5–8, *6*; and technological improvements, 5
innovation, implementation of: bottom-up implementation, 9, 11–13, 16, 184; framework for analysis, 16–20, *17, 18*; ideal conditions for, 4, 196–97; and institutional contexts, 1–29, 171; and institutional theory, 3–4, 13–16; joining innovation and implementation, 9–13; and policy entrepreneurs, 4, 8–9, 12, 183–84; practical lessons learned, 192–96, *193*; problems and challenges of innovative solutions to complex problems, 1–3; theoretical insights, 182–85; the three institutional perspectives, 15–16; top-down implementation, 9–11, 18, 178, 180, 181, 184. *See also* cultural factors in innovation; structural factors in innovation; individual factors in innovation
institutional contexts and implementation of innovation, 1–29, 171; building structural foundations, 4; challenges of, 3–4; and role of policy entrepreneurs, 4, 8–9, 12, 183–84; and tension between innovation and institutions, 3, 11

institutional theory and innovation, 3–4, 13–16; historical institutionalism, 13–14, 15–16, 18–19; operational, collective choice, and constitutional rules, 15, 29n74, 30–31, *31, 38*, 38–39; rational choice institutionalism, 13, 15, 16, 18, 183; sociological institutionalism, 13, 14, 16, 19
"iron triangles," 47, 48, 56

Jackson, Pat, 142–43
Janeck, Phil, 148
Jenkins-Smith, Hank C., 12
Jernejcic, Frank, 119–20

Kenney, Doug, 45, 47, 49
King, Paula J., 9
Kirkpatrick, Susan, 82–83
Kramer, Carveth, 143, 145, 146, 147, 148, 149, 157, 159
Kusel, Jonathan, 52

Lamm, Richard, 72, 85
Lancaster Farmland Trust, 43
land protection governance system (evolution of), 39–45; first era (1920s) and local land use regulation, 39–40; second era (1960s and 1970s), 40–42; third era (1980s and 1990s), 42–45; conservation easements, 44, 78; cooperative business efforts, 43–44; early federal land management agencies and constituencies, 31–32; grassroots groups, 37; habitat protection programs, 44; and initiative process, 44; land trusts and private conservation organizations, 37, 42–44; passage of NLUPA (1971), 41–42; population pressures and disappearing resources, 42–44; private property rights issues, 40, 42; public lands management and lan

protection governance system (*continued*)
  decentralization/shift in regulatory
  approach, 35–37; state and regional
  centralization of regulatory power,
  40–42; and tax laws, 44; and urbanization, 39–40; and zoning, 40, 41.
  See also Great Outdoors Colorado
  (GOCO) case study
Land Trust Alliance, 42, 43
land trusts, 37, 42–44, 80
Lead Partnership Group, 59, 69n138
League of Conservation Voters, 33
Leding, Chris, 82, 83, 90, 91, 93
Legacy Initiative, 78
legitimacy, *17–18*, 19; Camino Real
  and Collaborative Stewardship case
  study, 162–63, *164–65*, 166, 182,
  183; Friends of the Cheat/River of
  Promise case study, 114, 129–30,
  131, 134, 179, 183; GOCO case
  study, 85, 94, *95*, 174, 183; practical
  implementation lessons, 196; socio-
  logical institutionalism and organizational legitimacy, 14, 19, 179
Leo, Marshall, 107
Lindquist, Andy, 147, 161
Local Government Park, 78
Lopez, Henry, 144, 149, 150, 151–52,
  153, 154–55, 156, 166
Love, John, 72, 85
Lucero, Leonard, 147, 151–52, 156, 159,
  160, 161, 166, 181

Mackaye, Benton, 54
Macy, Sydney, 75, 86, 92
Maricopa Audubon Society, 147
Massachusetts Watershed Initiative, 50
Mathews, Kay, 151, 155
Mathews, Laurie, 76, 90, 92
May, Peter, 10–11
McCoy, Eli, 113
Mexican War, 57–58

Miller, Charles, 118
Mollohan, Allan, 119, 128
La Montaña de Truchas Woodlot, 149,
  153
motivation, 16, *17–18*; and bottom-
  up implementation theory, 12–13;
  Camino Real and Collaborative
  Stewardship case study, 156–57,
  163, *164–65*, 166, 179–80; Friends
  of the Cheat/River of Promise case
  study, 120–22, 130–32, *131*, 134,
  176; GOCO case study, 92–93, 95,
  95, 175; practical implementation
  lessons, 193–94
Muecke, Carl, 147, 148
Multiple Use and Sustained Yield Act
  (1960), 35, 37, 56

National Audubon Society, 33
National Environmental Policy Act
  (NEPA) (1969), 35, 37, 56, 61
National Fire Plan, 61
National Forest Management Act
  (1972), 35, 37, 56
National In-holders Association, 42
National Land Use Policy Act (NLUPA)
  (1971), 41–42
National Mine Land Reclamation Center,
  113, 125
National Oceanic and Atmospheric
  Administration, 3
National Park Service, 31–32, 36,
  61–62n2
National Pollutant Discharge Elimination
  System (NPDES), 48, 49
National Wetlands Coalition, 42
Natural Resource Conservation Service, 3
Natural Resources Defense Council, 33
Natural Resources Law Center at the
  University of Colorado, 50
The Nature Conservancy (TNC), 43,
  73, 75, 80

neo-institutionalism. *See* institutional theory and innovation

New England "tree wardens" (1900s), 57

New Federalism, 36, 49–52

New Mexico Environment Program, 150–51

New Public Management, 9, 183

Nixon, Richard, 33–34, 42

non-point-source pollution, 2, 35–36, 49, 151

norms and harmony, 16–18, *17–18*; Camino Real and Collaborative Stewardship case study, 157–58, 163, *164–65*, 166, 180, 184; Friends of the Cheat/River of Promise case study, 123, *131*, 132, 134, 177, 184; GOCO case study, 93–94, 95, *95*; practical implementation lessons, 194

North Carolina Division of Water Quality (NCDWQ), 1–3

Northern New Mexico Policy, 58–59, 142–43, 160–61

Northwest Power Planning Council (NWPPC), 49

"not in my backyard" (NIMBY) behavior, 37–38

NWPPC. *See* Northwest Power Planning Council (NWPPC)

Office of Surface Mining Reclamation and Enforcement (USOSM): agency structure and mandate, 114; and Appalachian Clean Streams Initiative, 111–12, 114, 121, 125; oversight of coal mining regulation and AMD pollution, 102–3, 111–12; and River of Promise, 112–13, 114, 115, 127

openings in political structure, 17–18, *19*; Camino Real and Collaborative Stewardship case study, 160, *164–65*, 166, 181; Friends of the Cheat/River of Promise case study, 125–27, *131*, 132, 134, 177; GOCO case study, 87, *95*, 174; practical implementation lessons about multiple openings, 195

Open Space Land Conservation Grant Program, 78

operational-level innovation, 15, 29n74, 30–31, *31*, *38*, 38–39; and forest governance, *139*; and land use governance, *71*; and watershed governance, *102*

Oregon Lands Coalition, 42

Oregon's watershed councils and watershed management, 50

Osborne, David, 12

Ostrom, Elinor, 14–15, 29n74, 181

O'Toole, Laurence, 5

Outdoor Recreation and Environmental Education Facilities Grant Program, 78

Owens, Bill, 74, 81

Pacific Forest Trust, 43

Pacific Northwest Electric Power Planning and Conservation Act (1980), 49

Pauer, Jennifer, 122, 123, 126

Picuris Pueblo, 149

Piedmont Environmental Council, 43

Pinchot, Gifford, 53–55, 61–62n2

Pitzer, Keith, 116–20, 121, 122, 124, 125, 126, 127–28, 129, 130, 177

Planning and Capacity Building Grant Program, 78

policy entrepreneurs: and bottom-up implementation theory, 12; and Friends of the Cheat/River of Promise, 177, 184; and GOCO, 95, 175–76, 184; and implementation of innovation, 4, 9, 12, 183–84; policy literature and emphasis on, 9, 12, 157, 177, 183–84, 185

policy studies literature: and hierarchical pressures, 30; institutional
theory and integration of literature,
3–4; and policy entrepreneurs, 9, 12,
157, 177, 183–84, 185
Powell, John Wesley, 45, 46
Progressive Era, 46, 53–55
property rights, 40, 42, 85
Public Health Service, 48
Public Works Administration, 46–47
punctuated equilibrium theory, 8, 19
Purkey, Andrew, 76

"quiet revolution," 41, 72
Quiveras Coalition, 150

Rails-to-Trails Conservancy, 43
rational choice institutionalism, 13, 15,
16, 18, 183; and GOCO, 175, 176,
183; and incentives, 18, 181; and
individual factors in innovation, 16,
175, 176, 179–80
Reagan, Ronald, 36, 49, 63n20
Reclamation Act (1902), 46
regulation: coregulation, 6, 6–7; and
decentralization/deregulation, 35–37,
63n20; and the EPA, 7, 34, 36, 49;
government involvement and legally
binding nature of, 5–8, 6; initiatives and initiative process, 6, 7; and
land use governance, 34–37, 39–42;
self-regulation, 5–6, 6; and stakeholder groups, 2, 6–7; voluntary, 2,
6, 7, 101–4, 139–40; and watershed
governance, 47–48, 49
resistance, 17–18, 19; Camino Real and
Collaborative Stewardship case study,
160–61, 164–65, 166; Friends of the
Cheat/River of Promise case study,
113, 127–28, 130, 131, 132, 133,
134, 178; GOCO case study, 76–77,
81–82, 87, 89–91, 92–93, 95, 96,

174–75; practical implementation
lessons, 195
Resources Planning Act (1974), 56
Rio Pueblo/Rio Embudo Watershed
Protection Coalition, 150
River of Promise. See Friends of the
Cheat/River of Promise case study
Roberts, Nancy C., 9
Robinson, Randy, 104–6, 107, 128
Robotham, Doug, 83
Rodriguez, Wilbert, 144, 156
Rogers, Everett M., 5
Romer, Roy, 74, 81, 87, 92, 93
Roosevelt, Theodore, 53, 61–62n2, 84
Roundtable on Communities of Place,
Partnerships, and Forest Health
(1995), 59–60
rules and communication, 17–18, 18;
Camino Real and Collaborative
Stewardship case study, 158–59,
163–66, 164–65, 180–81, 184;
Friends of the Cheat/River of
Promise case study, 123–24, 131,
132, 178, 184; GOCO case study,
91–92, 95, 174, 184; practical imple-
mentation lessons, 194; and top-
down implementation theory, 18

Sabatier, Paul A., 12
Sagebrush Rebellion, 42
Salazar, Ken, 76, 78, 83, 85, 86, 89, 90,
92–93, 175
Santa Barbara Grazing Allotment Re-
habilitation Project, 150, 154
Santa Barbara Grazing Association, 149,
150
Sante Fe National Forest (New Mexico),
58, 142, 153
Scenic Hudson Preservation Conference v.
FPC (1965), 34
Schiller, Mark, 146, 154–55, 157
scientific management, 32, 34–35, 54

Sea Shepherd Society, 33
self-regulation, 5–6, *6*
Seventh American Forest Congress
(1996), 59–60
Shafroth, Will, 78–79, 81, 83, 91, 93
shocks, *17–18*, 19; Camino Real and
Collaborative Stewardship case study,
162, *164–65*, 166, 182, 184; Friends
of the Cheat/River of Promise case
study, 128, *131*, 133, 178–79, 184;
GOCO case study, 84–85, 94, *95*,
172–74, 184; practical implementation lessons, 195; and sociological
institutionalism, 14, 16, 19
Sierra Club, 32, 33, 83
Sierra Club Legal Defense Fund, 33
Sierra Club v. Morton (1972), 34
Silver, Robin, 147
sociological institutionalism, 13, 14, 16,
19, 183; and concept of "embeddedness," 14; and framing, 14, 16, 19;
and organizational legitimacy, 14, 19,
179; and shocks, 14, 16, 19
Soil Conservation Act (1935), 47
South Carolina Department of Health
and Environmental Control, 2
Southwest, American: historical precedents for community forestry in,
57–59; landownership issues and
conflicts, 57–59, 139–44, 160–61;
Northern New Mexico Policy,
58–59, 142–43, 160–61; popular
unrest of the 1960s, 58; Truchas
Land Grant, 143–44, 167n7; and
Vallecitos Federal Sustained Yield
Unit, 58, 142, 160. *See also* Camino
Real Ranger District and Collabora-
tive Stewardship case study
Southwest Center for Biological
Diversity, 147
St. Vrain River and Trails Legacy Project,
81

stakeholder groups and regulation, 2,
6–7
stewardship contracting and
community-based forestry, 61, 150,
153, 154
Strand, Roger, 148
structural factors in innovation, *17–18*,
18–19, 182–83; alignment of factors in case studies, 172, 176, 179,
185–92, *186–92*; Camino Real and
Collaborative Stewardship case study,
158–61, 163–66, *164–65*, *173*,
180–82; Friends of the Cheat/River
of Promise case study, 123–28, *131*,
132–33, 134, *173*, 178; GOCO
case study, 87–92, 94–96, *95*, *173*,
174–75; and historical institutionalism, 18–19, 174, 177, 178, 181–82;
incentives, *17–18*, 18, 87–89, *95*,
124–25, *131*, 132, 159–60, *164–65*,
166, 175, 178, 181, 194–95; openings in the political structure, *17–18*,
19, 87, *95*, 125–27, *131*, 132,
134, 160, *164–65*, 166, 174, 177,
181, 195; practical implementation
lessons, *193*, 194–95; resistance,
17–18, 19, 76–77, 81–82, 87,
89–91, 92–93, *95*, 96, 113, 127–28,
130, *131*, 132, 133, 134, 160–61,
164–65, 166, 174–75, 178, 195;
rules and communication, *17–18*,
18, 91–92, *95*, 123–24, *131*, 132,
158–59, 163–66, *164–65*, 174, 178,
180–81, 184, 194
Surface Mining Control and Reclamation Act (SMCRA), 106–7, 118
Swarthout, John, 81

"takings," 40
Targeted Watershed Grant Program, 118
Tar-Pamlico River basin (North
Carolina), 1–2

Taxpayer Relief Act, 44

Tenneco, 44

Tennessee Valley Authority (TVA), 47

Thatcher, Margaret, 36

33/50 program (EPA), 7

Timmermeyer, Stephanie, 118

Titchnell, Troy, 121, 122

TMDL (total maximum daily load) determinants, 109, 135n27

top-down implementation theory, 9–11, 18, 178, 180, 181, 184; and forest governance, *139*; and incentives, 18, 181; and land use governance, *71*; and nested structures governance, 10–11; and state-level innovation, 11; and structural factors, 18, 178, 180, 181; and watershed governance, *102*

Torres-Horton, Luis, 149

total maximum daily load (TMDL) procedures, 49

Trail Grant Program, 78

Treaty of Guadalupe Hidalgo (1848), 57–58

"tree wardens" and community forestry in New England, 57

Truchas Land Grant, 143–44, 167n7

Trust for Public Land, 43

T&T Coal Operations mine blowout (1994), 104–6, 111, 128, 133, 178

Tucker, Donna, 23

Udall v. Federal Power Commission (1967), 34

Underwood, Cecil, 115–16

Uram, Robert, 111–12, 113, 114, 121

U.S. Army Corps of Engineers (USACOE): and Friends of the Cheat/River of Promise, 115, 119, 127, 128, 133, 178; Lick Run AMD project, 119, 127; and the NWPPC, 49; postwar water development projects, 47

U.S. Department of Agriculture, 61–62n2

U.S. Department of Energy, 3

U.S. Department of the Interior, 50, 61–62n2

U.S. Fish and Wildlife Service (US-FWS), 3, 36; establishment of, 61–62n2; and forest restoration work in Camino Real, 150–51; and Mexican spotted owl habitat protection plan, 147–49

U.S. Forest Service (USFS), 3, 31–32, 36, 52–61; broad organizational culture, 158, 160, 161, 163, 166, 181–82; changing relationship with Congress and the public, 56; and community-based forestry, 54, 59, 61, 138; custodial management and early conservation movement, 53–54; early responsibilities and legislation expanding scope, 54; Economic Action Programs, 61; and environmental era, 55–57; and forestry research, 54–55; legislation challenging power of, 55–56; and national forest system, 54–55; Northern New Mexico Policy, 58–59, 142–43, 160–61; Progressive Era, 53–55; and scientific forest management, 54; shift in regulatory approach (1980s and 1990s), 36; and state and private forestry, 54–55; timber production and commodity management, 31–32, 55, 56; and watershed management, 50. *See also* Camino Real Ranger District and Collaborative Stewardship case study; forest governance system (evolution of)

U.S. Soil Conservation Service, 47

USFS Economic Action Programs, 61
USOSM. *See* Office of Surface Mining
Reclamation and Enforcement (US-
OSM)
USX Corporation, 44

Vallecitos Federal Sustained Yield Unit,
58, 142, 160
Valle Grande Grass Bank, 149
Vermont Land Trust, 43
*Village of Euclid v. Ambler Realty
Company* (1926), 40
VISTA/AmeriCorps, 109, 117
voluntary regulation, 2, 6, 7, 101–4,
139–40

Walbridge, Charlie, 122
Walcher, Greg, 81
water pollution permits, 2
Water Resources Council, 47
Water Resources Planning Act (1947),
47, 49
watershed governance system (evolution of), 45–52; Progressive Era,
46; Depression era, 46–47; prewar
and postwar era, 47–48; the 1960s-
1970s, 48; the 1980s and 1990s, 36,
49–52; Clean Water Act and EPA
authority, 48, 49; community-based
and collaborative watershed councils,
49–50; conservation districts, 47;
cooperative federalism, 48; East-
ern/Western state differences, 51;
federal development projects, 46–47;
federal-state cost-sharing programs,
48; governmental and non-
governmental collaboration, 50–51;
grassroots groups, 37; initiatives and
state watershed management, 50–51;
interagency river basin committees, 47, 48; interstate development

projects, 47; pollution control and
federal regulations, 47–48; Powell's
vision, 45, 46; regional development institutions, 47; regional water
management, 46, 48, 49; regulation,
47–48, 49; state/federal agencies
and watershed management, 50–51;
states-rights and New Federalism, 36,
49–52; water resource commissions,
47. *See also* Friends of the Cheat/
River of Promise case study
Watershed Planning Act (1998)
(Washington state), 50
Webb, Wellington, 76
Western States Public Lands Coalition/
People for the West!, 42
West Virginia Abandoned Mine Lands
(WVAML) program: and federal
funding, 118–19, 128; and Friends
of the Cheat/River of Promise,
106–7, 115, 116, 118–19, 121, 123,
126, 127–28, 133, 178; water treat-
ment methods, 107, 119, 133
West Virginia Clean Streams program,
50
West Virginia Division of
Environmental Protection
(WVDEP), 112–13, 115, 125, 126
West Virginia Division of Mining and
Reclamation (WVDMR), 106–7,
111
West Virginia Division of Natural
Resources (WVDNR), 111, 112–13,
114, 119
West Virginia Rivers Coalition, 111,
112–13, 114, 124–25
West Virginia Stream Partners Program,
122, 126
Weyerhaeuser, 44
Wildlife Habitat Council, 44
Wise, Bob, 126

Wise Use Coalition, 42

Wise Use movement, 42

Works Progress Administration, 46–47

World Wildlife Federation, 33

Wunderlich, Karl, 21

Zon, Theodore, 54

zoning, land use, 40–41